PUBLIC ADMINISTRATION
AS POLITICAL PROCESS

JOHN REHFUSS

PUBLIC ADMINISTRATION AS POLITICAL PROCESS

CHARLES SCRIBNER'S SONS
NEW YORK

1 3 5 7 9 11 13 15 17 19 c/c 20 18 16 14 12 10 8 6 4 2
1 3 5 7 9 11 13 15 17 19 c/p 20 18 16 14 12 10 8 6 4 2

Printed in the United States of America
Library of Congress Catalog Card Number 72-11106
SBN 684-13319-9 (cloth)
SBN 684-13318-0 (paper)

ACKNOWLEDGMENTS

The quotation on p. 218 is reprinted from
*Tangle of Hopes: American Commitments and
World Order* by Ernst B. Haas. Copyright ©
1969; reprinted by permission of Prentice-Hall,
Inc., Englewood Cliffs, New Jersey.

CONTENTS

v

PREFACE

The primary emphasis of this book is to restore politics to center stage as the driving force behind most administrative behavior. Historically, public administration has placed entirely too much emphasis on organizational structure and on matters such as staff functions of the executive, budgeting mechanisms, and personnel issues. Contrary to the impression created by many introductory books on public administration, public executives do not deal with a sanitized, technical world safe from the swirls and uncertainties of politics. Administrative behavior is more meaningfully understood within a broader political process.

Technical questions are, of course, important. They are shaped, however, by the nature of the organization's political environment—or, as is often the case in the late twentieth century, the "technical" questions generate political issues. Politics—the struggle over the allocation of social values and resources—is intimately intertwined with administrative action. While few, if any, students of politics and of administration would deny this, the existing literature on public administration rarely deals with these questions.

This book represents a deliberate decision to write a concise study which, while not covering every aspect, attempts to capture the flavor and excitement of administrative life. Some choice among emphases had to be made. Little attention has been devoted to organizational structure, administrative techniques, or management principles. Instead this study places primary emphasis on political concerns, highlighting the intergovernmental nature of administration in the United States. State and local governments in America employ about three-quarters of all public employees. They are also the fastest growing sectors of government. Yet, most studies pay little or no attention to these levels. This book specifically devotes one chapter to these "lower" levels and takes many of its illustrations from state and local governments.

I have also devoted significant attention to the field of comparative administration, a relatively recent interest of political scientists. This interest has been spurred by the demise of colonialism which created new nations in control of their own destinies. The important role of government bureaucracies in national politics and in political and economic development has excited students of politics and administration. American public administration, disturbingly ethnocentric, has a great deal to learn by observing bureaucratic behavior in other societies. This is particularly true in terms of the impact of cultural patterns on administrative behavior, as the case studies dealing with France and the Philippines in Chapter 8 point out.

I would like to acknowledge those individuals who helped write and review the work. My family gave up many evening and weekend hours because of my love affair with the manuscript. The Political Science Department at Northern Illinois University was very generous in providing assistance. Professionally, some valued colleagues gave freely of their time. Ladd Thomas reviewed the chapter on comparative administration. Keith Henderson reviewed the entire manuscript. I am particularly grateful to Tom Murphy who made a painstaking review of the manuscript and a number of extremely useful suggestions. The pleasure of improving the work by accepting their comments is balanced by the burden of accepting responsibility for any defects which remain.

John Rehfuss
DeKalb, Illinois
September 1972

1

POLITICS, ADMINISTRATION, AND
BUREAUCRATIC POLICY-MAKING

Administrative behavior in public agencies is best understood as political behavior. The final solution to the Jewish question in Buchenwald was carried out by faceless bureaucrats. These acts were clearly political, even though the Nuremberg defendants pleaded that they were merely following orders.

These administrative acts effectuate the "authoritative allocation of social values" as no mere political pronouncement can do.[1] In the 1962 Cuban missile crisis, many of the key decisions were made, not by President Kennedy or Premier Khrushchev, but by the machinations and routines of large government agencies. These routines operated quite separately from overarching questions of whether or not the president should choose all-out nuclear war or what the United States posture toward Russia was. If war had resulted, it would have been at least partly, if not largely, caused by administrative behavior within the military and intelligence agencies of the two countries.

As suggested, administrative behavior has more than accidental or even substantial impact on political decision-making. Administrative acts create, in many ways, our expectations about what government should and can do. Citizen attitudes toward "law and order" are formed more by the behavior of the individual traffic policeman and trial judge than by political debates among candidates for office. What we, as citizens, see in everyday life largely shapes and determines our attitudes toward larger political issues. If citizens see venality and incompetence where government touches them directly, it is likely that they will develop quite different expectations toward government action than if the citizen perceives equity and consistency in the actions of government agencies.

In the long run, the creation of citizen expectations may be the most significant result of administrative behavior. In the short term, however, the intimate relationship between administrative behavior and political questions is extremely important and often quite obvious. The Nixon administration's views on school busing have resulted in tortured and twisted moves by the Justice Department, as the Civil Rights Division walks a path between Nixon's "Southern strategy" designed not to antagonize the South and the rulings of the courts requiring busing. The Division's less than consistent law enforcement behavior is hardly the result of administrative inefficiency, but rather the result of differing views on busing within the administration among political and administrative officials. Administrative practices and organizational policies have profound and immediate implications for public policy, and are political in every important way.

Not all administrative decisions are as dramatic as Buchenwald, Cuban missiles, or busing. They do, however, have the same basic impact on the political process. Patching a city street seems to be a most routine, almost tedious job best left to City Hall. However, a host of past and future policy questions surround the action. Whose street shall be patched and when? Should the city patch streets at all or require residents to maintain their own? Would the money be better used for police salaries or playground equipment? Understanding administrative behavior requires more than a technical knowledge of asphalt thickness in such cases. Even when the program is trivial, the implications for political decision-making are significant. This is the thesis of this book.

THE GAME OF BUREAUCRATIC POLITICS

One helpful way of viewing agency behavior is to regard it as a game. Officials who staff administrative agencies play a game of seeking to acquire, apply, and retain power. This game of bureaucratic politics is the ongoing administrative and political process which accounts for the life, rise, and fall of agencies, programs, and individual careers.[2]

Games are sets of roles associated with some kind of activity. The activity here is bureaucratic behavior, while the roles are generally associated with occupations and positions within administrative organizations. The concept of a game is common to Americans, as can be seen by noting the comments such as "play the game" or "stay on the team," which are applied to business as well as other occupational roles.

A game is a form of competition between individuals and groups in and among large organizations. Parties agree to abide by the rules, which determine and reward winners and penalize losers. Mutual dependence is required, since all parties must strive to win so that victory is not hollow.

Murray Edelman illustrates this process in a case study drawn from his Office of Price Administration experience during World War II.[3] The law, as is often the case, was largely a symbol to its constituency. The enforcement program was a contest, on essentially friendly terms, between administrators, lawyers, and clients. These figures played an important part in the war effort, at the same time participating in a game-like contest.

There are limits to the levels of conflict in bureaucratic politics. A game, not a war, it is played, in part, for fun and, more importantly, for a sense of program commitment, but *not* for ideological reasons. When the game becomes a trial of force and when sides become ideological, the game ceases. For example, the activities of the Justice Department's Antitrust Division, in connection with large corporations, are clearly a formal game and so understood by both sides. On the other hand, the activities of the federal government in rooting out suspected subversives in the McCarthy era of the 1950s were more like the Inquisition than a game. Losers were traitors to the country. Roles were far different, as were expectations. The Antitrust Division does not require merging corporations to sign a loyalty oath as federal employees were required to do.

A game requires mutual role-playing. Symbols and cues are used which evoke corresponding roles and behaviors in other actors. The budget director for the Bureau of Indian Affairs, for example, has a number of roles. He must cut, slice, and snip the requests of division heads and fit their requests into a budget that is always too small for their demands. Conversely, he is a salesman and advocate before the Office of Budget and Management whose analysts make up the president's budget. Before congressional committees he has a complex double role: he must officially support the president's budget not only as a team man, but also as a potential advocate of an increase for his department if a direct congressional question should call for such an answer. He must play all roles, taking his cues from the other actors and adapting his behavior as necessary to gain the maximum appropriation for his agency. His skill in this game contributes to the effectiveness of his agency in "Washington politics."

A final important element of games involves organizational socialization. Members of agencies must be convinced of the validity of their organization's goals and of the value of the political system in which it operates. If members don't believe the game is important they will not participate, and the administrative process slows to a drag. In most cases, those who are most successful in their governmental careers are those who enjoy the game most and are best at it.

These successful bureaucrats and their agencies gain rewards such as increased influence and power for the agency (usually measured in budget allocations), and personal and psychic income for the bureaucrat. Less successful contestants lose correspondingly. The game is not trivial, and it is not played merely for "fun." Nevertheless, the process is game-like and not a bitter struggle to the death.

Conceptualizing the administrative process as a game explains a considerable amount of behavior. A more formal analysis, however, is necessary before comparisons between agencies and administrators can be made. Francis Rourke's model will be outlined in some detail here and used thereafter to explain bureaucratic behavior.

ROURKE'S MODEL OF BUREAUCRATIC POWER

The model has two major elements: (1) the sources of bureaucratic power and (2) the way in which it operates, that is, who participates and in what ways.[4] Bureaucratic power comes from two major sources: the mobilization of support and expertise. These are essentially expert power and political power. The former must be developed, sought, and earned largely outside the agency. The latter is usually a function of bureaucracy and the specialization or functionalization of governmental services. Both are crucial.

Mobilization of Support. Agency support may be mobilized either inside or outside the government. Possibly the most common picture is the interest group walking hand in hand with the administrative agency in a symbiotic relationship. A good example of such a relationship might be state licensing boards, made up of members of the profession whose credentials they certify. While one might expect the general public to be represented on dental licensing boards, since the consumer has an interest, it is much more likely that the board will be made up predominantly, if not wholly, of dentists.

There is often conflict between the agency and its supporters. A typical case is the alumni association of a state university which ceases lobbying for increased appropriations when campus unrest causes unpopular student demonstrations.

Agencies pay a price for support. Cooptation, or the placement of supporting interest groups in the agency decision-making process, either openly or tacitly, is very common.[5] Advisory groups often may be involved in more than giving advice. Power is frequently, if not almost always, shared.

In terms of mobilizing outside support, the general public must also be considered. This kind of support is very diffuse and unreliable and is often written off by persons emphasizing the group basis of politics. Nevertheless, it can be a potent force, and the greater the propinquity of legislature and constituent, the stronger it is. The Parent-Teacher's Association in concert with the principal may influence many aspects of a specific school's program. However, more basic questions like taxes and curricula are largely determined by district-wide voter attitudes, which are reflected in the outcome of school board elections and bond referenda.

Inside the government, there are two major sources of support. In the legislature, individual legislators or legislative committees often become strong supporters of an agency program. This is most clearly seen at the federal level, but the same situation arises at the state level and in city councils large enough to have committees. This type of support is most helpful in considering specific legislation or authorizing new programs. It may be less helpful in providing the funds for operation since a separate committee or the legislature as a whole usually considers all appropriate requests together. Sometimes a specific legislator will "carry" an agency's legislative request or even a committee as a whole will support the agency if it is threatened. "To me, forestry has become a religion," said United States Representative Walter Horan. Protesting his own appropriation sub-committee report, he said "The items are totally inadequate and I do not care particularly which way we get them, but we do need funds. . . ." [6] The "we" indicates a most delightful source of support, but can be a mixed blessing. Legislators expect to be consulted and to have some measure of influence over agency decisions. The slightest request by a committee member must receive immediate consideration, and information channels must include the committee.

On occasion, the legislature as a whole will become dissatisfied with agency performance. A sympathetic committee can intercede and protect the organization to some degree. This type of conflict can be very serious to the agency and officials will go to almost any lengths to prevent it.

The other source of governmental support is the chief executive officer or his key representatives, such as budget bureau or staff aides. The governor, the mayor or city manager, or the school superintendent, are indeed key sources of support. They normally formulate the budget which often tends to place a ceiling on expenditures for the agency. In many cases, the executive's proposed budget contains the final figure, for the legislature may not care to or be able to change it.

Other support from the chief executive can involve the delegation of operational latitude sufficient to enable the agency to behave virtually autonomously. An example of this might be a city planning department obtaining permission from the city manager to present planning and zoning recommendations directly to the city council rather than relying on the manager's own summary of them. The department head can then frame discussion of the planning issues on his own terms or in terms of his relation with the council. This type of direct contact with the legislative body strengthens the planner's hand in dealing with planning issues and also demonstrates that he has the confidence of the city manager.

Expertise. The other major source of bureaucratic power in Rourke's model is expertise. Society is becoming more specialized and dominated by technological concerns, and now more is expected from government. Under these circumstances the possession of specialized and technical skills becomes a major source of information, and information means influence. Five elements when mixed together form the base of expert power. They are (1) full-time attention to the problem, (2) subpart specialization, (3) information monopolization, (4) the use of advice, both direct and indirect, and (5) the control of discretion.

Full-time attention to a problem assures complete information about the ramifications and thus is an advantage in framing policy questions. Politicians pay only sporadic attention to issues while agencies devote years of attention to specific problems.

Subpart specialization develops expertise by breaking the function, issue, or problem down into subparts. By putting part of the organization to work on a specialized subarea, very high levels of expertise can be developed. Streetsweeping, for example, in spite of the apparent simplicity of the operation, can be broken down into several specialized subparts: people responsible for the maintenance of specialized equipment (a job entailing knowledge of parts and how to get them on short notice), semiskilled operators who can move the sweeper around parked cars safely, and persons with the professional contacts to acquire information on sweeper usage in unusual weather. Even a city manager who is reasonably familiar with the procedure (compared to a legislator) will generally defer to the sweeping foreman who possesses specialized information.

Monopolization of information is not the province of glamorous, cloak-and-dagger operations of the Central Intelligence Agency. Routine, unclassified information accumulates in every organization. It allows the agency to develop and determine the facts of a case and to control the timing of information releases. Agencies often monopolize the professional competence which makes an attack on the problem possible, simply by being the only employer. If all state sanitarians insist on the need for state restaurant inspections, who may contradict them except restaurant owners? There is nothing conspiratorial or malevolent about information monopolization. Rather, it is the result of specialization and professionalization in organizations. Clearly, it is a source of power.

Since agencies tend to monopolize information, they tend to translate it into influence through the advice they give political decision-makers. While politicians may not entirely trust the bureaucracy, they have few other sources of information.

The influence gained by advice is limited by the extent to which the executive or legislator acts favorably on it or allows it to guide his actions. One agency may have a "good track record" and find its advice well-received, while other agencies have their advice liberally discounted. Institutionalized staff agencies such as the budget office, the personnel agency, or, in the case of the federal government, the Council of Economic Advisers generally carry a great deal of weight with legislatures. At the local level, commissions, ranging from human relations to traffic, advise the legislators and chief executive. Due to a lack of expertise and because they are often part-time, their advice does not carry quite the weight it might otherwise. If they do have a staff and the area is not too heavily value-infused, the commissions may gain in influence. Planning commission recommendations based on staff studies and public hearings in many cases do have weight.

Finally, a crucial variable in agency influence is the degree of discretion exercised. All agencies have some discretion, but some have more than others. The police department has more than the fire department, since the job is considered to require more judgment. Discretion may be considered direct when the decisions must be nonprogrammed, or indirect when they are programmed, but still involve discretion.

Nonprogrammed decisions include the activities of the National Guard or the State Highway Patrol in disaster situations or the activities of state licensing boards in setting regulations and standards for practitioners in the state. No guides can be set down by the nature of the job and the legislative body normally expects that the circumstances around each decision will be so unpredictable or require so much discretion that a specific guide becomes undesirable.

Not so clear are the programmed decisions where legislative or executive guides can be formed. The traditional difference between political and administrative decisions is breached, at least in theory, when agencies ignore or modify legislative intent; yet, such breaches or changes are necessary. Does a 70 mph-speed zone require the officer to ticket at 71, 75, or 85 mph? Is the use of radar permitted if it is not specifically disallowed? Does the required minimum coliform count in waste disposal waters require once-a-week or once-a-month samples? There are no simple answers to these questions, at least from the legislature, and so someone in the agency must decide.

Ultimately, bureaucratic power rests primarily on expertise. Many observers doubt this, however, believing that interest mobilization for program purposes is the primary, if not sole, source of agency support. Knowledge is fine, goes this argument, but in the end all that counts is politics, power, or who you know. This argument, I think, misrepresents the nature of administrative action and bureaucratic power. Agencies, to be sure, can be no less self-serving than elected politicians. But motives are not the crucial factor. Agencies are instrumental institutions formed for special purposes, whether they be program-oriented or purely symbolic, and they are expected to produce something. Some provide well-administered and perhaps noncontroversial programs, such as the Internal Revenue Service or the Social Security Administration. Others are involved in more controversial activities revolving about or touching interest-representation such as the constituent bureaus of the Department of Labor or the Office of Economic Opportunity. Other agencies have still different functions. All, however, are expected to develop specialized reservoirs of knowledge and information and to be expert in their areas. Weakening of the special skills of an agency will ultimately weaken its power base.

Variations in Power among Agencies. As we have seen, bureaucracies gain power by mobilizing support and, most crucially, by wielding expertise. What distinguishes among agencies in the total power they possess?

One major variation is in the strength of the constituency. Variations in the breadth and depth of the support are vital. Broad general support, as well as strong interest groups, may characterize universities, while a local building department has little general support since it is not particularly visible and often is in conflict with its client, the building contractors. These differences explain why certain agencies can expand their resource base and operations and others cannot. In terms of legislative support, committee support may or may not be matched through the legislature. Some agencies rely on executive, rather than legislative, support. Local programs involved in social relations, such as recreation departments and housing agencies, often fall into this area.

Divisions in constituency support can sap agency strength. Universities are torn by the polarization of public opinion in the 1970s, and public support for higher (and secondary) education is much weaker now than in years past. Specific groups such as alumni are split in their support and oppose some educational policies.

Similar disunity is being experienced by the police. Students, as well as certain liberal and moderate groups, join with highly antagonistic groups such as Black Panthers in their negative appraisal of law enforcement agencies, thus rupturing traditional support for law enforcement in the United States. Other law and order groups may spring to its defense, but the net effect of polarization and the appearance of organization enemies sooner or later must weaken the agency.

Another variable in agency influence is the nature of an organization's expertise. Some specialties and professions which may play a leading role in an agency have more prestige, which can often be transformed into influence. College professors have high occupational status, as do doctors and engineers. Other things being equal, higher education, public health, and public works departments will do better than competing agencies if their performance can be evaluated in terms of occupational prestige of the organizational elite. The task of convincing legislators to act on this sort of premise is, of course, not always easy. Even so, these agencies can use their professional base to avoid criticism or outside supervision of their operations. The inability of nonspecialists, such as legislators and executives, to come to grips with actual operations puts them in the position of either concurring with the agency definition of the problem or acting arbitrarily by cutting the agency budget and/or placing severe restrictions on its programs. If political forces concur, the agency has achieved its goal, at least in the short run. If the political forces behave arbitrarily the agency may be able to blame them later for any shortcomings due to lack of funds and program restrictions.

Internal organizational variables often make a difference in agency power. Some agencies seem to seek power as an end in itself and consciously bend every attempt to strengthen themselves. This does not seem to be attributable to any one type of agency or function but rather to a complex amalgam of individual member drives, organizational structure, and opportunity. This drive for power may be merely an honest desire to improve medical care or police protection or win increased appropriations; in other cases, there is less concern for service and more for power as an end in itself.

A drive for power should be distinguished from organizational vitality or élan. At the federal level, the Peace Corps was a classic example of what Amitai Etzioni calls a "normative" organization, in which members served with fervor and enormous commitment.[7] Certain agencies with a service orientation and fewer ties to prior commitments may manifest this vitality, and this may again transmit itself into power. Small experimental schools and research agencies might fall into this category. Larger, more traditional agencies that are able to manifest a strong sense of member identification with their programs will tend to have more influence, largely because of the favorable impression created by this attitude.

Leadership, or administrative statecraft as Rourke calls it, is a critical organizational variable. Rarely will organization vitality develop to any large degree unless it is nurtured by effective leadership. Charisma helps but is not required; at a minimum the leader must have a profound sense of commitment and a keen understanding of what the organization is and can be. He must inspire organizational zeal and commitment within and be an effective spokesman to the world outside. Far from a harkening back to the now discredited "great man" theory, this argument merely asserts that many differences in organizational influence are due to effective leadership. Cultivating outside interest groups, providing quick and accurate information to legislative committees, and opening organizational communications to new ideas are examples of effective leadership. Few administrators have the ability and favorable set of circumstances to effect a Charles de Gaulle type of leadership, but most of us can visualize organizations in which poor or ineffective leadership held back progress.[8]

Operation of Bureaucratic Power. Operation of bureaucratic power is the second half of Rourke's model. There are crucial variables in the ways that policy is made within public bureaucracies, and the administrative process is no less a political struggle because it takes place largely within agency itself.

A key question in determining agency operational policy involves the question of participation in the decision. There are three broad areas of conflict over policy-making control—professionals versus administrators, political versus career executives, and outsiders versus insiders.

Professionals tend to dominate decision-making on the nature and focus of specific programs. This is due to their near monopoly of information since they are often trained in specialized occupations such as a social worker or city engineer. Interested in effectiveness or the accomplishment of a satisfactory end product, they are less concerned with the cost of the service. Administrators, on the other hand, tend to be concerned with efficiency and with concerns such as the relative strength and maintenance of the organization and with "business as usual." Professionals will usually concern themselves with the absolute "correctness" of a decision, while administrators will be more willing to find a "satisficing" (satisfying them and sufficing for the job) solution. The professional is often on the cutting edge of policy, deeply concerned with the impact it has and if it meets professional standards, whether they be those of law, medicine, or engineering. The administrator normally found in staff agencies such as budget and finance is often the cautious mediator, aware of outside political pressures and the need to maintain the viability of the organization. The agency decision process will tend to mirror the sorts of policy suggested here to the extent that either of these two groups dominates an organization.

Another competing set of policy participants is composed of political executives and careerists. In democratic theory, political executives are responsible for determining agency policies in accord with the preferences of the victorious political party and chief executive. However, bureaucratic theory implies that political dilettantes such as short-term political executives cannot control or resist the overwhelming expertise, knowledge, and secrecy of the bureaucracy.[9] The real picture is considerably more complex. In most cases, respect for norms based on electoral control and organizational authority causes careerists to defer to political executives. This deference is also due to the substantial influence the executive bears as head of the agency. Conversely, most political executives learn to use the expertise of the career officials and rarely attempt massive changes of the established agency order. A sort of accommodation is reached since both groups need each other. The political executive is the visible symbol of sovereignty, a legitimized authority figure, and he also is necessary to persuade decision-makers to support the agency program. Likewise, careerists cannot be pushed too far or they will resort to either bureaucratic "sabotage" or withdrawal of services by resigning or reducing their efforts.

Outright bureaucratic sabotage is relatively rare. Rourke notes that it usually takes the form of informal leakages of information to outside enemies of the political executive. Sometimes it is nullification of new laws or policies, or continued foot-dragging and reluctance to implement new or different programs. A case indicating this type of action in reverse was Inspector Goldberg's insistence on enforcing New York City laws outlawing bingo in churches and private clubs. Goldberg was eventually demoted by the chief of police, who could not resist the outcry from Catholics and club members. Even so, fearful of other groups, the chief was unable to specify in a written statement that the law should not be enforced. The uproar over Goldberg's demotion compelled the chief to crack down on bingo, forcing the games to go to Newark, New Jersey and ultimately causing the law to be repealed.[10] Both political and career executives normally will go to almost any lengths to avoid this kind of open conflict which damages both participants and the agency. Some accommodation is usually reached between the dramatic changes often desired by political executives and the past practices of the agency which careerists may prefer. This is not to imply that all policy initiation comes from political executives, nor all resistance to change from careerists. It depends on the type of leader, the agency members, and the particular situation. Often careerists who favor policy changes welcome new political executives as providing an opportunity for a program review which could be resolved in their favor.

The last set of competing participants, insiders and outsiders, is perhaps less significant than the first two, but in certain cases the nature of the conflict can be quite important. Bringing in outsiders is normally one way to receive objective, expert views of agency issues and programs. Most commonly, outside views are given by either consultants or advisory committees. With the former, there is a contractual agreement and a disinterest on the part of the consultant which is normally desired by the agency. Advisory committees are more institutionalized. They provide a chance to get the best thinking of experts in the field without hiring them or committing them to a specific policy. Sometimes they are used to obtain outside opinions and to penetrate the bureaucracy with the values of society as a whole. In certain cases, the outside groups may be "coopted" into supporting the insiders' policy and providing a veneer of respectability for it. This even may occur unintentionally, as in the case of advisers who through familiarity with the agency program become committed to it and thus lose the ability to view it critically.

The participation by outsiders in agency decision-making can be highly divisive, as the present struggle over civilian review boards for police departments indicates. In state and local government the use of committees varies greatly and probably less formalized use is made of them than in the federal establishment.

Bureaucratic versus Legislative and Executive Policy-Making. Three major elements stand out in comparing the bureaucratic policy-making process to that of the legislature and perhaps the chief executive level. The first is hierarchy. The head of the organization has a great deal of control over the decision process in the organization and his position of authority is generally sufficient to compel deference. Hierarchical patterns mean that negotiations take place among persons unequal in power. Decisions dominated largely by those at the peak of the pyramid tend to be more consistent and take into account more varied views both within and outside the organization. They also tend to be based on less complete exchanges of information since the tendency is to advise a superior of the things he would like to hear.

Hierarchies are not monolithic—sub-agencies and agents sometimes work autonomously and have many chances to leak information or contrary views to the outside. Also, the functional responsibilities of agencies have been fragmented and over-extended thus building pluralism into the administrative architecture. This guarantees competing sources of information to final policy-makers. Nevertheless, the existence of hierarchical decision-making imparts a special flavor to bureaucratic policy-making.

Bureaucracies differ from other political institutions in a second major way, that of specialization. Legislatures and political executives specialize in a rough way, by committees and staff assignments, but nothing like administrative agencies. Specialization is the major way in which agencies maintain expertise. Police ballistics laboratories are a purely professional, scientific function. They have to be or arrests would not hold up in court. Designing streets for maximum traffic flow and safety must be done by trained, expert draftsmen—failures are not only professionally humiliating but may be politically painful. This is not to say that political considerations are unnecessary as a supplement to professional judgment in a most functional way. For example, it often becomes necessary to overrule a less expensive freeway route through a housing area in favor of a more costly path with fewer social dislocations.

A final difference between bureaucratic and legislative policy-making concerns secrecy. Legislatures are rather public places. Legislators usually vote publicly, are interviewed frequently, seek publicity, and often gain from controversy. The bureaucracy operates largely in secrecy. They control information, avoid public controversy for fear of suggesting division over an issue on which they wish to present a united front, and attempt to pursue discussion without having individuals being publicly accountable for their ideas. Usually, this is functional. Fact gathering and alternative analysis are not always best done in the glare of publicity, and many of the alternatives can be discarded without commitment that later could prove embarrassing. However, when combined with hierarchical organization forms, problems can arise when divergent views are not strongly expressed or are shouted down in private. There is often a tendency for a like-minded group of policy-makers to agree on a one best plan that receives, in reality, little scrutiny. A case in point is the Chicago police raid on Black Panther headquarters in which two blacks were killed in December 1969. A grand jury investigation revealed that police shot in the middle of the night without provocation, told conflicting stories, and did very sloppy, if not deliberately false, laboratory work which led to charges against the black survivors which later had to be dropped. Subsequently the state's attorney and a number of policemen were indicted for conspiracy for attempting to "cover up" the police errors. The whole story cast considerable doubt on the veracity of the police department and the state's attorney who sponsored the raid. Lack of divergent views while planning the raid seems to have prevented alternative plans from being considered seriously.

A summary of Rourke's model is in order. Bureaucratic power comes from the sources and mobilization of power and expertise. Agency mobilization includes both interest groups outside the government and the legislative or executive inside the government. Expert power comes from control over discretion, monopolization of information, specialization in problem subparts, full-time attention to problems, and the use of advice. Differentials in agency power are based on strength, breadth, and lack of divisions of support, the lack of organizational or interest enemies, the relative prestige of their expertise base, and organizational variables of leadership, vitality, and drive for power.

The operation of bureaucratic power is best viewed by looking at the relationships between three groups: political versus career executives, professionals versus administrators, and insiders versus outsiders. It differs from purely legislative policy-making by the influence of hierarchy, the professionalization of policy, and the secrecy with which it is carried on.

COMMUNITY ACTION PROGRAMS: A CASE STUDY

A relevant case study to illustrate bureaucratic politics and the model outlined above is the federal antipoverty program of the mid-1960s. The program dealing with Community Action Programs (CAP) was unusual in that it attempted to alleviate poverty by directly involving the poor in designing and operating programs for their own benefit. To the extent that it attempted to make poor and powerless persons a separate political force operating at the local level, it was a revolutionary idea designed to federally finance opposition to local political leaders in city hall.[11]

Initiation of the program began outside the traditional executive branch bureaucracies. The ideas bubbled out of the minds and internal fires of a group of "guerrillas" who infiltrated the new Kennedy administration in the early 1960s. Headquartered in a new agency called the President's Committee on Juvenile Delinquency, the group was made up of people who were passionately committed to social reform and who did not share, through years of experience and socialization, the values of the old-line bureaucracies. They wanted to change the welfare-administrative-political system, not to work within it. Many of the group's members were originally connected with the Ford Foundation's work in urban areas in the late 1950s, and were heavily oriented toward social science research and analysis as well as a certain social work point of view. Essentially, they believed that poverty was becoming a structural part of the economy and that many poor people would not move out of poverty in the near or foreseeable future, by the working of the economic system. This view was adopted by President Kennedy at a later date after considerable study by economists in his administration.

Confusion and misunderstanding that ultimately upset the whole program resulted from differences in opinion over how community action could be a force for change. Some felt that the federal government could stimulate reform from the top by giving grants-in-aid and establishing performance requirements, just as most traditional programs did. Another group favored letting the poor move into the bureaucracies and modifying policies that way. While the first two still preferred to work within the system, a third group wanted community organizers to establish new and relevant organizations to replace the existing arrangements. The last approach stressed conflict between the old and the new organizations. These three views argued for by persons who were not in the Kennedy administration mainstream of bureaucratic power seemed in retrospect to have had a strange air of unreality among the power relationships in Washington. But for a number of reasons, the differences were never reconciled, and the particular constellation of political power led to the establishment of the Office of Economic Opportunity in 1964, with CAP a major program, with no basic agreement on the purposes of community action. First, however, the whole process of program formulation needs further examination.

After Kennedy gave the antipoverty program the go-ahead in 1963, interbureaucratic struggles over the program began. An early and influential force was the Bureau of the Budget. The bureau was the fiscal watchdog for the president and also the agency largely responsible for effective management oversight of federal operations. Budget analysts, according to Richard Blumenthal, ". . . were appalled by the paucity of comprehensive planning, the fragmentation of authority, and the bureaucratic small mindedness that pervaded the welfare establishment." This jaundiced view resulted in rejection of most of the old-line agency proposals and the insistence on newer approaches. The older agencies were jockeying for position hoping to control whatever funds and proposals would be forthcoming. Their suggestions were largely rehashes of earlier programs which would maximize the influence of each agency by limiting the antipoverty program to areas within their jurisdiction. For example, the Labor Department suggested youth-oriented, job-creating and job-training programs, while Health, Education and Welfare wanted mostly adult programs related to Medicare and vocational rehabilitation.

The Bureau of the Budget, disappointed by the traditional responses of these established agencies, turned back to the Juvenile Deliquency Committee and toward a set of proposals revolving around community action. It hoped that new institutions would avoid the ineffectiveness of traditional welfare programs and might coordinate the varied programs in such a way as to focus them more directly toward the poor.

The ways in which coordination was to occur were vague, at best. The bureau wanted coordination of federal programs while the guerrillas really sought conflict with them on behalf of the poor. These are mutually contradictory, but apparently none of the participants were aware of it.

Calculations changed dramatically when Lyndon Johnson became president and embraced antipoverty as "my kind of program." It was, or at least became, clear that while Johnson regarded antipoverty programs as economically beneficial to poor people, he had to obtain political benefits for his administration by securing middle-class support. He wanted money spent, mostly on traditional programs, and had little time for the complexities of community action theories involving relative deprivation or maximum feasible participation. Johnson wanted an impressive program on behalf of the poor, but did not want to spend a great deal of money since he was emphasizing frugality in executive branch activities.

These conflicting desires were united by classifying a number of traditional single purpose proposals already before Congress as "antipoverty" and adding the CAP and a few other ideas such as the Job Corps and VISTA. Thus small business loans and job training also came under the antipoverty umbrella. The stage was set for bureaucratic infighting over the division of the potential spoils. The struggle was fierce since it was apparent that Johnson was likely to get his program and the traditional agencies wanted "a piece of the action."

The traditional agencies were as critical of the "go-slow" planning approach of CAP as they were ignorant of the meaning of community action. (The reformers wanted small, trial programs.) Action programs geared to maximum public visibility, rather than experimental prototypes, were the aims of old-line agencies. Their views—developed over years of experience in guarding power in Washington—were based on a sense of historical resistance to drastic changes and an acute awareness of what Congress might do to new and/or ill-conceived programs. They sought to advance their own agencies in a not unfamiliar pattern of bureaucratic infighting. Their sentiments were strengthened by a tradition of government service which emphasized "doing things for people," rather than giving power to their clientele. Power is guarded rather than given away in Washington, even for worthy causes.

In short, traditional agencies resisted making CAP the major emphasis of the war on poverty, and some even resisted the idea of community control. They also fought among themselves. Labor wanted job-creating and job-training programs. Agriculture wanted money for the rural poor and marginal farmer. HEW wanted the money for education and health programs. Commerce wanted to expand Area Redevelopment Administration, and Interior wanted money for Indian reservations.

President Johnson selected Sargent Shriver, fresh from his triumphal reign of the Peace Corps, to head the new agency. It seemed likely that Shriver was the only person with sufficient stature to pull outside support together and knock heads together inside. Certainly, it did not take him long to make some basic decisions. He cut back CAP funds and expanded allocations to traditional programs particularly in the Labor Department, shaping the proposed program in ways more congenial to the president and the operating agencies. The final total came to nearly $1 billion, of which CAP had $300 million. He also was able to get the Office of Economic Opportunity established in the Executive Office of the President, a place usually reserved for staff functions such as advising the president and budgeting. The Executive Office represented a hierarchical level above other cabinet departments. It was necessary perhaps to indicate that the president personally backed the agency and to protect it from the attacks of traditional agencies.

Drafting the legislation was relatively simple. Interestingly, the crucial question of what CAP or community action really represented was still hazy. A provision was added about "maximum feasible participation" of the poor in the formation of community action programs. This famous clause was the legislative justification for the controversy that marked CAP programs. It was apparently added only to prevent discrimination against blacks in the South. No one saw the use that civil rights groups would make of it.

Congress did not review the proposed legislation very carefully. Democrats were anxious to pass the president's program, and to force the Republican opposition into an "anti-poor" position. In fact, Adam Clayton Powell's House Committee on Education and Labor did not even allow Republicans the traditional right of sharing in marking up the final bill before passage. Congressional reaction was limited to a few ad hoc changes which modified the bill very little. Congresswoman Edith Green, exasperated with the original Juvenile Delinquency Committee for its emphasis on planning, succeeded in amending out comprehensive planning requirements. She and others were tired of plans and programs and wanted action.

Adam Yarmolinsky, Shriver's assistant, was drummed out of any role in administration as a gesture to the North Carolina delegation. He was considered too liberal, progressive, and pro-black. Other congressional concerns over administrative or organizational matters were limited to the power of the OEO head. Fear of a "poverty czar" led both parties to write in an apportionment formula for grants to states, based on factors such as number of welfare recipients and children in poor families. This, along with the "governor's veto" which gave state executives veto power over CAP contracts with the federal government, was designed to limit the OEO head's discretion.

Nowhere did Congress consider the political and social implications of "maximum feasible participation" nor even vaguely suspect that the poor might be administering their own programs. They can hardly be blamed, for neither President Johnson nor most of the executive branch had such ideas.

Shriver referred to OEO, after enaction of the legislation by Congress, as "the business corporation of the new social revolution." To him, and most federal officials, it was mostly rhetoric, justified by the language of the act. To those administering the CAP program, however, they were not idle words.

A number of ironies had occurred. The original guerrillas, whose views had been overridden when CAP became only part of the antipoverty umbrella of OEO, were now in a position to install their original views as part of the task force established to plan implementation of the program. The vagueness of the legislation led these men to develop guidelines for CAPs which stressed not only "maximum feasible participation" but "broadly representative" phrases. These guidelines, to say the least, were not true to the view of Congress or of the president. The guerrillas wished to assist the poor in obtaining power, not merely to dispense money and services from a position of federal power. The poor were to be mobilized.

CAP programs quickly became controversial. In many cities the poor did gain control of CAP. In many cases a new kind of professional directed the programs. In too many cases to please Democratic mayors of cities, or congressmen, or Lyndon Johnson, the poor actually began to demonstrate and organize. Much of the activity was a struggle for power among spokesmen for the poor or even among groups of poor. Even so, it was directed rhetorically against local officials. Syracuse, New York City, Los Angeles, and many other cities were wracked with controversy. One incident involved a busload of poor singing sarcastic antipoverty Christmas carols at Shriver's house in 1965. The program was not coordinating, as the Bureau of the Budget had hoped; it was unpopular with congressmen and with the president, and it pitted big city mayors and urban blacks against each other, dividing two elements of the Democratic party.

A political liability and administrative disappointment, OEO had its funds cut back in 1965. While OEO programs have continued, each appropriation of money has been a struggle, and the program has been rather restricted.

Analysis: CAP, Poverty, Politics, and Power. The CAP program is an interesting federal program to illustrate the bureaucratic power model for several reasons. A "radical" rather than "incremental" departure from existing programs, it was originated and passed as a result of unusual circumstances. First, the program emerged at a time when political alignments and forces allowed it to be enacted without the normal agonizing and extended review by congressional committees, and, because of the timing, even without the normal amount of interdepartmental critique. Secondly, it was the creation of outsiders with quite different aims than old-time bureaucrats. Normally federal programs are developed within a federal agency and aimed at constituencies already served by that agency. This was not the case. The goals of CAP were more visionary and less pragmatic than those generally developed by other agencies. The bureaucratic mind seeks order, predictability, and maintenance of power—the academic or social-work mind is less tied to such temporal matters.

In terms of the game of bureaucratic politics, the actions of the other federal agencies were highly predictable. Used to a role of advancing their own organization and jockeying for power and position, they did just what they always have done—engaged in a game-like process which gives meaning to their life. Used to the game, the old-line agencies banded together to resist the new community action program and to advance their own. Through years of experience, they had a fixed idea of political reality in Congress and were completely baffled by the idea of disbursing rather than accreting power. The protection of power is so universal a phenomenon in Washington that it has become a guiding rule of the game of bureaucratic politics. Older game players have been socialized to maintain power and influence within their agencies and they wanted larger appropriations instead of social change. The guerrillas sought power and influence also, but it appears that their orientation was essentially programmatic. They wanted the CAP program to be enacted so that a social experiment, one which dispersed power and espoused conflict, could be attempted. It is likely that the old-line bureaucrats would have been reluctant to interpret the CAP legislation as broadly as the guerrillas did. Much more aware of the dangers of exceeding congressional intentions (the law was too vague for anyone to violate specific provisions) and more fearful of controversy in an administered program, they simply would not have tolerated some of the peccadillos of the CAPs. They were in the game for the long haul and could not afford to be associated with revolutionary activity. To them the process of game-playing was the important matter; to the guerrillas it was a unique chance to change society. It is unlikely that OEO actually wanted CAP to be so controversial that it caused political problems. It is clear that they were willing to take risks to activate the poor and this risk a more seasoned bureaucrat would not take.

Community action was an important idea representing a heightened social consciousness on the part of middle-class Americans. It also supported the thrust of the civil rights movement in activating previously powerless minorities. If traditional bureaucrats had administered OEO, there would be fewer controversies, less life, more order, and little or no social revolution. Given the goal of reform, the accidental, stumbling way that circumstances gave social experimenters large sums of money to mobilize the poor may have been providential.[12] The point is that mobilization would not have occurred if bureaucrats socialized to the game of bureaucratic politics were administering it, or even if they were creating the program or writing the legislation.

CAP experience further illustrates the model of bureaucratic power in several ways. In developing the legislation and in obtaining congressional approval, perhaps less mobilization of support than usually occurs outside the government was present. The only major effort reported by Blumenthal was Shriver's work in selling the program to labor, big city mayors, and dubious congressmen. Although the outside work may have been greater than reported, it appears that the whole-hearted backing of Johnson, heading a united party facing an election, made it somewhat less necessary to scrape up support outside the federal establishment. The poor were not an articulate group which could provide major support and most of the interest groups associated with the old-line agencies either were not likely to oppose it, or could be easily convinced by Shriver to support it.

Most of the agencies within the government had been bought off by including some of their categorical programs within the proposal. Others were quiet in deference to the strong wishes of the president. In any case, Democrats were not interested in looking for opposition, so the bill passed easily.

The question of expertise is a bit more complex. The control of discretion and of information monopolization enabled OEO to involve the poor in program operation to a greater degree than Congress or the president would have liked. No one told the president or Congress directly how the program was to operate (doubtless the OEO was not clear itself). The guidelines for CAP operation were distributed to communities and to congressmen in June of 1964, and elicited little comment. Until OEO began to administer them, no one could tell what might happen and what types of orientations would guide the grants and operation of the local CAPs. In short, the administrative discretion of the OEO could not be evaluated until it was used, and until then there was little use for presidential or congressional oversight.

It was mentioned earlier that partisan political objectives expedited OEO legislation. In addition, it seems that Congress assumed that the legislation was completely thrashed out, that at least the Executive Branch understood the meaning of "maximum feasible participation," and that administration of the program would be in a traditional, centralized manner. None of this was true, but it seems reasonable to suspect that Congress tacitly assumed the bureaucracy would take care of the details.

It is interesting to note that Congress was willing to make this assumption for it suggests that agencies are automatically given credit for being "expert." This is a most important base of power.

It is also interesting that the CAP program was administered by an unusual group of people. They were professional social workers or academics rather than career administrators. They were outsiders, in the sense that they had little career commitment to either the OEO or the federal government. They were also politicians in the sense that they advocated policy positions rather than being concerned with administrative feasibility. Under these conditions, one should not be surprised that the CAP did not run smoothly.

NOTES

1. Graham Allison, "Conceptual Models and the Cuban Missile Crisis" in *American Political Science Review* 63 (September 1969), pp. 689–718.
2. Norton Long, "Power and Administration" in *Public Administration Review* 9 (Autumn 1949), pp. 257–64.
3. Murray Edelman, *The Symbolic Uses of Politics* (University of Illinois Press, 1960), pp. 45–47.
4. Francis Rourke, *Bureaucracy, Politics and Public Policy* (Little, Brown, 1969).
5. See Philip Selznick, *TVA and the Grass Roots* (University of California Press, 1949).
6. Aaron Wildavsky, *The Politics of the Budgetary Process* (Little, Brown, 1964), p. 48.
7. Amitai Etzioni, *A Comparative Study of Complex Organizations* (Free Press, 1961). Apparently this organizational pride can be lost rather quickly, as the present distress of the Corps indicates.
8. Rexford Tugwell, "The Moses Effect" in Edward Banfield, ed., *Urban Government and Administration* (Free Press, 1961).
9. H. H. Gerth and C. Wright Mills, *From Max Weber: Essays in Sociology* (Oxford University Press, 1948). Chapter 4 develops this theme in greater detail.
10. John Logue and Edwin Bock, "The Demotion of Deputy Chief Goldberg" in Edwin Bock, ed., *State and Local Government: A Case Book* (University of Alabama Press, Inter-University Case Program, 1963), pp. 229–62.
11. Most of the information is from Richard Blumenthal, "Anti-Poverty and the Community Action Program" in Allen Sindler, ed., *American Political Institutions and Public Policy* (Little, Brown, 1969), and Daniel Moynihan, *Maximum Feasible Misunderstanding* (Free Press, 1969).
12. See Moynihan, Chapter 8.

2

THE BUREAUCRACY IN ACTION—
POWER, ORGANIZATIONAL GOALS,
AND THE POLITICAL
ENVIRONMENT

In Chapter 1 the interrelationships of politics and administration and the basis of administrative power were described. In this chapter, power will be examined in some detail and related to organizational goals. The discussion will then link these goals to the political environment of agency operations by examining the relations of the agency to the chief executive, the legislature, interest groups, and other agencies. Particular attention will be paid to the relationships between federal agencies, the president and the Congress.

THE NATURE OF POWER

Power and influence are the medium of exchange in the administrative process. They delineate the success or failure of programs, policies, and persons. Success usually breeds success, as a popular program translates a favorable position into additional resources to expand the program further, thus accreting more power. Conversely, an agency saddled with an unpopular program may see its influence wane and power diminish. It may become, in Norton Long's words, "an object of contempt to its enemies and despair to its friends." [1]

Power is simply the ability of an individual or agency to enforce compliance with their wishes. Power is accreted by accumulating support, goodwill, ability, expertise, money, or any other resource which other persons or agencies value or respect. A professor's ability to give a student a "D" grade is power, as is Congress's ability to investigate the Federal Aviation Agency (FAA). The ability of the FAA to mobilize pilots' associations and airline companies in opposition to such an investigation is administrative power.

Influence is generally defined as the likelihood that another party will be guided in his actions or decisions by values or premises held by another. A subordinate official in the Antitrust Division of the Justice Department may have the view, based on years of experience, that certain types of holding corporations will not be judged illegal in court. The new attorney general and his assistant attorney general for the Antitrust Division may accept his advice despite campaign promises of the new administration. We say, then, that the subordinate had influence over the decisions of his political superior. He had no power, for the attorney general was under no compulsion to accept his advice.

Power represents the ability to compel some sort of action or to punish noncompliance. It involves the possession of resources and sanctions that can be applied on behalf of desired ends. In one sense, influence is also power since it often results in changing behavior to the same degree. However, it involves the absence of sanctions and suggests the effect that expertise, friendship, and proven judgment can have on decisions.

Authority is based on the legitimacy of organizational position or formal office. A superior generally has the authority to discipline an employee, to give orders and assign work. Authority becomes actual power when sanctions can be applied—if the superior can dismiss a recalcitrant employee or at least severely punish him. However, organizational authority and effective power are *not* always the same thing. The president appoints cabinet officers and many lower ranking officials, but he may not have the effective power to dismiss them even if he keeps undated resignations in his desk. Each appointee may represent a commitment to some interest, to some region, or to some program, and the president simply may not feel free to ignore this. President Nixon's appointment of Roy Farmer, a noted black leader, to the position of Assistant Secretary for Administration of the Department of Housing and Urban Development was not made because Mr. Farmer was an effective administrator. It was, purely and simply, an attempt to get blacks into high level administration positions. The choice as secretary for administration was probably dictated by previous commitments for other assistant secretary positions. Regardless of his performance or the length of his stay (Mr. Farmer has since resigned), it was extraordinarily unlikely that he would ever have been dismissed. He was a visible symbol and the effective power to dismiss him, save at unacceptable political cost, was not there.

The same principle applies at a lower level, when a bureau chief is staunchly supported by a particular interest group. Orders by the secretary of the department to change agency priorities and programs may be stub-

bornly resisted and a stalemate may develop. The realities of power dissi-
pate the weaker ties of authority.

There are limits to authority at all levels. A "zone of indifference" per-
mits most orders from a superior to be routinely accepted.[2] When unusual
or inappropriate orders are seen by subordinates as invalid, the "zone of indifference" shrinks and resistance occurs. If the superior has the organizational sanctions to compel official compliance, quiet resistance may occur
by foot-dragging, misplaced papers, and so forth. However, if the superior
persists, he will usually win. If he does not have sanctions (e.g., if the employee cannot be disciplined for some reason), in all likelihood his order
will be ignored.

Hereafter, the term "power" will be used to denote the ability to force
compliance or to accumulate political resources for use in the pursuit of
desired objectives. "Authority" will refer to the formal sanctions of an
office holder whether or not he has the power to compel compliance. "Influence" will be used to describe the process of advising, briefing, and in-
forming those in a position of power or authority.

ORGANIZATIONAL GOALS

While power is often sought for its own sake, it is also sought for the sake
of some program end. Even when sought for its own sake, power is invoked in the name of those programs. This legitimizes the organizational
accumulation of resources or individual demands for control in the name of
an altruistic program goal such as "better service for citizens" or "more
housing for poor persons." Most power seekers have a mixed set of motives; some include policy or program questions while some primarily revolve around personal considerations. Whatever the source of these program ends, however, agencies over time become committed to them. They
become the aspirations and ambitions of the organization as a whole. Once
these ends are developed and articulated, resources are devoted to achieving them. Subsequently, these goals shape the ambitions and orientations
of organization members who hold policy-making positions, and thus shape
future organizational policies in similar directions.

Since goals do provide the primary rationale for seeking power, and are
the basis for almost all purposive action, the question of goal formation is
an important matter. The process of goal formation and the way members
internalize goals is not well understood, however. Ideally, organizational
goals incorporate consistent, clear guides to action for all organizational
members. If this ideal were met, the struggle for power would be a good
deal more organized and predictable. Clearer organizational goals might

result in higher conflict levels, as each actor saw clearly the set of rewards and punishments.

Goals, however, are frequently unclear, often in conflict with each other, and not always linked directly to program ends. Administrative behavior is correspondingly less predictable.[3]

Most discussions of organizational objectives refer to formal and informal goals. Formal goals indicate the legitimized, sanctified set of rules and standards established by the legislature and chief executive. Informal goals are the objectives which the actual application of organizational resources and energies indicates are being pursued. Informal goals may or may not be formal goals. For example, the Army's formal goal is to defend the nation in time of war. Its informal goal may be to maintain technological superiority in military hardware, to support non-Communist countries, or even to provide a mechanism to reform and mature potentially difficult young persons.

There is a tendency for the general public to pay excessive attention to formal goals, ignoring the informal ones. Often the real objectives are not clear even to the leaders of the organization, and leadership rhetoric is unrelated to actual application of resources. In the case of the Army, excessive concern with a narrow definition of national defense without an appreciation of the complexity of the informal goals and their impact on military behavior could be dysfunctional for the agency. Simple deterrence power against any aggressor, for example, cannot be the only concern for Army leaders.

One common type of informal goal is symbolic in nature. The agency, bureau or special title allegedly exists to perform a certain function, but in reality only serves to dramatize the success of its prime movers. An example of this is the president's consumer council. The official goal of this office is to advise the president on consumer affairs, but the informal goal is to indicate the president's support for "consumerism."

Often, informal goals are completely unintended, at least initially, and arise out of social action as the agency adapts to the demands of its members and clients. Many regulatory commissions formally regulate a particular industry in the public interest. Over time, they come to serve, in effect, as the promoter of industry interests.[4] With no overt intention of aiding the regulated interests they serve, their efforts are deflected to reach an accommodation with the interest.

Informal goals arise from the exercise of social power in ways that cannot be justified publicly or are seen as undesirable. These goals may be intended, or may be unintended results of social actions. Power relationships cannot be ignored, but neither can they be officially sanctioned. This is especially true when they involve government actions on behalf of private interests. For example, the net impact of the Labor Department's efforts is primarily to benefit organized labor, but the department cannot make such a statement. It must be coated with more laudable statements about the "public interest" or some other broadly acceptable generalization. The Labor Department must justify its existence in terms of formal goals such as employment security programs to make available job openings. It may have the informal goal of representing the labor movement in government councils and the even less formal goal of preserving a balance of power among competing large unions.

One major informal goal is the maintenance of the organization. Robert Michels' classic work on political parties notes that the original aim of socialist parties was to serve as a force to change society, but that over time the interest was deflected to organizational maintenance.[5] This phenomenon was called "The Iron Law of Oligarchy" to suggest that a small group always seizes control of an organization, displacing the official goals with unofficial ones. While it is not clear that this iron law always comes into play, goal displacement very often does occur. It usually operates to rigidify organizations, to work against rapid change, and on behalf of the survival and growth of the organization. Survival generally involves an emphasis on strengthening the organization, developing support groups in the environment, and maintaining effective relations with the legislature and executive. A newer organization with fewer commitments will devote a higher amount of resources and energies to its program aims. Only later will a commitment to the organization, as a valued object in itself, develop among organization members and outside interests. Then, the organization will likely pursue more limited goals, develop its organizational infrastructure, specialize its subparts, and generally settle into a more or less routine pursuit of more limited goals, one of which is organizational survival.

Perhaps no better example of organization survival could be found than the National Foundation for Infantile Paralysis. By the end of the 1950s, after nearly two decades of work, polio was largely eliminated through development of the Salk vaccine. Having completely accomplished its goal, the organization was a success. However, the foundation was also valued for itself and employees found many rewards in working with it. Thus, rather than abandoning the organization structure, the foundation took on the new goal of combating arthritis and birth defects. Members found a new goal to service the needs of the organization and in this case goal replacement rather than goal displacement occurred.[6]

Goals and Environments. Mere survival alone as a reason for existing rarely shows itself so vividly. When organizations must change, incremental goal adjustments through the acquisition of new executive leaders and recruitment of new members with special skills or different perspectives are much more common methods. Blockages occasionally occur to new programs and to goal adjustments. These are most dramatic when seen at the top level, but somewhat more frequent among lower level employees. When Federal Bureau of Investigation Director J. Edgar Hoover died, he was replaced with Patrick Gray, who seems committed to changing some of the traditional practices of the FBI. In the process, Gray has had to discipline severely some senior agents who were not in sympathy with modified dress codes or more restricted limits on wiretapping.

A classic example of organizational adaptation to meet a special environment (in this case, a hostile one) was the Tennessee Valley Authority's adaptation to entrenched agricultural interests in the Tennessee Valley region.[7] The TVA was a New Deal agency created to develop the Tennessee River Valley, an eight-state, impoverished region. Among its aims were improved navigation and flood control, expanded irrigation, and the selling of nitrogen fertilizers to help farmers increase crop yields. As the first regional agency to unite both government and private interests in the development of private lands, it was regarded with considerable suspicion and even thought by many to be socialistic. Wealthy agricultural interests in both Southern and Border states viewed government intervention as a distinct threat to private enterprise. The TVA soon found that to succeed in many of its programs it was necessary to enlist the cooperation of wealthy farmers and the land grant universities. Poorer tenant farmers and sharecroppers, who in the initial design of the TVA were to be the prime beneficiaries of its endeavors, obviously lacked the influence of the wealthy landowners. In order to achieve its aim the TVA, therefore, was forced to align its policies with the preferences of the individual landowners. One result of this realignment was the TVA's selling the owners of land abutting the new reservoirs enriched land near the new water line which was originally intended for public purposes. Another was the discrimination against blacks in hiring practices.

Since most New Deal agencies tended to centralize authority at the federal level, the adaptation to local views was considered by many to be a major breakthrough in federal-state-local relations.[8] One's view on this matter largely depends upon whether he feels that the TVA should have maintained a nationalizing influence. This was not the question faced by the agency in the late 1930s, however. Survival in a rather hostile arena appeared to the three commissioners to be the question.[9]

One of the ways that the TVA adapted its goals to survive was through cooptation. Cooptation is a way of transferring power to determine organizational goals. Formal cooptation transfers official stature to groups by placing representatives in positions of authority, generally on the decision-making body. The power is generally used to legitimize present practices since the new member is generally unable to change policies or help set new goals. He often bears collective responsibility and credit for the official practices, however.

Unofficial cooptation results when new leadership is taken into power arrangements and actual power realignments occur. This is how the TVA modified its goals in return for support from the dominant forces in the valley. These new power relationships are not always considered legitimate and so the consultation process is informal. This process occurs many places. On some campuses the addition of a few students to the academic senate may serve as official cooptation, while at others private conversations with dissident leaders and agreements over policy matters may serve as unofficial cooptation or actual power-bearing agreements.

Like the TVA, regulatory commissions, and private foundations, public agencies are in a constant struggle with their environments. These struggles broadly represent attempts to set goals for the agency and thus direct its actions for the future. One aspect of administrative power is creation of a favorable or more favorable environment, thus enhancing support for its programs vis-à-vis other agencies. In this respect, the crucial difference between different agencies becomes the nature of each one's environment. Knowledge of environmental conditions affecting an agency could help predict the nature of its power drives, the behavior of key executives, and the nature of many decisions that might not be explained otherwise.

There are essentially three kinds of environmental settings—agency controlled, environmental dominant, and unstable. The latter category includes the vast majority of agencies. The former two types perhaps do not exist as "pure types," but many agencies appear to be similar to them in their interaction with the environment.[10]

Burton Clark notes an example of an agency largely, if not almost entirely, dominated by its environment—the California adult schools. These schools, whose sole function is adult education, are organizationally marginal because their function is seen as less legitimate than educating the young. They rely entirely on their clientele, adult enrollees, for support

since their appropriations are based on attendance. Courses must please
the clientele rather than meet professional standards. There is a strong
tendency for this clientele to demand courses which are not considered
substantial by professional educators, but these must be offered or the students will not enroll. Adults freely determine whether courses are desirable and they generally demand the weaker or less difficult courses. This
trend results in professional disdain for the courses which in turn threatens
long term goals of professional respectability. "The crux of the matter is
that the adult schools labor under incompatible needs." [11]

In a pluralist socialist system there are perhaps no good examples of
public agencies which dominate the environment. The best examples
might be party bureaucracies in totalitarian states, such as the U.S.S.R. or
Nazi Germany, and to a lesser degree, one-party bureaucracies in developing countries. In the latter case, the scope of government power over
citizens is sufficiently limited to reduce environmental dominance. In totalitarian countries, the only effective challenge to the party comes from
within, in the form of internecine power struggles. This was the case in
1955 when Khrushchev and his followers did away with Beria, leader of
the secret police. To the extent that these internal struggles reflect outside
pressures for policy changes, the party organization is not truly dominant.

The case of unstable environments requires slightly more analysis since
the category covers an enormous range of organizations. The concept includes those organizations that have largely come to grips with their environment. There is little need to mobilize resources since their function is
now considered noncontroversial and accepted. These agencies are no
longer in the limelight and barring major changes in societal preferences
can expect to survive and continue their programs with no dramatic
changes. Perhaps the Bureau of Labor Statistics is a good example. It might
be considered unstable only because major changes or controversies do
occur from time to time, and a hard struggle to retain position is called for.
The Bureau of Labor Statistics has in the past been involved in just such a
struggle and perhaps in the future will be again.[12]

At the other extreme are those agencies so convulsed with controversy
that every act and every consideration has critical political implications.
The Office of Economic Opportunity is in such a position, as discussed in
Chapter 1.

James Thompson and William McEwen classify strategies for dealing
with organizational environment as either competitive or cooperative, with
the latter category including three subtypes—bargaining, cooptation, and
coalition.[13] Competition is a struggle between two or more parties with a

third party mediating. In the case of public organization, the legislative committee allocates funds and the president may provide support in a number of ways, based on the outcome of the competition with other agencies for outside and inside support. The legislature and the executive are not neutral referees, of course, but they do bestow rewards largely based on interagency struggles for public support. In this way, the environment partially controls the organization's choice of goals and prevents unitary or unilateral goal setting.

Bargaining, cooptation, and coalition do not directly involve third party controls and are primarily relationships between two or more organizations for their mutual advantage. Bargaining is negotiation of an agreement for an exchange of goods, services, or other resources. Universities bargain the name of a hall in return for the donor's contribution. The Attorney General's Antitrust Division signs consent decrees with firms who promise not to pursue actions further without admitting guilt. To the extent that either party exercises a veto over the other's action, he shares in the decision and thus helps to set goals.

Cooptation has already been discussed. McEwen and Thompson suggest that one of its functions is to provide overlapping memberships on the decision-making group (they seem to be primarily referring to formal cooptation), and thus increase the likelihood that organizations related in complex ways will find compatible goals. Cooptation reduces the likelihood that organizations will pursue antithetical goals and thus serves to unite parts of a heterogeneous society.

A coalition is a combination of two or more organizations for a specific purpose. It involves a commitment to a joint decision or series of decisions, again preventing unilateral one party decision. The Navy and the Air Force may form a coalition to urge nuclear carriers in conjunction with another air wing rather than opposing each other's programs. Universities may form consortiums for social science research or astronomical equipment.

To this point, the relation of environmental interaction, goal setting, and the search for power have been discussed. None can be viewed in isolation, and their interplay is the essence of administrative politics. Let us consider some of the institutional forces and roles which are involved in this complex process.

THE CHIEF EXECUTIVE AND HIS AGENCIES

It is routinely agreed, among citizens and among some political scientists, that the president, or other chief executive such as governor or mayor, is or should be the actual head of the bureaucracy. He should control it, outline broad policy goals if he cannot directly serve as its head, and be held responsible for bureaucratic performance. This view is based on the need to ascribe legitimacy to bureaucratic action by subjugating it to the political responsibility of a directly elected chief executive. Since the bureaucracy is mentioned in neither the United States Constitution nor in most state constitutions, it suffers from a fundamental lack of legitimacy. To remedy this, it is argued that the president should act as chief administrator and direct executive branch agencies in accordance with the policies blessed by his popular mandate. The same argument largely applies at the state and local levels of government. This is an appealing view, centralizing authority and responsibility in a visibly elected executive. It is particularly compelling in developing nations where a strong executive most obviously manifests the spirit of nationalism and is perhaps the only person or institution who can unite groups into a cohesive whole. In the United States, however, popular mandates do not automatically result from electoral victory. The successful candidate may not have support for all his programs, indeed may have been elected in spite of them or in ignorance of them. The mandate argument assumes that every chief executive should centralize the policy-making aspect around his program. This is obviously too simplistic a view of the United States political process.

Even if the president has complete centralized administrative authority, in a presidential system the legislative branch is also strong, and legislators may join with bureaucratic agencies against the chief executive on behalf of one policy or another. Eliminating this source of conflict would strengthen the president vis-à-vis Congress and his own executive branch agencies. But the experience of the Vietnam war suggests that too strong a president may be a mixed blessing, and that conflict and competition among the various actors in the political process may result in better, if slower, decisions.

Practical reasons against executive centralization are even stronger. Holding the president responsible for some one hundred executive branch departments or even for the cabinet departments places an intolerable burden on him and on his personal staff. The president can concentrate only on a fairly limited number of major issues at any one time. He cannot, to take a ridiculously simple example, concern himself with admission rates to the Smithsonian Institute. At the other extreme, he may not wish to be associated, either favorably or unfavorably, with the way the Office of Economic Opportunity operates the Community Action Programs. Lyndon Johnson became involved only when big city mayors protested that their political base, which was the same as Johnson's, was threatened. To act early was either to offend part of the Democratic party's political base, or to offend the "liberal" elements who strongly supported "community action." It was good politics, and perhaps good administration, to let Sargent Shriver take the heat of OEO's peccadillos as long as possible.

The president or other chief executive is a major factor in the program calculations of every federal or state and local agency. Each department seeks, in Richard Neustadt's words,[14] to make the president a clerk for its programs: that is, it wishes him to assent to its budgets, support its programs, and leave policy-making in its area to the department. Like every bureaucracy, a department desires to "use" the president for its own programs and power goals. It also instinctively resists policy innovations which come from the White House which are or seem to be contrary to existing policies. The experience of Eisenhower's conflict with the Agriculture Department and longstanding New Deal programs is well known. Such conflict is played down by the agency because open conflict is more likely to damage it than the president. These disagreements are usually muffled by inaction and foot-dragging, and fought out in memos and conferences between and within the department and the White House. The president can, if he chooses, dramatize the issue by publicizing it and thus tip the balance of power in his favor. By using his resources of popular legitimacy, publicity, and sanctions such as appointment, dismissal (in extreme cases), and the budgetary power, he can normally win any particular struggle. However, the president also has an interest in keeping conflict muted. One reason is that the agency has resources of its own in Congress and in its constituency outside the government. It also can afford to wait since presidents come and go. The most crucial reason, however, is that the president cannot afford to let his public standing be weakened by warfare over what are, ultimately, small matters. The damage to the president's prestige by a losing struggle will imperil his legislative or international goals as well as weaken his power in future battles.

The president also will look, on occasion, to the departments or bureaus for support for his programs. These agencies with linkages to independent power bases can be major sources of support. Their quiet opposition can defeat major policy initiatives while their mere assent may be sufficient to let the White House carry the day.

The Department of Transportation. Lyndon Johnson's successful attempt to create the Department of Transportation (DOT) illustrates the need for agency support.[15] By 1966, even though the federal government was spending billions of dollars on various programs related to transportation, there was no agency or person to consider overall policy. Agencies such as the Interstate Commerce Commission, the Maritime Administration, the Civil Aeronautics Board, the Bureau of Public Roads, the Corps of Engineers, the Coast Guard and the Federal Aviation Agency were all subsidizing, regulating, and administering programs related to transportation. Logic called for a unified Department of Transportation, but opposition from three areas had blocked its creation for many years. The concerned agencies naturally preferred autonomous stature to being submerged in a larger agency. Congress was lukewarm, at best, since many members looked to these agencies for "pork barrel" projects such as roads, waterways, dams, and airports and were not sure that a unified department would be so amenable to congressional demands. Finally, opposition came from the interests themselves. For years the airlines, railroads, and truckers had dominated the agencies created to regulate them. Economic groups with specific interests tended to develop close, symbiotic relations with the regulating agency. Obviously, these groups were not interested in reorganization, unified viewpoints, or efficiency.

Although much more than intrabureaucratic negotiations were required, recounting some of them may explain how essential departmental support was gained for the president's plan. Joseph A. Califano, Jr., Johnson's assistant in charge of the plan, found the Federal Aviation Agency opposed the plan initially because its administrator was afraid of a new level being placed between himself and the president and was fearful of losing authority for the development of the Supersonic Transport plane (SST). Assured that he could retain his salary level and authority for the SST under the new DOT, he assented. The administrator was a former Air Force general with contacts in Congress, and his opposition would have endangered the plan in congressional hearings.

The Civil Aeronautics Board retained its rate-fixing and route-setting authority, surrendering only its authority to investigate safety violations and accidents. Even this modest change took a great deal of negotiation, with the chairman going along only after President Johnson committed himself to the program. His support, as a power in the Democratic party, was necessary to head off potential opposition within the Congress and the party.

The secretary of commerce was reluctant to lose the existing Office of Transportation, preferring to make the Commerce Department the focal point of transportation. He also initially resisted the loss of the Bureau of Public Roads which administers a $3 billion federal highway construction program.

The $130 million urban mass-transit program became a struggle between the proposed DOT and the Department of Housing and Urban Development (HUD). When Secretary Weaver refused to lose the program, President Johnson evaded the issue by appointing a high-level task force which, after a year, ruled in favor of DOT.

After some time it became apparent that DOT would be formed, although it would not include some functions such as the Maritime Administration which had been in the original proposal. At this point, the opponents switched their tactics from opposing the creation of DOT to weakening it by granting internal autonomy to the constituent elements. Concessions which Califano made (1) granted increased autonomy to the major internal administrative units, i.e., the Federal Highway Administration, Federal Railroad Administration, and the Federal Aviation Agency, and (2) delegated DOT's safety authority to a five-man, virtually autonomous, National Transportation Safety Board. This latter decision prevented expert safety decisions from being overruled by political considerations of the DOT secretary.

Within eight months of the initial presidential request for a Department of Transportation, the final act was passed establishing a 90,000-employee department that united most federal agencies in the transportation area; its budget was approximately $6 million a year. Even though the original bill was seriously weakened, its passage was still something of a minor miracle. Without the support, or at least the assent, of the bureaucracies affected, this could not have been accomplished successfully. In this case, the president needed agency support and by negotiation and compromise was able to gain it. The picture is hardly that of the president invoking his statutory power, hierarchical authority, and moral suasion on behalf of his policies. It more clearly resembles that of an equal invoking national necessity and straining to convince another set of equals (Congress, the bureaucracies, and the interests) to assent.

Reorganization. One of the most traditional and time-worn means of attempting to assert presidential control over the bureaucracy is through reorganization. Dramatic reorganizations such as the new DOT require considerable congressional support but lesser combinations of functions and programs can be done by the president alone, subject to disapproval of either house of Congress. The historical reasons for reorganizations revolve around the value of efficiency and the role of the president as coordinator of the federal establishment. Thus, similar programs should be in the same department, linked cheek to jowl in order to establish departmentalization by major purpose.[16]

Under this rationale, the Forest Service should be in the Interior Department instead of Agriculture since it relates more closely to national parks and the use of recreational areas. Similarly, the already mentioned decision to put urban mass-transit grants under DOT seems to centralize transportation functions in one area.

If the multitude of federal programs were reorganized into some rational system, presumably the cost of doing government business would be reduced through the elimination of duplication and overlapping. It would also simplify the task of coordination by program area, such as when three or four federal agencies make grants to local units for the construction of sewage treatment facilities for different purposes and under different funding requirements.

"Eliminating overlapping and duplication" and "straightening lines of command" are among the phrases used to rationalize reorganizations on the basis of efficiency and economy. Some persons argue that program leadership and coordination will be improved without claiming dollar savings (which are always hard to prove), but the official reasons can always be reduced to a base of efficiency.

The unofficial reasons are equally consistent. They are to increase the power and effectiveness of the president, department head, or bureau chief. This is as true at the state and local levels as in Washington. If transportation programs are chaotic, raise them to the cabinet level where the president has more visible leverage and centralize them so that the president's appointee can effectively set policies. If a function has outlived its usefulness and becomes troublesome politically, downgrade its status in the name of efficiency and program rationality.

Reducing an agency's organizational level and official status is a severe blow in rank-conscious Washington. To a bureau or department head, formal access to high level persons or to Congress is an important source of influence. Successful reorganizations are proof that the agency demoted has lost clientele, power, or respect for one reason or another. If it has not, Congress would probably not approve the change. In the case of DOT, Lyndon Johnson's extraordinary legislative majority, as well as his personal political skill, and a national crisis in transportation proved sufficient to subordinate powerful interest group and agency coalitions.

Reorganizations almost always increase the potential influence and power of one agency or interest over others. Justified on the basis of economy, efficiency, logic, and coordination, they actually reflect changes, proposed or existing, in bureaucratic and presidential power alignments. No senior bureaucrat ever forgets this. The president and his staff ignore it at their peril.

The White House Staff. The president has little direct contact with executive branch departments. One recent study of twenty bureau chiefs indicated they had met with the president an average of only once every other year.[17] These bureau chiefs represented a total of 170 years of service and had met with the president only seventy-nine times. Twenty-five of these meetings were with the Internal Revenue commissioner. Disregarding the latter official, the average was only once every three years. The president, of course, is not particularly concerned with many routine functions, although in other cases he will deal directly with the cabinet head. Nevertheless, since the bureau is the key element in most Washington agencies, these figures indicate that there is not a great deal of communication between two key actors in the governmental process. The study concluded that the president might put forward his programs by a personal sharing of his interests with the chiefs. This leaves the strong implication that the bureaus feel no commitment to, or even interest in, the president's program except as it may directly affect them. Since they are in constant contact with congressional committees and with private interests, the president may be losing a chance for some indirect support.

Bureau chiefs form a heterogeneous group composed of both career employees and political appointees whose length of service ranges from zero (in the case of new appointees) to more than thirty years (the late J. Edgar Hoover, for example). They are usually of major help to the president only in areas close to their own programs. Even then, however, there is little contact between them and the president.

Even cabinet officers do not always have access to the president. They have their own programs, he has his. Only when the two join or when the president needs the support of a cabinet member in a matter outside his departmental role do contacts become frequent.

Most presidential-executive branch contacts are between agencies and the president's personal staff or the budget examiners of the Office of Management and Budget (OMB). The president's personal staff and the budget office have become the major arms of the president in dealing with Congress and the executive agencies. As a result, in 1972 OMB had over 600 employees and the president's personal staff (White House Office and special assistants) totaled nearly 600. Henry Kissinger, President Nixon's foreign affairs adviser, has a small bureaucracy of an estimated one hundred persons, all of whom work full-time feeding information to the president through Kissinger. Prior to the Kennedy administration, this function was performed in the State Department; the weakness of the department's analysis, however, caused Kennedy to maintain his own staff.

For better or worse, the White House office has been institutionalized and bureaucratic relations have become stabilized in this manner. Ad hoc intervention by the president is less frequent—rather presidential involvement takes the form of contact between the various agencies and both the budget office and the president's personal staff on programs and policies. The increase in size of the White House staff illustrates Anthony Downs' view that any attempt to control bureaucrats results in the formation of another control bureaucracy[18]—in this case the OMB and the president's personal staff.

Dealing with the White House staff rather than the president or a few persons directly responsible to him has certain implications. First, on fiscal and general management matters, negotiations are conducted with the OMB, an agency with somewhat separate status even in the White House. Dealing separately with Congress on the budget as it does, the OMB may upon occasion find itself with differing views from the president.[19] Merely by being a large office and an institutionalized staff arm, the White House staff leads a life of its own. This may make agencies closer to the White House, but further from the president.

Often the personal assistants to the president do not always speak for the president. There are too many of them and they either cancel each other out or struggle with each other for power. Furthermore, they do not always know what is in the president's mind. Under Lyndon Johnson, there were "a dozen Special Assistants and three or four dozen Assistants' assistants. . . ."[20] Even if a special assistant knows the president's mind and has a true "passion for anonymity" (no longer possible because the Washington press corps has made special assistants better known than most senators), he will nonetheless develop a power base of his own. This occurs simply because he does know the president. Bureaucrats who wished the president of yesteryear to clerk for them and forward their requests to Congress now use the special assistants for their own necessities. This is inevitable, perhaps, but the bureau chief is still no closer to the president. The result, paradoxically, could be that the development of a control bureaucracy in the White House serves to maintain the isolation of the bureaus and assure the insulation and continued fragmentation of federal programs.

Executive Branch Control Agencies

FISCAL CONTROLS. There are two agencies in the executive branch that have significant control responsibilities over other agencies. The first of these has been mentioned—the Office of Management and Budget, located in the White House office. Traditionally, the powers wielded by this agency have been primarily related to its work in developing the president's budget, but they also extend to responsibilities of management improvement and legislative clearance.

Management improvement is aimed at strengthening federal programs and coordinating the many overlapping responsibilities of various federal agencies, particularly those making grants to local jurisdictions. The Nixon administration appears to be very concerned about the inability to rationalize many of the new programs authorized during the legislative triumphs of the Johnson administration's "Great Society."

The budget office of OMB has for many years been responsible for legislative clearance. Agencies are required to submit to the bureau any proposed legislation before it goes to Congress. The bureau circulates the proposal to all concerned or potentially concerned agencies for their views. Only on legislation which is considered "part of the president's program" will the agency be allowed to testify before Congress as a favorable witness. This procedure prevents formal bypassing of the president by agencies. Practically speaking, of course, Congress need pay no attention to the president and can informally discuss legislation with the agencies, although most bureaucrats are careful to observe the clearance procedure.

The states have been active in expanding the budget powers of the chief executive and thus bringing more state programs under his formal powers. Many states have a Department of Finance and Administration, or the equivalent, which exercises most of the centralizing functions associated with the budget process and fiscal-accounting-purchasing controls. Legislative clearance does not appear to be so common at the state levels, and neither does any concerted interest in management improvement. At least part of this is due to the number of individually elected officials and constitutionally separate agencies. The trend, however, is in the direction of greater executive control. Since programs require funding, even modest financial controls over accounting systems and budget programs will tend to increase the governor's strength at the expense of department autonomy.

At the local level, larger cities have moved in the same direction as states. The City of Los Angeles, for example, created a City Administrative Officer post after World War II. The position has major responsibility for preparation of the mayor's budget and has a number of associated fiscal and personnel powers associated with it. Budgetary and fiscal management powers generally have been centralized in cities and school districts with managers and superintendents. In smaller cities, the manager's budgetary authority is one of his major sources of administrative influence. Many managers have been able to force their councils to consider proposals or review previous actions in the light of "financial stewardship." This is a means of transforming political questions into administrative matters upon which the manager has a great deal more weight.

In general, however, neither local nor state governments have moved as far as the federal government in centralizing management-budget-fiscal powers in the hands of the chief executive and departments tend to remain more autonomous.

PERSONNEL CONTROLS. If there is a central personnel agency in the government, it will most likely be a civil service commission or department. Agencies are generally headed by a group of commissioners who govern the agency, hear appeals, and rule on all kinds of personnel transactions. They are normally established by statute to be independent of the chief executive. If there is a civil service or merit system, the central agency generally is responsible for centralized recruiting of personnel, training, transfers between departments, examinations for appointment or promotion, and often for employee-management relations. In a small state or city, one office may suffice for the entire system, while at the federal level most of these functions are delegated to the agencies with the federal Civil Service Commission overseeing them through periodic audits.

Generally, these kinds of personnel controls are not of the same nature as centralized financial/fiscal powers. Their impact is less direct, and unless the chief executive has direct access to the commission, their controls involve procedures rather than policies. They serve an essentially negative function, keeping out unqualified employees and assuring that merit, or at least lack of partisanship, is the primary criterion for personnel practices.

Instead of control, it might be more appropriate to think of central personnel agencies as an obstacle to be surmounted in the game of bureaucratic politics. They often operate as a hindrance to management and offer only modest employee protection. This anomaly arises out of the historical context in which reform took place. Civil service reform arose from the abuses of patronage in the nineteenth century and commissions are still constituted independent of the chief executive as a protection against the spoilsman rather than a positive aid to either the chief executive or the agencies in achieving program aims. While their role and function is changing rapidly, they are still seen in negative terms by both the chief executive and the agency head. The latter struggles against regulations which bind him on promotions, appointments, and dismissals. His concern for "getting the job done" often conflicts with the civil service commission orientation toward assuring perfect equity in personnel transactions. The chief executive is often aligned with the departments against the commission since the commission's interests are not his. He may want political appointments in lower positions than permitted to staff program areas with his own men. Frequently he wishes the commission to take a management orientation focusing on training and top level staffing, while the commission is committed to traditional concerns of recruitment examinations. He rarely cares about equity on a service-wide basis.

On occasion the central personnel agency can become a significant factor in executing public policy if that policy is directly related to personnel practices. The federal Civil Service Commission is responsible for overseeing service-wide policies regarding increased hiring of minorities, handicapped persons, and women. It is a major control agency in this respect, and agencies worry a good deal about quotas.

The only real personnel controls of the chief executive in a large jurisdiction come from his appointive and dismissal powers. This is not a particularly significant source of strength. With exceptions, appointments generally are made to satisfy certain wings of the party or interest groups rather than to advance program goals of the executive. Dismissals are generally messy situations hardly worth the trouble. President Roosevelt tried to dismiss Commissioner Humphrey of the Federal Trade Commission over a conflict of views, but was rebuffed by the courts who ruled that Congress had created the regulatory commissions so that removals could only be for improper acts, not policy differences.[21] Many cases of city managers attempting to dismiss department heads such as police chiefs have resulted in the manager himself resigning or being dismissed. Generally in a civil service system powers of appointment and dismissal by the chief executive have not proven very helpful.

The case is different in a patronage system or in a system with no central personnel program. Here the chief executive may be able to command policy support from the bureaucracy through liberal appointment of friends and supporters after election. Patronage may have no relationship to policy or program questions, of course, but if it is a major factor it still provides political support for the executive. Then the departments will have to deal with him and the executive assumes a larger role in the political calculations of the bureaucracy.

LEGISLATIVE-BUREAUCRATIC RELATIONS

At one time the legislative branch stood preeminently above the executive and the judiciary. This was at a time when the thought of a powerful independent bureaucracy was beyond men's imagination. This dominant position was based on the power of Congress to appropriate money and to authorize new programs or eliminate older ones as well as on the generally shared belief that the legislature was the most representative. Congress has long since lost its preeminence to the president in international affairs (a casualty of the cold war) and to the bureaucracy in many domestic affairs (a casualty of the need for expertise). Even so, Congress is fighting a strong battle to maintain its prerogatives. However, it is losing to the bureaucracy in program initiation as most bills come from the executive agencies and the president initiates most important legislation.

In recent years the practice of "legislative oversight" has developed, which essentially places Congress in the position of overseeing the effectiveness of governmental action. In effect, the role of policy initiation has passed to the president and the bureaucracy, while Congress has assumed the role of policy evaluation. The policy evaluation process takes many forms of checking administrative action and forcing agencies to justify their actions. Sometimes committees even mirror the views of interest groups least influential with the agency to provide a counterbalance to the agency's policies.[22]

These changes have significant effects on relations between the bureaucracy and the legislative branch. The agency still must obtain authorization for any new programs or significant legal modifications to existing ones and must run the appropriation gauntlet each year. In addition, the agency must cope with the legislature's interests in its program—that is, the way it is administered and a host of what the agency would like to consider internal matters of concern only to management.

Most bureaucratic contacts with Congress are between the individual bureau and the congressional committees most concerned with the bureau's program. There remain many informal contacts as the bureaus process requests from individual congressmen, answering letters and preparing reports for them. The more formal and institutionalized contacts involving legislation, oversight, and appropriations are with committees, however. To the extent that these contacts establish enduring relationships between bureau, committee, and interest group, a substantial amount of the bureau's policies become established. However, the president, through his staff, can and will often impose his will on major policy issues, and the Office of Management and Budget exerts a continuing influence through formulation of the budget. In more cases than not, however, the primary relationships affecting the bureau's program come from the triumvirate of agency, committee, and interest groups. The bureau chief generally stands out as the principal mover in this group.

Actual or potential conflict marks many legislative-agency relationships. An important element which underlies much of this conflict is the extensive legislative discretion delegated to administrative rule-making. This has been a factor for many years as Congress has been forced by the complexity of a modern society to grant more discretion to the agency. For example, the 1914 Federal Trade Commission Act states that "unfair methods of competition in commerce, and unfair or deceptive acts or practices in commerce are hereby declared unlawful." The act then goes on to provide that the commission may "prevent persons, partnerships or corporations . . . from using unfair methods of competition. . . ." [23] The act does not, nor could it, say what unfair competition is. Only a specialized agency could make such a determination. At the local level, an equivalent act is the council ordinance requiring all new construction to be conducted in such a manner as to reduce unnecessary noise. The building or planning departments will have to determine what "unnecessary noise" is, when it is necessary, and how to enforce such a nebulous ordinance.

Although congressmen recognize the inevitability of the process, they do not like to relinquish power and are thus very sensitive to administrative exercise of discretion. For this reason they seek legislative control over the administration, largely through contacts with bureaus involving congressional attempts to specify administrative policies and programs.

Cultivating Congress. There are a number of techniques and practices by which a federal bureau chief can attempt to maximize the influence of his bureau or withstand attacks.[24] They are quite similar to the practices of local and state agencies when dealing with their respective legislative committees.

The first is the use of top level support. This is an attempt by the bureau chief to gain support from his department head or other higher administrative official. This is, of course, not always possible since cabinet officers or high ranking administrative officials do not want to become involved in every legislative skirmish. When they can, bureau chiefs trade on the influence of their hierarchical superiors and try to enlist the administration on behalf of the bureau. This is a two-edged sword, however, since higher officials will likely demand bureau backing for other administration programs or demand greater influence in bureau policy in return for support. Involving the administration will enlarge the scope of conflict, and committee members neutral or favorable toward the bureau may be antagonistic toward the cabinet office of the administration in general. Bureau chiefs using this tactic thus run the risk of increasing potential opposition as well as support.

Every bureau engages in what is called legislative liaison. It is nothing more than routine contact with the interested committees and with Congress to assure that information is shared and that the bureau is open to suggestions. It includes bill drafting, arranging testimony, and taking care of miscellaneous complaints and questions voters send to their representatives. Much of this work is designed simply to eliminate as much unintended conflict as possible and to use congressmen in such a way as to maximize their support for and understanding of the bureau.

Social and personal ties are likewise important. These ties involve relationships between bureau officials and both congressmen and interest group leaders. Over years of service strong ties develop between bureau chiefs and those with whom they work, and committee members are more likely to ascribe competence to someone they have seen in action and in whom they have gained confidence. Selection of officials for the bureau from interest groups is another way of assuring Congress that preexisting relationships will not be disturbed, or that future relationships will be more closely joined. Often these are direct ties between the agency and specific congressmen. *The Nader Report on The Federal Trade Commission* specified some circumstances as in the following example.

John W. Brookfield (GS-15), the chief of the Division of Food and Drug Advertising in the Bureau of Deceptive Practices is the nephew of the former Chairman of the House Rules Committee, Representative Howard W. Smith. Fletcher Cohn is now a GS-16 earning $24,477. According to Richard Harrington of *The Washington Post*, March 27, 1966, Mr. Cohn is "the FTC's lobbyist and Ambassador to Capitol Hill." Cecil G. Miles (GS-17, $26,900) is a close acquaintance of a fellow Arkansan, Representative Wilbur D. Mills. He is also bureau chief in the Bureau of Restraint of Trade. The list goes on, but the conclusion is obvious—if you want to float to the top of the FTC, a political friend is the most beautiful buoy in the world.[25]

The circumstances differ in degree rather than kind from agency to agency although the regulatory commissions are notorious for these relationships.

Occasionally, a bureau chief can play one congressional committee against another. Each house has at least one committee dealing directly with the bureau, and each house also has an appropriations committee which considers budget requests. The Senate substantive committee may not agree with its House counterpart, or the budget amounts may vary. Often the authorizations (maximum spending limits) recommended by the substantive committee may be used to justify requests to the appropriation committee for increased appropriations (actual budgets, usually lower than the authorization).

Committee hearings can be used to further bureau interests. This is particularly true if the committee is sympathetic and the bureau has an opportunity to make an effective case for its programs. Even if the committee as a whole is hostile, the presentation makes it possible for a record to be made which gives individually favorable members documentation with which to support the bureau. Aside from the written record, the hearings let the chief demonstrate that he is competent and understands the role of the bureaucrat while deferring to his legislative superiors. This involves giving honest, short answers, acting straightforwardly, accepting legislative suggestions, and demonstrating knowledge of the field. This latter point is extremely important for politically appointed bureau chiefs who are generally assumed to be less knowledgeable than their civil service counterparts.

Committee members can have a significant impact on bureau policymaking. The most obvious way is, of course, by committee disapproval of legislative proposals or by proposing laws or amendments disagreeable to the bureau. In the case of appropriations committees, the budget may be reduced or eliminated (rarely), or padded in places where the bureau is not anxious to expand or undertake programs. The agency can also have its appropriation tied in knots by specific spending limits on small items or by requirements to report back before taking action on certain matters.

Above and beyond these factors is the influence committees have in determining the application of laws. Certain field office locations may be required and others frowned on. The views of certain groups regarding field action may be urged on the bureau and others played down. Legislative preference for massive, selective, or even nonexistent enforcement cannot be written into law, but bureaus are keenly aware of "legislative intent."

Another aspect of legislative-bureau interaction takes place between the committee staff and the agency bureaucrats. For major committees, the staff, working with the chairman, largely sets the agenda for meetings and hearings, follows up complaints, does necessary research, and often shapes committee decisions. The congressman often finds himself as dependent on his own staff as he would be on the bureau without them, and in either case is forced to operate on information given him by bureaucrats. His staff members, of course, are congressionally-oriented and counterbalance the information from agencies. However, they are normally in close contact with the bureau and other executive branch agencies, and some modus vivendi is reached over time. Leiper Freeman states, "Consequently, well-entrenched, well-trained and astute committee staff members are often in quite favorable positions to be 'powers behind the throne,' insofar as committee members transfer their dependency to them." [26] If this is the case, many bureaus should (and do) spend as much time cultivating staff members as committee members. Merciless staff investigations into a bureau can reveal any agency weaknesses more thoroughly than any other process, although this does not seem to be as common a practice as mutual accommodation.

Formal Legislative Controls over the Bureaucracy. Two other devices for legislative control over administrative agencies include the post-audit and congressional investigations.

THE POST-AUDIT AND THE GENERAL ACCOUNTING OFFICE (GAO). The GAO was created in 1921 when the Budget and Accounting Act first established a national budget system. The comptroller general, head of the GAO, is appointed by the president for a fifteen-year nonrenewable term, is confirmed by Congress, and removable only by a joint resolution. He is clearly independent of the executive, operating as a staff arm of Congress. The GAO was originally designed to post-audit government expenditures, determine their legality, and disallow illegal spending, and in performing these duties, it became a check on the stewardship of the executive branch. The GAO later moved into pre-audits, disallowing proposed expenditures to prevent error. This role has been a source of conflict and confusion, since it may take considerable time to approve an expenditure while the program languishes. It also mixes the legislative and executive functions, although it does maximize congressional control. The GAO, since post-World War II days, has also prescribed accounting systems—a major potential source of conflict, although the actual procedures and practices have been mutually agreed upon between GAO and agency.

Since 1950, the GAO has been moving into what might be called "management audits." These are policy-oriented, seeking to determine what the bases for agency decisions and actions were, and go far beyond the question of legality. In 1959, the GAO criticized the Secretary of Agriculture for his actions in setting higher than desirable export prices for cotton. Agriculture was refraining from dumping cotton on world markets, but the GAO regarded the pricing policy contrary to congressional policy. In 1962, the GAO told the Secretary of Health, Education, and Welfare that drug-product testing procedures were not consistent between the Food and Drug Administration and the National Institutes of Health. To emphasize its point, the GAO then reported to Congress what it had done.[27]

The movement toward management/policy audits further strengthens the role of Congress in overseeing policy. As mentioned, the increasing dominance by the bureaucracy and the executive of the policy-making function forces Congress into this role, and in years to come it is very likely that the GAO will see its duties expanded.

At the local level the post-audit is normally performed by an outside auditor in the same way that records of business firms are audited. If the jurisdiction is large enough, the outside firm may specialize in municipal finance and become fairly familiar with a city's accounting and funding system. In almost all cases, the examination is limited to questions of legality, and policy questions do not arise.

INVESTIGATIONS. Congress from time to time has embarked on investigations of one or more executive branch agencies. These are essentially extensions of the overseeing function routinely carried on by regular committees. They differ primarily by the way they are carried on in the white glow of publicity and the partisanship or showmanship manifested by members. The purpose is rarely to uncover facts. Early investigations of the conduct of the Civil War were designed to advance the aims of radical Republicans and little was done to help Congress legislate on military matters. As a consequence, Lincoln was severely hampered in his efforts to conduct the war.[28]

Not much has changed in the intervening years. The McCarthy hearings of the early 1950s played on the cold war fears of the populace and fed the ambitions of the junior senator from Wisconsin. Many security investigations were launched and many persons were dismissed or discredited through the loyalty investigations carried out in all agencies. While some Communist "fellow travelers" were probably ferreted out, many innocent persons were also injured. The impact on executive agencies varied considerably, with some, such as the State and Defense departments, virtually incapacitated. Again, the use of the investigatory power of Congress proved to be a strong control device with which to bludgeon the bureaucracy.

Investigations can have policy implications although they rarely reflect the will of Congress as a whole. Key members have been able to use the threat of investigation, or actually initiate investigations to force an agency to adopt or delete policies favorable to interests represented by the congressman. The Forest Service has been periodically investigated when it has attempted to initiate regulations and policies which stockmen and grazing interests oppose. Senator McCarran of Nevada used the threat of investigation through much of the 1940s to keep the Grazing Service from increasing fees to stockmen.[29] When the Federal Trade Commission adopted a 1964 regulation requiring a warning on cigarette packages, an immediate investigation by the Senate-House Commerce Committee resulted in legislation amending the Commission's rule and prohibiting it from further consideration of a health rule for three years. Final action to strengthen warning labels came after this period when the position of the tobacco lobby weakened.[30]

A favorable investigation can help a hard pressed agency prove its worth by dispelling unfounded charges. If a clean bill of health is given, the agency may emerge stronger than before. Even so, the costs in time, psychic energy, and money in responding to congressional demands for information are heavy. Investigations are inevitable in a system where the legislative body is responsible for reviewing administrative action. Perhaps the best that can be said for investigations is that they are a necessary evil.

NOTES

1. Norton Long, "Power and Administration" in *Public Administration Review* 9 (Autumn 1949), p. 247.
2. Chester Barnard, *The Functions of the Executive* (Harvard University Press, 1938).
3. Charles Perrow, "The Analysis of Goals in Complex Organizations" in *American Sociological Review* 26 (December 1961), pp. 854–65.
4. Samuel Huntington, "The Marasmus of the ICC" in Francis Rourke, ed., *Bureaucratic Power and National Politics*, 1st ed. (Little, Brown, 1965).
5. Robert Michels, *Political Parties* (Dover, 1959). Originally published in 1902.
6. David Sills, *The Volunteers* (Free Press, 1957).
7. Philip Selznick, *TVA and the Grass Roots* (University of California Press, 1949).
8. David Lilienthal, *TVA—Democracy on the March* (Harper and Brothers, 1944).
9. This matter is still subject to interpretation since at least one of the original commissioners was strongly in favor of local mores, and the board make-up eventually reflected his views. It is not clear if a "nationalizing" board would also have felt compelled to adopt the same policies.
10. James D. Thompson and William McEwen, "Organizational Goals and Environment" in Amitai Etzioni, ed., *Complex Organizations* (Free Press, 1961), pp. 177–86. Also see Perrow. Thompson and McEwen note that the only controlled agency may be a commuter railroad which can neither cover costs nor cease operation, while gigantic industrial monopolies such as the Japanese Zaibatsu or the New Jersey Standard Oil may have truly controlled their environments, but these are very rare.
11. Burton Clark, "Organizational Adaption and Precarious Values" in Etzioni, pp. 159–67. Quotation from p. 167.
12. Kathryn Arnow, *The Attack on the Cost of Living Index* (Bobbs-Merrill, Inter-University Case Program, 1951).
13. Thompson and McEwen, pp. 180–86. This outline is largely based on their work.
14. Richard Neustadt, *Presidential Power* (Wiley, 1964).
15. This account comes from Patrick Anderson, *The President's Men* (Doubleday Anchor, 1969), pp. 425–33.
16. This is the primary criterion of Luther Gulick in "Notes on the Theory of Organization" in L. Gulick and L. Urwick, eds., *Papers on the Science of Administration* (Institute of Public Administration, 1937). This article is the basis for and the definitive statement of the efficiency rationale for organization. Chapter 4 covers it in more detail.

17. David Brown, "The President and the Bureaus: Time for a Renewal of Relationship?" in *Public Administration Review* 26 (September 1966), pp. 174–82.

18. Anthony Downs, *Inside Bureaucracy* (Little, Brown, 1967).

19. Aaron Wildavsky, *The Politics of the Budgetary Process* (Little, Brown, 1964).

20. Anderson, p. 476.

21. Humphrey's Executor v. United States [295 U.S. 602 (1935)].

22. Leiper Freeman, *The Political Process: Executive-Bureau-Legislative Committee Relations*, rev. ed. (Random House, 1965).

23. This example is from Peter Woll, *American Bureaucracy* (Norton, 1963), p. 121.

24. Freeman relates these techniques in detail.

25. Edward F. Cox et al., *The Nader Report on the Federal Trade Commission* (Richard Baron, 1969), pp. 136–37. Mr. Cohn is described earlier (p. 132) as a protégé of the Crump machine in Tennessee who was sent to Washington after being defeated for reelection to the state legislature.

26. Freeman, p. 29.

27. Both examples are from Joseph Harris, *Congressional Control of Administration* (Doubleday Anchor, 1964), pp. 166–67.

28. Harris, pp. 282–83.

29. Harris, p. 302.

30. Lee Fritschler, *Smoking and Politics* (Appleton-Century-Crofts, 1969).

3

STATE AND LOCAL
BUREAUCRACIES IN ACTION

THE INTERGOVERNMENTAL NATURE OF PUBLIC EMPLOYMENT

If there is a typical government employee, he (she) does not shuffle papers in Washington, but rather grades them in a Little Rock or Duluth school district. Three-quarters of all American civilian public employees work for state and local governments, over half of them in educational activities. The post-World War II growth in state and local services and in their expenditure and employment capacities has been nothing less than astounding. The demand for public services has resulted from urbanization, population growth, and affluence. Increased levels of expectation combined with higher service standards set by professionalized public officials to increase further the number of government employees. Finally, societal crises such as war and the growing awareness of poverty and discrimination have added impetus to the growth of public payrolls.

Most domestic services such as education, police protection, and welfare have traditionally been provided by cities and states. This explains why the expansion of public services has been considerably greater at these governmental levels. While state and local officials are influenced heavily by national or federal standards and supported by funds from Washington, they nevertheless meet the public and perform the service that the public demands. Citizens are more intimately familiar with local officials and services than with any other level of government, although the morning paper headlines may focus their attention on the president and Congress.

Consider some figures about public employment and spending. Table 3-1 indicates government employment levels in 1952 and eighteen years later in 1970. Several conclusions stand out. While federal civilian employment has increased slightly over 10 percent in this period, state and local employment has more than doubled. The number of employees engaged in educational services has nearly tripled in this eighteen-year period. The population explosion and the increase in social expectations is shown most dramatically by the higher enrollments of school children and college students. The inevitable result is more teachers, more administrators, and more service personnel.

TABLE 3–1

Civilian Employment by Level of
Government and Function, 1970 and 1952
(In thousands)

Function	1970			1952		
	Total	Federal	State-Local	Total	Federal	State-Local
National Defense	1,200	1,200	—	1,342	1,342	—
Post Office	731	731	—	525	525	—
Education	5,316	19	5,297	1,884	11	1,873
Highways	612	5	607	460	4	456
Hospitals and			—	589	157	432
Health	1,202	193	1,009	—	—	—
Police Protection	538	30	508	254	16	238
Natural Resources	404	221	183	292	171	121
Public Welfare	259	—	259	—	—	—
Corrections	146	—	146	—	—	—
Local Utilities	277	—	277	—	—	—
Financial Administration	334	94	240	—	—	—
General Control	412	43	369	—	—	—
Other	1,567	317	1,252	1,959	358	1,042
Total	12,998	2,851	10,147	7,105	2,583	4,522

SOURCE: United States Bureau of the Census, *Historical Statistics on Government Finances and Employment*, pp. 60–61 (1963); *Compendium of Public Employment*, p. 20 (1969); and *Public Employment in 1970*, p. 7 (1971).

Other functions have shared in these increases. The health-hospital service system has more than doubled. This service area may increase even more rapidly than education in the future as people live longer and as young people demand better medical care. Police protection has also more than doubled in this period, and increases were noted in the staffs of courts and in corrections facilities.

Certain large jurisdictions employ a very high percentage of state and local officials. Table 3-2 gives the employment totals in the nation's largest state, California.

TABLE 3–2

California State Employees as of October 1970

Fulltime Equiv	180,604
Education	73,139
Higher Education	69,221
(Teachers only)	26,262
Highways	19,541
Natural Resources	12,203
Hospitals	23,355
Police (Highway)	8,300
Corrections	10,290
Financial Administration	10,435
Welfare	2,502
Other	21,785

SOURCE: United States Bureau of the Census, *Public Employment in 1970*, p. 19 (1971).

California may seem small in relation to the federal government, but all fifty states employ approximately 2.5 million persons, almost as many as the federal government. California's 195,000 employees, some in rather large bureaucracies, such as the University of California, the State Department of Natural Resources, and the California Highway Patrol, pose major administrative, management, and personnel problems. Certainly they have a major impact on the formulation and execution of public policy.

The major employers outside of federal agencies, however, are not the states but the large urban governments. Here is the cutting edge of the urban crisis. If students at a university burn their draft cards, city police or county sheriff's deputies must arrest them for this federal crime. If a federal order desegregates city schools, local school district buses drive students to their new teachers. Federal and/or state moneys may finance most county hospital expenses, but the county staffs and operates them. Table 3-3 gives a view of some of the largest local employers.

Local governments come in varied sizes, shapes, and forms. Cities and counties are general purpose units of government, while smaller, more localized systems are normally restricted to one function. School districts, for example, concentrate their energies on the one broad function of providing education. Similarly, hospitals and transit authorities are single function

TABLE 3-3

Selected Local Government Jurisdictions with Large Numbers of Employees, October 1967

Jurisdiction	Total	Employment in Selected Functions						
		Health	Public Welfare	Hospitals	Police	Highways	Education	Fire
Los Angeles County	52,465	2,013	9,147	12,344	3,017	2,014	21	—
Cook County	20,486	93	5,167	6,955	1,239	1,407	—	—
New York City	348,448	—	—	38,213	31,839	5,234	93,233	13,885
Boston	24,996	—	—	5,094	3,757	791	6,881	2,092

Jurisdiction	Students	Total	Teachers*
Detroit School District	298,027	20,408	13,178
Los Angeles School District	632,498	43,888	29,455

Jurisdiction	Total
Chicago Transit Authority	12,482
Port of New York Authority	8,129
Fulton-DeKalb Hosp. Auth. (Atlanta, Ga.)	2,398

* Full-Time Equivalent

SOURCE: United States Bureau of the Census, 1967 Census of Government: Employment of Major Local Governments, Vol. 3, No. 1 (Washington, D.C., 1969).

units, although in the case of the latter (especially in large cities like New York), services may include a wide variety of activities ranging from maintenance of bridges and tunnels to modernizing subway, train, and bus systems.

These are crucial public services. The quality of education, transportation, and police protection is largely determined by these local governments. If urban life is to be made more attractive, the effort will have to begin at the local level.

Professionalization and Merit Systems. Not as much is known about state and local bureaucracies and bureaucrats as is known about their federal counterparts. Most academic discussions rely on broad generalizations or specific case studies. Good comparative, empirical data is rarely found. Even so, the information we do have is sufficient to gain an overview of subnational bureaucratic politics. Generally, the interaction between bureaucrats and politicians at the state and local level is very similar to that at the federal level, given differences in scale.

Professionalization is perhaps the major variable when comparing federal to state and local bureaucrats, and in distinguishing between agencies, states, and localities in the capacity to carry out public policies. Without highly skilled professionals such as engineers and public health sanitarians, agencies cannot develop the expertise necessary to provide services at an acceptable or desired level. Great variations of professionalization exist at the subnational level. One major differentiating element involves the existence of a merit system in a particular agency. Professional occupations are much less likely to be attracted to a non-merit system. As merit systems develop, professionals are attracted to the state or local agencies and staffs expand. Since large, expert bureaucracies contend for power more successfully than small or weak agencies, the development of professionals in an organization is often a prelude to influence and ultimately power.

Merit systems, then, have greater significance for the political process than their status as merely a "good government" reform would indicate. These implications are most clearly seen at the state and local level, where patronage or weak merit systems are still common. Focusing on this point first requires a review of the merit principle at all levels of government.

MERIT SYSTEMS. Most persons expect that government employment will be based largely on objective merit, that is, a rational matching of personal qualities with a particular job. Usually, overt failure to accomplish this has serious political repercussions although there are major pockets of irregularity that still remain. These expectations are of recent origin in the

United States as it was not until fairly recently that merit replaced patronage as a major criterion for choice at all levels of government.

Merit is a subjective term. It could be demonstrated in other ways than by a pencil and paper test, or by advanced educational degrees in a certain field. Service to a man, to a party, or to a policy is often reason enough for employment. So is need. In other countries, religion and kinship are often criteria. In the United States, veterans receive absolute preference, and certain other groups such as racial minorities, women, and the physically handicapped are eagerly sought in an effort to achieve quotas. These examples are all infringements on the merit principle and represent deviations deemed necessary to meet social problems greater than a "pure" merit system. Other than veteran's preference, these infringements indeed indicate a relatively new demand for representation of all groups within the bureaucracy. No matter how great the social problems, however, defenders of a "pure" merit system resist these infringements. If Americans really wanted to redress discrimination against blacks, for example, we could give them the same benefit points (normally 5 to 10) on their qualifying entrance exams that are extended to veterans.

A modern merit system emphasizes, as mentioned, "objective merit." In the 1970s, this means that subjective questions, such as party loyalty or friendship with an office holder, are irrelevant, if not disadvantageous. When applying for a government position, most persons take an examination which may be written and/or involve an evaluation of their credentials. Scores on the examination and an oral interview generally are used to rank candidates on a list in order of demonstrated ability to perform the work (to the extent that a test can measure this ability). The agency or department head then chooses a person from this list, usually from among the three highest scorers. The recruit then must complete a probationary period as part of the examination, generally six months to a year, before he or she receives a permanent appointment. Removal is then only for specific cause. This prevents political meddling with the service and protects the employee from abuses of discretion by his supervisor. Barring unusual changes in the agency's mission or appropriation level, the employee can expect to remain with the agency as long as his work is satisfactory and can, therefore, establish a civil service career. Civil service systems are merit systems monitored by a civil service commission, while merit systems refer broadly to any system emphasizing objective merit. They are virtually synonymous.

Patronage systems were dominant for much of our history and still are a basic part of many jurisdictions. Not until well into Franklin D. Roosevelt's administration were many federal positions "blanketed in" with civil service status. Until 1969, first-class postmasters were generally appointed on a partisan basis with service to the political party or congressman in power a dominant criterion. By 1970, about 90 percent of all federal employees were subject to merit personnel policies.

In the case of FDR, apparently the New Deal agencies were to be staffed initially by adherents of the service, men fired with the zeal to remake America through these new agencies. Later, the positions were placed under civil service regulations. This illustrates a primary argument for staffing agencies with political supporters. Only then can a newly elected executive be assured a supply of personnel fully committed to the success of his administration and not wedded to previous policies. The argument has considerable merit, but it is normally carried to the extreme of demanding that most lower level, nonpolicy-making positions be vacated for a new cadre of party faithful. Uncontrolled, the inevitable results are inefficiencies and the breakdown of agency morale and quality of traditional services.

As government grows more specialized and technical, and citizens desire a higher quality of service, patronage systems simply do not work. However, for low-level or unskilled jobs, elements of patronage systems are still somewhat common. In other cases, the political ethos of a state or local unit may be "job-patronage" rather than "program-issue" centered. Citizens in these patronage-oriented units prize availability of jobs rather than quality of service. Certain states such as Kentucky and Tennessee have achieved a reputation for patronage consideration although it is by no means limited to them, and Chicago appears honeycombed with political adherents of the dominant Democratic party machine. Frequently political behavior which seems strongly "job-oriented" is simply a matter of economics—in a poverty culture, such as Appalachia, the availability of employment is a major policy question. There, to argue for professionalization is to ignore reality.

Patronage systems are more likely to exist where government is not highly visible and where the political culture does not prize honesty or efficiency. Certain states, on this basis, may be more resistant to merit systems than large cities. About thirty states have comprehensive merit systems although federal requirements for a merit system in grant-in-aid programs have established partial merit systems in all states. Many special districts do not have merit systems, nor do many small cities. Bureaucratic development in the United States has always depended upon legislative sanction, which comes slowly after public opinion has formed. Thus, the type and quality of public employment has tended to mirror public opinion although there is an inevitable political lag. This characteristic is in contrast to many other nations where the executive branch and its bureaucratic tradition developed before a strong legislature. At the national level in the United States, the shape, orientation, and efficiency of public bureaucracies generally have been subjects of keen interest, particularly to groups with a special interest in the program. At the state and local level, this is not so true and while concern has developed over executive power and the role of the chief executive, the actual operation of state and municipal services has not always been a highly salient issue.

PROFESSIONALIZATION. There is relatively little empirical evidence regarding the professionalization of state and local government employees. Ira Sharkansky has estimated variations in professionalization among states and found that the states differed widely on two factors, salaries and fringe benefits. Large, highly industrialized and urbanized states such as California, Ohio, and New York tend to pay high salaries but give low fringe benefits, while low salary states such as Idaho, Mississippi, and Louisiana provide relatively high fringe benefits.[1]

There was little relationship between spending for functions such as welfare or education and quality of state professionalization. There was some association of spending and professionalization where the highest salaries were paid in the most urbanized counties, suggesting that upgrading of state government may begin in large urban centers, possibly because of the demands of urbanization.[2]

Measuring professionalization by salaries has limits. Another approach is merely to count those persons in key occupations.[3] One study indicated that there were nearly 900,000 persons in professional or managerial positions in state and local government in 1964, of whom 441,300 were professionals. While this was only 6.1 percent of the over seven million total employees, it is an important figure because it represents the professionals who provide many of the crucial public services (see Table 3-4).

To the extent that key social functions of government are rendered by organizations largely built on professional expertise, this small group exercises influence out of proportion to its numbers. A great deal of social power rests in the hands and on the judgment of the heads of these agencies, particularly when they are "professionals" also. Martha Derthick found, for example, that almost all variation between Massachusetts city welfare agencies was due to the attitude of the welfare administrators. Mandated program levels and state-federal funding were certainly the cru-

TABLE 3-4

Professionals Employed in State and
Local Governments, 1964

Profession	Number Employed
Accountants	20,000
Dentists	1,500
Engineers	70,000
Foresters	4,500
Lawyers	14,200
Librarians	24,000
Physical Therapists	2,500
Physicians	10,000
Planners	4,000
Psychologists	5,000
Public Health Nurses	37,000
Recreation Workers[a]	30,000
Registered Nurses	125,000
Rehabilitation Counselors	2,700
Sanitarians	8,000
Social Workers	75,000
Vocational Counselors	2,900
Other[b]	5,000
Total	441,300

[a] Full time only.
[b] Includes other occupations such as purchasing agents, medical records librarians, pharmacists, speech pathologists, audiologists, mathematicians, statisticians, actuaries, artists, historians, economists, sociologists, etc.

SOURCE: United States Department of Labor, *Occupational Outlook Handbook*, Bulletin No. 1450 (Washington, D.C.: 1966).

cial factors. But a good deal of spending variation remained and attitudes of program directors toward recipients accounted for it.[4]

Likewise, major variations between Massachusetts cities in traffic citations are largely if not entirely accounted for by the individual police chief's attitude toward speed limit enforcement. City policies changed radically on a number of occasions when new chiefs were appointed.[5]

The influence of these agencies and their leaders is largely dependent on environmental forces. Welfare and police decisions rest ultimately on broad public support. Variations between states and most local units, accountable partly to organizational leadership and professionalism, are most dependent on the political cultures of each state or local unit.

Political Culture. The use of the term "political culture" as a surrogate for the political environment of state and local bureaucracies has intuitive advantages as well as some empirical basis. Bureaucracy in Illinois, where the influence of political leaders pervades, differs greatly from that in Minnesota or Oregon, where individual merit and skill are prized more than influence. The differences and their implications for political and administrative behavior are obvious.

Daniel Elazar has developed the concept of political culture to the point of defining three types of political culture and applying them specifically to states and regions in the United States. The cultures developed originally from religious and ethnic minorities merging with political ideologies (e.g., the Progressive movement) or with economic subsystems (e.g., southern plantations).[6] These three types are individualistic (I), moralistic (M), and traditionalistic (T). See p. 62.

The individualistic political culture holds politics to be just another means by which individuals may improve themselves socially and economically. In this sense, politics is a "business" like any other that competes for talent and offers rewards to those who take it up as a career. . . . The I political culture is ambivalent about the place of bureaucracy in the political order. In one sense the bureaucratic method of operation flies in the face of the favor system that is central to the I political process. . . . In the end, bureaucratic organization is introduced within the framework of the favor system; large segments of the bureaucracy may be insulated from it through the merit system but the entire organization is pulled into the political environment at crucial points through political appointment at the upper echelons and, very frequently, the bending of the merit system to meet political demands.[7]

Under most circumstances the widest variations in professionalization would be found in individualistic political cultures which generally include the major industrialized states in the belt from Illinois to Massachusetts. Here, we would expect to find highly professional, merit-based agencies cheek to jowl with agencies dominated by patronage and personalistic considerations. Likewise, one would expect to find agencies stratified by levels, with lower ranking employees carefully selected by civil service procedures and higher ranking employees (not merely the top policy-making positions) selected for particularistic, nonprogrammatic concerns. Generally, the administrative process in I cultures will represent the range in values of the culture itself and certainly will not reflect any monistic view of the public interest.

The moralistic political culture is quite different. Politics is considered a struggle to determine the good society and is valued as a worthwhile process: ". . . Both the general public and the politicians conceive of politics

as a public activity centered on some notion of the public good and properly devoted to the advancement of the public interest." [8]

Issues play a major role in M politics, and while views of the general
welfare may vary greatly, the political process is usually "programmatic"
with the victor having a greater or lesser mandate to implement these programs.

> The M political culture's major difficulty in adjusting bureaucracy to the political
> order is tied to the potential conflict between communitarian principles and the ne-
> cessity for large scale organization to increase bureaucratic efficiency. . . . Other-
> wise, the notion of a politically neutral administrative system creates no problem
> within the M value system and even offers many advantages. Where merit systems
> are instituted, they tend to be rigidly maintained.[9]

Moralistic states generally correspond to the major thrust of the Progressive movement earlier in the century.[10] Civil service or merit systems are
stronger in these areas. States such as Wisconsin, Minnesota, Michigan,
Oregon, and some of the New England states manifest the M culture most
strongly. These are generally less urban states. Their smaller population
and lower per capita incomes may make the development of professional
bureaucracies more difficult. Even with their apparently more congenial
attitudes toward government action, they may be less able to meet the pay
schedules and social attractions of more urban states.

Traditionalistic cultures are associated with the old South and border
states, and are related to a preindustrial social order such as a plantation or
sharecropper economic system. The T political culture ". . . is rooted in
an ambivalent attitude toward the marketplace coupled with a paternalistic and elitist concept of the commonwealth. . . ." [11] This culture tends to
reflect a hierarchical or stratified social structure as part of the given order
and an expectation that the social "elite" will rule. Thus family and social
ties are very important.

> . . . traditionalistic political cultures tend to be instinctively anti-bureaucratic be-
> cause bureaucracy by its very nature interferes with the fine web of informal inter-
> personal relationships that lie at the root of the political system and which have
> been developed by following traditional patterns over the years. . . .[12]

Although several of the states, such as Mississippi and Louisiana, tax themselves very heavily, T culture states have the lowest levels of government
services. The generally low level of industrialization in these states has resulted in a very low per capita income which in turn restricts the states'
ability to provide services. Highly professional bureaucracies are not likely

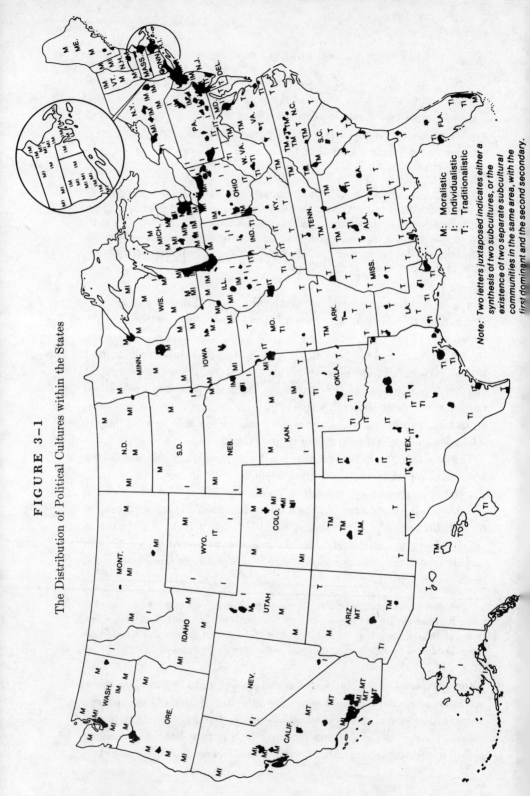

FIGURE 3–1

The Distribution of Political Cultures within the States

M: Moralistic
I: Individualistic
T: Traditionalistic

Note: Two letters juxtaposed indicates either a synthesis of two subcultures, or the existence of two separate subcultural communities in the same area, with the first dominant and the second secondary.

SOURCE: Daniel Elazar, *American Federalism: A View from the States*, 2nd ed. (Crowell, 1972), pp. 106–107. Copyright © 1972. Reprinted with permission of Thomas Y. Crowell, Inc.

to be found here due to lack of resources and the cultural antagonism toward them.

These differences among regions and within states based on political culture appear to have some effect on bureaucratic attitudes and structures. One study found that bureaucratic structural elements such as hierarchy, professionalization, and specialization were more related to behavioral characteristics of state executives in Minnesota than in Iowa.[13] Minnesota is characterized by a very strong M culture, while Iowa is relatively more individualistic. This is the direction that Elazar's concept of political culture would predict. Minnesota created a civil service system in 1939, whereas Iowa enacted a civil service system only in 1965. Lack of such a system in Iowa might have retarded bureaucratic development. Later civil service system installation in less moralistic cultures is normally to be expected. Other studies indicate different variations from region to region.[14]

Another form of political culture, at the local level, involves types of city governments. The categories include amenities cities, which stress a high level of urban services; development cities, which emphasize growth; caretaker cities, which stress a low level of services and taxes; and arbiter cities, which primarily resolve group conflict.[15] Amenities and development cities are most congenial to city managers and hence to a professionalized local bureaucracy, size being held constant.

Political culture explains only a portion of bureaucratic behavior. Most public executives place program expansion and agency autonomy near the top of their value structure. The classic, and typical, response to reorganization proposals was made by the head of a Mississippi agency:

I think this is one of the best things that has ever been done in the state of Mississippi and I have long been of the opinion that this work should have been accomplished in the past. However, my department is of a type, character and kind that cannot be consolidated with any other agency, as its duties and functions are unique, and a reduction of personnel or a transfer of any duties of this department would work a hardship and prevent certain citizens from receiving benefits to which they are entitled.[16]

Forces other than culture have a powerful impact on professionalization and, ultimately, on power. After a certain point, organizational size results in sufficient expertise to influence or actually dominate policy-making. These large institutions usually are found in large urban centers, and their sheer size demands, or at least is associated with, highly professional employees (see Table 3-3). At this point in our history, bureaucratization and professionalization seem to be associated more with large local governments than with small local units or states.

State and Local Bureaucracies and the Chief Executive. Sooner or later, professionalization becomes translated into power. The professional group eventually will feel compelled to mobilize its clientele to support the agency. Agency heads, because of their role as agency representatives and because they support professional norms, usually find it necessary to become involved in the political process. Their activities in mobilizing support, servicing legislative committees, interacting with clientele, and carrying on an uneasy love-hate relationship with the chief executive are much the same as their federal counterparts'. The power they wield varies largely with the size and professionalization of the jurisdiction, as well as with the strength of the chief executive.

LARGE URBAN GOVERNMENTS. The largest units of local government are marked by a high level of bureaucratization. They vary somewhat in relation to the strength of competing political institutions, such as the executive and interest groups. Large cities have fairly strong political institutions. Political parties are active, there is a separately elected executive, the political system is highly visible, and the individual bureaucracies must contend among themselves for power and appropriations.

In some cities, relationships between the bureaucracies and the chief executive resemble cautious sparring between political equals. In cities like Chicago, where the party and mayor are all-powerful, all policy matters must be cleared personally with the mayor or his aides. This is rarely a problem, since there is little policy initiation by the bureaucracies. Most major urban functions continue today in much the same way as in the past. Police work, fire protection, and sanitation are labor-oriented. Short of money as cities are, modest pay hikes for employees and perhaps the hiring of a few more employees are the best that can be expected. Occasionally on a major policy issue, such as police review boards, there may be severe differences, but in these matters the bureaucracies frequently are successful.

New York may be a more representative example than Chicago. There, power within the city itself is hopelessly divided among different agencies. The budget bureau rules financial matters and the functional bureaucracies rule their own empires. The mayor must make his peace with these agencies which have split the administrative process into unrelated bits and arrogated the policy-making process to themselves. From the agency's point of view, the mayor's job is to get them additional funds, if not from Washington, then by wrenching a few more pennies from the local property tax. Agencies act, the mayor and/or council reacts. Even political tickets are balanced with the leaders of these agencies.[17]

The result, according to Theodore Lowi, is that cities like New York are better run, but worse governed. The fragmentation of power has increased expertise through specialization, but the task of governing has been rendered almost impossible. There is insufficient executive power to accomplish urban goals or any set of coherent ideals and programs.[18]

Other large urban units tend to be less visible but often have as large and powerful bureaucracies as cities. Large school districts often fuse the bureaucracy and the superintendent. The governing board may or may not play a policy-making role. The single function nature of school districts leads to relatively high levels of bureaucratization, with less administrative and political pluralism than in large cities. This is a major factor in the power of professionalized, unionized teacher bureaucracies. The recent situation in New York where the teachers' union confronted city desegregation policy in the Ocean Hill-Brownsville battle was a good example of the increasing influence of large school bureaucracies.[19]

Very large, special districts, such as the Port of New York Authority (which controls bridges, subways, airports) and the Metropolitan Water District of Southern California are somewhat similar to school districts in fusing legislative, executive, and administrative functions. They are even less visible although the services they provide are crucial to urban life.

Large urban counties such as Westchester in New York or Los Angeles in California, have competing bureaucracies of welfare, police, and health, as well as greater differentiation of legislative and executive functions. Even so, bureaucracies there are not always as visible to the public as those in large cities. Even the more urban counties still retain rural vestiges. Thus, demands are often not transmitted because of the lack of political party influence or competition.

Urban bureaucracies comprise the upper portion of Figure 3-2. These agencies are most highly bureaucratized and, to the extent that other political institutions are weak, they suggest major imbalances in bureaucratic-political relationships.

SMALLER UNITS. Smaller units of government present greatly reduced dangers of bureaucratic domination. Here the problem is achieving a satisfactory level of professionalism.

Smaller local jurisdictions with a separately elected chief executive include mostly cities with rudimentary bureaucracies. Issues between the agency and chief executive usually are settled around a table on an informal basis. The underlying consensus is based on propinquity, deeply shared values about grass roots control, and acceptance of most urban functions as routine and technical. In many cities of moderate size, ranging

FIGURE 3-2

Bureaucratic Power in Local Government Institutions

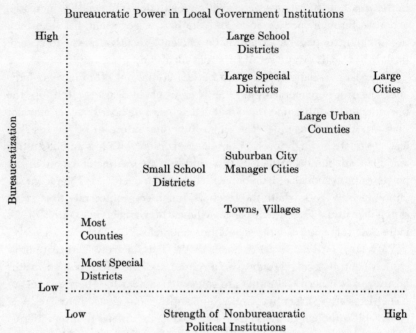

generally from 50,000 to about 250,000, urban tensions are mounting. The mayor may have public visibility and be expected to launch an attack on some urban problems. In contrast to the position of the large-city mayor, the office of a mayor of a city of moderate size usually politically overwhelms the modest size and professionalism of the bureaucracies. Consequently, this mayor *can* provide program leadership unlike his larger city counterparts, although such leadership varies considerably from city to city and issue to issue. In water fluoridation issues, for example, his support is generally crucial to success, whether through council action or referendum.[20] His position on busing or quality education may be irrelevant, however, because school districts generally control educational policies.

The remaining local governments (with few exceptions) do not have a separately elected executive. The 3,000 or so counties rely on control through the chairman of the board of supervisors, plus direct election of many department heads, such as sheriff or commissioner of education. The small size of most counties makes most interaction personalistic, and policy leadership by a county board chairman is relatively rare.

Other small urban units include city manager cities, school districts, and special districts. In these cases, the executive largely operates as part of the bureaucracy. Most special districts are so small and their authority limited to so few areas that the legislative board of directors and the chief engineer or semi-professional manager casually and informally settle program matters among themselves. The board of directors is usually intimately familiar with insect control or irrigation and develops a close relationship with the executive that mutes political conflict. In any case, special districts operate in virtual secrecy, due in part to public ignorance and the non-controversial nature of the function.

The city manager and the school superintendent are career professionals who usually move from city to city and district to district. They serve at the pleasure of the council and the school board, with superintendents generally under contract for a specified period. They not only control and coordinate departmental programs, but represent the bureaucracy before the executive body. To a large degree, they are in but not of the local bureaucracy. As they are experienced and professional, their views are normally accepted by legislators. The job of career agency personnel is thus to convince the manager or superintendent that programs and policies are meaningful and are being carried out properly. They generally speak to a sympathetic ear. However, the executive is familiar with the departmental programs, and he is likely to want his own type of programs and to be able to get the legislative body to support him. Unless the department heads are long-time local residents with some standing before the council or school board, city managers and school superintendents will prevail; they do, after all, have appointive and budget powers in their control. City managers have been dismissed because local police chiefs resented their "meddling" with their departments, and superintendents have left after struggles with their boards over curriculum. However, these cases are generally less frequent than ones where the appointed executive is able to change existing programs and policies of the council and/or school board.

Figure 3-2 indicates graphically some of the points made in this section. Most smaller units of government fall into the low part of both axes, since these political institutions are not highly developed or visible, and the bureaucracies are not professionalized. Small cities and towns are more likely to have some established political leadership than other units. Medium-sized cities with professional city managers are in an intermediate position. They have potentially powerful bureaucracies, but also have separate executive and legislative controls able to exercise countervailing power over departments. In all cases involving small units of government, bureaucratic power seems unlikely to develop to the level of New York City.

State Bureaucracies and the Governor. When considering agency-governor relations, it quickly becomes apparent that the enormous variations between states prevents easy generalizations. Furthermore, the various states have not been the subject of intensive study as has the subject of presidential-executive branch relationships. Probably even less is known about state agency-chief executive relations than at the local level. Even so, certain cautious statements can be made.

State government bureaucracies cannot easily be identified or evaluated. Probably only the highway patrol and the university system loom large in the eyes of citizens.[21] In addition to the lack of visibility of the state bureaucracies, many are rather small. Under these circumstances, personal relationships between the governors and the bureau chiefs or even lower ranking officials flourish. Personal relationships, the perquisites of rank, and a private club atmosphere—all combine with the lack of visibility to cause wide fluctuations in bureaucratic power vis-à-vis the governor.

In most states, there is elected competition for such positions as state auditor, secretary of state, attorney general, and superintendent of education, as well as many heads of agencies with specific program orientations such as the university regents or the commissioner of agriculture. There is a tendency toward eliminating election of department heads, but the pace is slow. In states where these offices are elective, it is obviously more difficult for the governor to control and intervene directly in agency programs.

In general, the longer a governor's term and the more terms he can be reelected, the greater his influence. Nelson Rockefeller of New York will have served at least sixteen years by the end of his term in 1974, while G. Mennen Williams served six two-year terms in Michigan during the 1950s. Conversely, New Mexico and South Dakota allow their governor only one reelection to a two-year term, while fifteen other states limit their executives to one four-year term.[22] Obviously, the "short-termer" has less time to make his mark on state administration and can be outwaited by recalcitrant bureaucrats.

The governor's formal power is another variable. His ability to make appointments to key executive positions ranges from almost complete authority to appoint all sixteen major functions and offices in Tennessee to almost complete powerlessness in Colorado, where most departments are headed by civil service appointees or are separately elected.[23] Appointment powers may or may not mean much in terms of actual power, given variations in removal power or whether an elected executive ran with the governor's ticket.

Deil Wright found, in a study of 900 state executives, a slight tendency for the formal powers of the governor to be associated by administrators with greater controls over agencies. This tendency was very strong when appointive powers were considered. The more the governor is involved in appointments, the more he is perceived as having influence.[24]

In any case, a majority of administrators believe the governor to be more sympathetic than legislators to their particular agency: 55 percent mentioned the governor and only 20 percent the legislature, with 25 percent saying "about the same." Wright indicates that this finding supports the argument that the governor is the primary institutional means through which new or expanded state programs are advanced, advocated, and accepted.[25]

A more important variation in formal power is the budget power. Most states now give their governor full responsibility for preparing the budget. The power to allocate funds may be the most important weapon the governor has even though prior budget claims and fund shortages usually cramp any initiative he may wish to undertake. Most state legislatures are much weaker than Congress, making legislatively initiated changes in the chief executive's budget unlikely. When the governor also has the power of the item veto, he is able to put almost absolute maximums on agency spending by eliminating what he believes to be excessive legislative appropriations. States with these characteristics, Illinois and California, for example, have seen agency programming become largely dependent on the governor. The bureaucracy must come to terms with him, particularly in those states where the chief executive can be reelected for an indefinite number of four-year terms. Governor Ronald Reagan of California, in particular, has used the item veto and budget power to whip the state university system into his line of thinking. Reagan's actions, however, indicate that formal powers do not prescribe all the limits of gubernatorial power, since it is highly unlikely that he would slash as deeply as he did if he were not confident of popular support. Conversely, Joseph Schlesinger notes that the governor of North Carolina lacks a veto but appears no weaker than other Southern governors.[26]

Political variations within each state in all likelihood account for most variations in governor-agency relationships. Concern over reelection may divert a governor from program concerns, or the ineligibility for reelection may give him the luxury of concentrating on administrative matters to the pleasure or consternation of the affected agency.

Patronage is another consideration since many states still lack a general merit system. Where the system has patronage positions, jobs can still be used for a variety of reasons.

Since governors do come and go, in all probability, the crucial variable in governor-agency relations is the professionalism and strength of the agency. A strong, competent agency can normally count on gubernatorial support. A weaker agency is less likely to receive support and more likely to have the governor concern himself with modification of its programs.

CARROTS, STICKS, AND THE INTERGOVERNMENTAL SYSTEM

Federalism is one of the major structural elements in the United States political system. It affects the nature and complexity of the political and administrative relationships between and among state, local, and federal officials. Federalism is a method of distributing power between the national and subnational levels in such a way as to protect and assure the existence and authority of both levels. In the United States, both levels share national decision-making and policy execution processes. National unification is enhanced by this complex, dual system.[27] In America, states have a great deal more constitutional and actual or real power and sovereignty than in many other federal systems. Cities are legally creatures of the states, although they have independent authority granted them by their respective states, and they can deal directly with the federal and state levels as equal partners. This results in far different outcomes and public policies than if a more centralized federal system, or a unitary system, existed.

The result of this three level "marble cake"[28] is a complex, shared relationship in which all levels initiate both national and subnational public policies and share in their performance. This characteristic is in contrast to a more specialized system of providing a specified set of duties at each level—the entire political system is not three layered, as in a cake, but marbled throughout. As noted, national unity is enhanced and the system is generally functional for a large, heterogeneous society. At times, however, it has had unfortunate results, as in the case of racial discrimination.[29] Since subnational units of government have real sovereignty, they are able to maintain behavior patterns or policies which are dysfunctional for the nation as a whole although obviously popular in a particular state or city.

Since federalism has resulted in sharing between levels of government, largely through a weak party system feeding local preferences into the national legislative process, local, regional, and particularistic preferences have always been important in the United States. These preferences have made important impacts on the provision of public services, on governmental policy-making, and on administrative behavior.

Federalism strengthens the interrelationship between politics and administration. Every public official deals, at one time or another, with a different level of government, and he will need the cooperation of each to accomplish his goals. Many officials spend much of their time with counterparts at other levels, and some spend almost all their working hours in intergovernmental relations. A public health officer in a small city, enforcing state and local laws required by federal standards and financed by federal funds, is a common example. So is an urban renewal specialist in the Department of Housing and Urban Development who spends his days explaining the program to local officials and in inspecting local plans and programs.

Morley Segal and Lee Fritschler identify four types of political interactions between state-local and federal officials in the intergovernmental arena.[30] *Joint policy-making* is marked by cooperation and sharing, usually between program specialists and professionals at different levels. Conflict often occurs between agencies at the same level competing for funds.

Mutual accommodation is marked by competition and bargaining. "Decisions are made within functional subsystems, including congressional delegations as well as appropriate interest groups, congressional committees, and executive agencies. It is in the type 'mutual accommodation' that the federal aid coordinators might make interventions in the process on behalf of or in spite of those within the functional hierarchies." [31]

Innovative conflict is characterized by deliberate manipulation of the intergovernmental system to accomplish the goals of one or more of a set of actors. An example is a federal agency's refusal to wink at guideline violations of, say, the 1964 Civil Rights Act. The "feds" lack political power to compel requirement, so they are forced to bargain, persuade, and negotiate within the intergovernmental system. The tension is creative, or it can be, for participants are forced to innovate and develop new means of accomplishing goals.

Disintegrative conflict represents a breakdown in cooperation between the federal and state and/or local government. For example, when, in 1963, Governor George Wallace attempted to bar the entrance of a black student to the University of Alabama, he was representing the state's defiance of a federal law.

Conflicts, cooperation, and shared duties are not limited to domestic affairs. Mayor Daley and the Chicago Police Department were much more lenient with 10,000 demonstrators against French President Georges Pompidou on a visit following his decision to send jets to Libya in 1969 than they were with youthful demonstrators at the 1968 Democratic National

Convention. In the former case, it was necessary for President Nixon to make a special visit to Pompidou in New York to smooth Franco-American relations. Pro-Jewish sentiment ran high since it was widely assumed that the jets would be used by Arabs against Israel. Thus the Mayor overlooked more than he might have otherwise. Another classic example was Los Angeles Police Chief Parker's veto of a Khrushchev visit to Disneyland in the early 1960s merely by asserting that he would not assure the Russian Premier's safety. The State Department was dismayed, but under the circumstances able to do little but assent.

Even an examination of the frequent contacts between officials at all levels of government over various issues and programs does not reveal the depth of the sharing relationship. The process is built so deeply into administrative operations that it is largely unconscious, like the act of breathing. There is hardly a function, service, or activity at the state and local level that does not involve the federal government in one way or another, as Table 3-5 shows. Benton, Arkansas, located near Little Rock, was a town of 10,148 in 1957. It has no particular or unusual relationship to the federal government or the state of Arkansas, and was selected by Morton Grodzins as a typical small town. It shows clearly the complexity and pervasiveness of the shared functions in the American governmental system.

Intergovernmental Finance. The present intergovernmental system is a complex blend of historical, social, and political factors. The glue that keeps it together is money. The carrot for lower levels of government[32] is the subvention or grant-in-aid. The stick is the requirement for state and/or local performance at a level set by the federal government and the matching of the federal grant with state or local funds. This is the best known example of intergovernmental finance and usually is the primary basis for a higher level of government to obtain compliance by a lower level.

Much intergovernmental finance involves shared revenues where a higher level of government, usually the state, makes money available to a lower level for unrestricted use. The state collects the taxes and remits them to local units on the basis usually of population or of point of collection; this is the case with many sales taxes and motor vehicle taxes. In some cases, a higher level of government has a semi-contractual agreement with a lower level regarding provision of certain functions which are necessary for the convenience of the higher, such as local maintenance of a state highway. Sometimes the higher level pays for costs it imposes on the lower as in the case of federal payments to impacted school districts, where large federal installations have burdened the school system.

TABLE 3-5

Governmental Services in Benton, Arkansas, 1958

1. Activities for which city government has little or no responsibility.[a]

Service	City of Benton	Special District	County of Saline	Special Local Government Engineered by U.S.	State of Arkansas	United States
Agricultural conservation and stabilization				**	*	**
Agricultural extension			**		**	**
Bank examinations and deposit insurance					**	**
Education		**	**		**	**
Employment security					**	**
Farmers Home Administration						*
Industrial safety					**	*
Inspecting boilers, weights and measures, other commercial inspection	**		*		**	**
Inspecting food and drugs			**		**	**
Labor relations					**	**
Postal service						**
Public health	*		**		**	**
Public welfare			**	*	**	**
Selective Service				**	*	**
Soil Conservation Service			*		*	**

2. Activities for which city government has important responsibilities.

Service	City of Benton	Special District	County of Saline	Special Local Government Engineered by U.S.	State of Arkansas	United States
City planning and zoning	**				**	(b)
Civil Defense	**		*		**	**
Fire protection	**				**	
Garbage disposal	**				*	
Library	**				**	(c)
Parks	**					
Police	**		**		**	**
Public utilities	**d	**			*	**
Recreation	**					**
Sewage disposal	**		*		**	(b)
Streets and highways	**				**	**

** Major role * Minor role

ᵃ This section of the table is abbreviated and is only meant to be illustrative

ᵇ Federal aid pending

ᶜ Federal aid under discussion

ᵈ Utilities are operated under a three-man commission appointed for life by city council.

SOURCE: Morton Grodzins, *The American System* (Rand McNally, 1966), p. 75. Copyright © 1966. Reprinted with permission of Rand McNally and Company, Chicago.

Another form of relationship is a tax forced upon the lower level. The higher level gives a credit to the taxpayer for the amount paid to the lower level, or takes the full amount if the lower unit does not levy the tax. This is the way the federal government forced Florida and Nevada to enact estate and inheritance taxes. It is also the way that some states force localities to add a penny or so to the sales tax, thus making it partly a local tax. There are many other arrangements similar to these. However, the primary interest here is on the grant-in-aid relationship between the federal government, on one hand, and the states and/or local units on the other.

At the turn of the century, states and localities provided services from the property tax or other miscellaneous levies that they collected. The federal government was concerned mostly with international and military affairs, which it financed with tariff revenue. However, the property tax now consumes each year over 3 percent of the value of the taxable property in many urban areas, precisely at the time when demands for urban highways, housing, welfare, and education have also reached a peak. Some localities pay even higher percentages. State revenues, even when expanded to include sales and income taxes, are also reaching taxpayer limits. Because the relatively regressive state and local tax systems simply are not providing sufficient revenues, states and cities now look to the federal government for financial help.

The income tax, which the federal government initiated in 1913, has become the most lucrative source of federal income. Although states are increasingly instituting their own income tax systems, the revenue that will accrue to them will never match that which the federal government earns. As helpful as property and sales taxes are to the states and localities, they are not nearly as elastic as the income tax since revenues from the latter increase more rapidly as individuals move into higher brackets.

Thus, the federal treasury is potentially a major source of new revenues for the hard-pressed cities and states. Another reason for looking to Washington is that it is much easier to enact a tax from a distance than in a crowded city council chamber or in a state legislature subject to close scrutiny or immediate citizen access.

Another reason that federal grants-in-aid have expanded over eightfold from 1948 to 1967 is that these grants have been used largely to obtain state and/or local cooperation in national programs which must be operated where lower levels have traditionally provided the services (see Table 3-6). The Federal Highway Program is a good example. It was apparent that Washington would have to finance a huge part of it (90 percent) through a federal tax. However, state and local cooperation was essential,

TABLE 3-6

Expenditure for Selected Major Civil Functions
by Level of Government, 1967 and 1948
(In millions of dollars)

Function	1967				1948			
	Total	State-Local	Federal Grants	Federal Direct	Total	State-Local	Federal Grants	Federal Direct
Education	$40,214	33,999	3,920	& 2,295	7,721	4,961	418	& 2,342
Highways	14,032	9,873	4,059	100	3,071	2,718	318	35
Public Assistance	9,592	3,984	4,234	1,374	2,144	1,375	724	45
Hospitals	6,951	5,440	119	1,392	1,398	937	—	461
Health	2,506	791	290	1,425	536	292	—	244
Police	3,331	3,048	1	282	724	664	—	60
Total	76,626	57,135	12,623	& 6,868	15,594	10,947	1,460	& 3,187
Percentage	100.00	74.6	25.4		100.00	70.2	29.8	

SOURCE: United States Department of Commerce, Bureau of the Census, *Historical Statistics of the United States—Colonial Times to 1957* (1964), pp. 723–29; *1967 Census of Governments* (Vol. 4, No. 5, *Compendium of Government Finances,* 1969), p. 32; *1967 Census of Governments* (Vol. 6, *Historical Statistics on Government,* 1969), pp. 37, 40, 52.

so federal grants financed (and continue to do so) state-built expressways which must adhere to federal standards. Public housing is another example where it was apparent that only federal funding could hope to make a somewhat unpalatable and controversial program locally acceptable.[33]

Without federal support, welfare payments in many poorer states would be even further below the present minimum level. As it is, most of the state and local spending is concentrated in areas already funded by the federal government so as to match federal grants in these areas, rather than apportioning it where the real need may be. Aid to families with dependent children is relatively well-supported; general assistance is often neglected.

Federal grants have not only financed badly needed services, they have upgraded the personnel involved in providing the service. Since 1940, all states receiving grants under the Social Security Act have been required to place their public employees under a merit system. Similar requirements apply to grants for public health, vocational rehabilitation, and child welfare. For many states these are virtually the only employees under a merit system.

A more significant factor than the merit system in upgrading state and local bureaucracies has been the acquisition of more highly qualified professional employees in the expanding areas. Social workers, airport managers, sanitarians, highway engineers, and many other occupational professionals have been attracted to state and local public service. Many of these occupations are primarily found in state and local public services, which are in turn largely federally funded.

Closely related to the development of professionalized staffing in federally funded areas has been the increase in service standards. This was the primary intention of federal funding in the first place, and the development of merit systems or professional staffs was only the means to an end. In the case of fish and game departments, federal research funds aim to develop wildlife programs based on rigorous field research rather than intuition or past experience. Therefore, it is necessary to employ professional biologists to assure accomplishment of this goal.[34]

Frequently, functional linkages of specialists between levels of government develop. A state wildlife specialist may feel closer and more responsive to his federal counterpart in the National Forest Service than to his administrative head in the state capital. This speeds the dissemination of information, increases cooperation, and generally improves the quality of a state wildlife program. It also reduces the influence of immediate supervisors, slows agency reaction time to state political issues, and tends to fragment state and local organization practice. Functional linkages are both a bane and a blessing.

The federal system has never been without strains. Still today, as in the past, race relations and desegregation divide the American public. Struggles over busing children to overcome school segregation are only the latest controversy. A new dimension has been added, however, as the "urban crisis" of the 1960s and early 1970s threatens to engulf us. At heart it is a crisis of expectations. Americans expect higher standards of public service, the elimination of poverty and discrimination, and a higher quality of life in our central cities and older suburbs. The triumph of President Lyndon Johnson's "Great Society" legislative program in 1965 promised an attack on poverty, medical indigence, discrimination, and assorted urban and societal ills. But race riots and urban unrest developed at the same time and were intensified by weaknesses in the national economy. At this writing, there is severe polarization within the United States. On the surface, it is embodied in the continuing Vietnam war, but there are deeper feelings that much of American society, particularly in cities, is out of control. There is sober academic discussion over whether New York City and perhaps other large cities are "ungovernable." [35]

Most larger cities and many suburbs are indeed plagued by a number of very serious problems. These include, but are not limited to, drug abuse, racial polarization, shrinking tax bases and increasing demands on the budget, increasing welfare rolls, declining educational quality provoking teacher militancy leading, in some cases, to strikes, and blight in the central business districts matched by traffic congestion as people drive downtown to work, but do not shop. Despite great public concern, federal legislation, and the spending of considerable sums of money, urban problems seem to be growing worse. The shared relationship between levels of government does not seem to be working well. The infusion of federal moneys into state and locally administered programs has not brought relief to urban problems—indeed, sometimes it seems to exacerbate them.

Oakland, California, may be taken as a reasonably typical example. A study of the federal government's impact on Oakland revealed a multitude of programs within the city. Most of them were aimed at a specific urban problem and associated with one of the thirty-seven federal agencies active within the city. Some of these programs had more direct impact than others, but all reflected a "federal presence" which, according to high level directives, was to concern itself with urban problems.[36] A list of the agencies follows:

Department of Agriculture
Department of Commerce, Economic Development Administration
Department of Defense
Defense Contract Auditing Agency
Department of the Army, Sixth Army Headquarters
Department of the Army, U.S. Army N.W. Procurement Agency
Department of the Army, South Pacific Division, Corps of Engineers
Defense Supply Agency
Department of the Navy, 12th Naval District
Department of the Army, Office of Civil Defense
Department of Health, Education, and Welfare
Department of Housing and Urban Development
Department of Interior
Bureau of Outdoor Recreation, Pacific Southwest Region
Geological Survey
Federal Water Pollution Control Administration
Department of Transportation
Federal Highway Administration
Department of Labor
Executive Office of the President, Office of Economic Opportunity
Small Business Administration
Department of Justice
Immigration and Naturalization Service
Community Relations
Treasury Department
Bureau of Customs
Post Office Department
National Labor Relations Board, Region 20
Federal Power Commission, Regional Office
Securities and Exchange Commission, Regional Office
Civil Service Commission, San Francisco Region
Veterans Administration
Veterans Regional Office
Veterans Canteen Service Field Office
Railroad Retirement Board, Regional Office
Interstate Commerce Commission
Atomic Energy Commission

The study attempted to analyze the federal role in Oakland and to assess the impact of federal programs.[37] The complexity and variety of these programs, however, largely defied analysis. In reality, there was no federal role or presence in Oakland. Rather, there were many unrelated and uncoordinated agency programs, sometimes working at cross purposes. Coordination was variously referred to by researchers as a "rare occurrence" or "a peripheral happening." For example, HEW-supported hospital construction grants were not coordinated with California's comprehensive health-planning process, even though parts of this process were being funded by another federal program. Potentially related programs of federal job training and development also were not considered.[38] There was no consensus among federal regional officials regarding any federal role—only a generalized feeling that more emphasis on their own agency programs was necessary. City officials were likewise unable to identify and set priorities. Lacking any overall goals, they set aside scarce local funds to meet whatever federal grant required the least matching. The entire process was essentially random in its impact on urban problems. Local officials were unhappy with the process, the rigidity of federal programs, and the lack of coordination between federal agencies as well as between agencies and the city.

It also proved impossible to identify specific outputs and results from federal programs, particularly those involving human resources. There was little data available to measure the impact of these programs on the recipients, partly because of the complexity of program goals and partly because a demand for follow-up data had not been made. Reporting systems among agencies were not consistent, and most agencies made little attempt to assess costs and benefits.

> The absence of clear and precise data regarding the federal presence in Oakland . . . poses a number of serious difficulties with respect to the analysis of federal urban assistance programs. . . . It becomes highly difficult, if not impossible, to gauge the real effectiveness of federal programs in specific cities, let alone on a national basis. . . .[39]

In terms of local income generation, the nine programs studied in depth varied from $0.22 per federal dollar for an urban renewal project to $1.10 for a neighborhood youth corps program. Generally, "software programs" such as job retraining generated more local income, on a short-term basis, than "hardware programs" such as public works or housing. The inability of federal agencies to produce relevant data on funding and processing procedures made it impossible to develop a long-term model for evaluating impact.[40]

The general conclusion that emerges from the report is that federal program impact has a largely undetermined effect, despite the noted rough estimates. It seems almost impossible under present regional arrangements and decision-making processes to analyze this impact more carefully. Decentralization through large blocs or unrestricted grants poses an alternative arrangement, but there is little reason to believe that local officials have much better guidelines for their own programs.

There is serious question about how well public officials understand the nature of urban problems. The Oakland report and the example in Chapter 1 of the antipoverty program raise the next logical question: can programs be effective if no one understands the urban system? The Report of the National Advisory Commission on Civil Disorders (the Kerner Commission Report) had this to say about the impact of federal programs in urban areas:

The spectacle of Detroit and New Haven engulfed in civil turmoil despite a multitude of federally-aided programs raised basic questions as to whether existing "delivery system" is adequate to the bold new purposes of national policy. . . .

. . . There are now over 400 grant programs operated by a broad range of federal agencies and channeled through a much larger array of semi-autonomous state and local government entities. Reflective of this complex scheme, federal programs often seem self-defeating and contradictory; field officials unable to make decisions on their own programs and unaware of related efforts; agencies unable or unwilling to work together; programs conceived and administered to achieve different and sometimes conflicting purposes.

The new social development legislation has put great strain upon obsolescent machinery and administrative practices at all levels of government. It has loaded new work on federal departments. It has required a level of skill, a sense of urgency, and a capacity for judgment never planned for or encouraged in departmental field offices. It has required planning and administrative capacity rarely seen in state-houses, county courthouses and city hall.

Deficiencies in all of these areas have frustrated accomplishment of many of the important goals set by the President and the Congress.

In recent years serious efforts have been made to improve program coordination. During the 1961–65 period, almost 20 executive orders were issued for the coordination of federal programs involving intergovernmental administration. Some two dozen interagency committees have been established to coordinate two or more federal aid programs. Departments have been given responsibility to lead others in areas within their particular competence—OEO in the poverty field, HUD in Model Cities. Yet, despite these and other efforts, the Federal Government has not yet been able to join talent, funds and programs for concentrated impact in the field. Few agencies are able to put together a comprehensive package of related programs to meet priority needs.

There is a clear and compelling requirement for better coordination of federally funded programs, particularly those designed to benefit the residents of the inner city. If essential programs are to be preserved and expanded, this need must be met.[41]

Questions have been raised for many years about the effectiveness of federal grants and their alleged rigidity. The Oakland Task Force Report verifies these deficiencies and the Kerner Commission Report publicizes them in light of a national emergency. The belief of most administrators, federal, state, and local, is that urban problems are soluble if enough money and talent are applied. This assumption has been severely called into question.

NOTES

1. Ira Sharkansky, "State Administrators in the Political Process" in Herbert Jacob and Kenneth Vines, eds., *Politics in the American States*, 2nd ed., (Little, Brown, 1971), p. 264.
2. Sharkansky, pp. 264–70.
3. The following information is from Edward Seidler, *An Investigation into the Relationship of Professionals and State and Local Governments* (unpublished Master's thesis, San Jose State College, 1967), pp. 5–8.
4. Martha Derthick, "Intercity Differences in Administration of the Public Assistance Program: The Case of Massachusetts," in James Wilson, ed., *City Politics and Public Policy* (Wiley, 1968), pp. 243–66.
5. John Gardner, "Police Enforcement of Traffic Laws: A Comparative Analysis," in Wilson, pp. 151–72.
6. Daniel Elazar, *American Federalism, A View from the States* (Crowell, 1966), pp. 85–116.
7. Elazar, pp. 87–89.
8. Elazar, p. 90.
9. Elazar, p. 92.
10. See p. 106, "Public Administrative Model" for a discussion of the political and administrative implications of this movement.
11. Elazar, pp. 92–93.
12. Elazar, p. 94.
13. Catherine Papastathopoulos, "A Bureaucratic Model for the Comparative Study of Administrative Behavior" (unpublished paper, Louisiana State University, 1970).
14. Deil Wright, "Executive Leadership in State Administration" in *Midwest Journal of Political Science* 11 (February 1967), pp. 1–26.
15. Charles Adrian and Oliver Williams, *Four Cities* (University of Pennsylvania Press, 1963). For an attempt to apply these types, see John Rehfuss, "Political Development in Three Chicago Suburbs," a paper presented to the American Political Science Association in Chicago, September 1971.
16. Karl Bosworth, "The Politics of Management Improvement in the States" in *American Political Science Review* 47 (March 1953), p. 90.
17. Theodore Lowi, *The End of Liberalism* (Norton, 1969).
18. Lowi, p. 204.
19. It has been argued that in New York school teachers have never really chosen either professionalization or unionization, and that their behavior is not "professional" nor atypical of large districts as a whole. This may be true, but their behavior seems typical of New York City public agencies. In any case, the organization possessed expertise, since no one else could teach school, and power, since they blocked undesired city action in many cases.

20. Donald B. Rosenthal and Robert Crain, "Structures and Values in Local Political Systems: The Case of Fluoridation Decisions," *Journal of Politics* 28 (February 1966), pp. 169–96.

21. Joseph Schlesinger, "The Politics of the Executive" in Jacob and Vines, Chapter 6. He suggests that state politics is not particularly visible to the citizen compared to the national and local levels (pp. 208–9). My own views coincide with his. Harmon Zeigler and Kent Jennings come to somewhat different conclusions using survey data. The responses they report, however, merely mark a form of psychological-ideological commitment to the concept of "state level" rather than any ability to evaluate state services or hold the governor or bureaucracy responsible for programs. See their "The Salience of American State Politics" in *American Political Science Review* 64 (June 1970), pp. 523–36.

22. Schlesinger, p. 220. Data as of 1960.

23. Schlesinger, p. 224.

24. Wright, p. 16.

25. Wright, p. 7.

26. Schlesinger, p. 228.

27. This brief discussion of federalism is largely from Elazar, p. 2.

28. Morton Grodzins, *The American System* (Rand McNally, 1966).

29. William Riker, *Federalism* (Little, Brown, 1965), attributes the continuation of segregation almost wholly to the federal system.

30. Morley Segal and Lee Fritschler, "Policy-Making in the Intergovernmental System: Emerging Patterns and a Typology of Relationships," a paper delivered to the American Political Science Association in Los Angeles, September 1970.

31. Segal and Fritschler, p. 26.

32. It is customary to refer to the national level as the highest level of government and local units as the lowest. Thus funds go "down" to localities from Washington much as orders go "down" the hierarchy of an organization. The bias of terminology is evident.

33. See Martin Meyerson and Edward Banfield, *Politics, Planning and the Public Interest* (Free Press, 1955) for a classic study of the controversial nature of public housing.

34. John Owens, "A Wildlife Agency and Its Possessive Public" in Frederick Mosher, ed., *Government Reorganizations* (Bobbs-Merrill, 1967), pp. 116–49.

35. See, for example, "Focus on New York," a special issue of *The Public Interest* 16 (Summer 1969); and "Governing the City: Challenges and Options for New York" in *Proceedings of the Academy of Political Science* 24, no. 4 (1969).

36. While I am not aware of specific memoranda or directives, the development of regional Federal Executive Boards with Critical Urban Problems Committees suggests this high level of interest. These FEBs are made up of every head of a program in a region. The San Francisco FEB was a co-sponsor of the Oakland Survey.

37. Oakland Task Force, San Francisco Federal Executive Board, *An Analysis of Federal Decision-Making and Impact: The Federal Government in Oakland* (Praeger, 1968).

38. *Ibid.*, p. 78.

39. *Ibid.*, p. 55.

40. *Ibid.*, p. 137.
41. *Report of the National Advisory Commission on Civil Disorders* (Bantam Books, 1968), pp. 411–12. This commission, known as the Kerner Commission, was in 1967 charged by President Johnson to look into the causes of the racial disorders in American cities, starting with Watts and spreading into some dozen or more cities in the summer of 1967. The section on federal programs is instructive in the context of this book, but only incidental to the main thrust of the work in analyzing "white racism" in America.

4

THE NATURE OF LARGE ORGANIZATIONS AND TRADITIONAL VIEWS

BUREAUCRATIZATION OF LIFE IN MODERN SOCIETY

Patterns of life in the United States, as elsewhere in the world, are changing rapidly. Many of these changes result in more and more individuals working for fewer and fewer organizations. The number of small farms is declining while corporation farms flourish. The professions expand and an individual is more likely than ever to be working for an organization, rather than self-employed. Technology and urbanization are now the dominant forces in our lives, rather than church and neighborhood. The old sacred myths have been replaced by new secular realities and the change is unsettling, as much of the current turmoil over pornography, drugs, and social justice amply indicates.

Both the rationalization of society, as the German sociologist Max Weber termed it, and the modernization process, as political scientists call it, refer to the same thing—a change in cultural values to more universalistic, predictable, demystified patterns of behavior. These changes then support the development of social institutions which we now see as large bureaucracies in both the public and private sphere.[1] Bureaucracies require a certain impersonal, other-directed type of behavior, a concern with the application of specialized means toward given goals and a devotion to non-family or non-kinship affairs. These attitudes are found most commonly in modern, rationalized societies, such as Western European countries and particularly the United States.

Large Organizations in the United States. The study of organizations is of vital importance to us. They determine where we work, often where we live, what kind of people we will meet, and other vital personal questions. In addition, the study of organizations can be justified in itself as being a necessary contribution to social knowledge. A final reason concerns the social power of bureaucracies. In some cases it is so great that it (and thus, the bureaucracies) may pose blockages to democratic policy-making by their possession of vast political resources and their demands on both the government and citizens. Secondly, organizational demands for employee conformity and passivity raise basic questions about individual freedom and individualism.

Most Americans work for a large bureaucracy; General Motors, the United States Post Office, and American Telephone and Telegraph (AT&T)—each employ more than 700,000 people. See Table 4-1 for the personnel figures of fifteen large American organizations.

TABLE 4-1

15 United States Organizations Employing
the Largest Number of Employees

Organization	Number of Employees
General Motors	793,924
American Telephone and Telegraph	735,856
U.S. Post Office	730,977
Department of the Army (Civilian Only)	486,859
Ford Motor Company	436,414
Department of the Navy (Civilian Only)	430,205
General Electric	400,000
Sears, Roebuck, and Company	355,000
International Telephone and Telegraph	353,000
City of New York	348,448
Department of the Air Force (Civilian Only)	316,230
International Business Machines	258,662
Chrysler Corporation	234,941
State of California	213,488
United States Steel	204,941

SOURCE: For private corporations: "The Fortune Directory," *Fortune* (May 1970), pp. 182–218. Data as of 1969. For federal agencies: United States Civil Service Commission, *Challenge and Change, 1968 Annual Report*, p. 66. Data as of June 30, 1968. For California and New York City: United States Bureau of the Census, *1967 Census of Governments* (Vol. 3, Nos. 2, 10, *Employment of Major Local Governments*), 1969, pp. 28 and 106. Data as of October 1967.

When non-civilian organizations are considered, the Air Force, Army, and Navy must, of course, be added to the list. The United States Department of Defense employs a total of four million persons.

The size of these huge organizations, particularly of the private ones not so subject to public scrutiny, poses most of the alleged threat to democracy to be discussed here. They have a powerful influence over the lives of millions of citizens as they set prices, negotiate among each other, pressure government agencies for legislation, and contend with other giants in the marketplace. When the United Auto Workers Union sits down with General Motors for contract renewal talks, the outcome affects the entire economy and millions of persons in related jobs. Yet, except for moral suasion or jawboning by the government to urge a quick, non-inflationary settlement, there is no one to speak for the public or for the consumer. Despite the magnitude of the issue, it remains legally a private matter between two large private organizations.

The government is deeply involved in regulating the economic affairs of these giants. Often the response has resulted in accentuating the growth of other large organizations. A supposed balance of economic interests exists in the cabinet among labor, commerce, and agriculture. Other agencies, such as the Veterans Administration, also serve to represent their clientele. Interest-group pluralism may keep each major private organization from politically overpowering the other. Because federal agencies are created to check public and private interests and to represent various groups, the result is still the addition of large public bureaucracies generally representing a partial rather than a general interest.

Direct regulation of large private interests when they seem to dominate a crucial public concern has been attempted through such regulatory commissions as the Federal Communications Commission (FCC) and the Interstate Commerce Commission (ICC). The effectiveness of these commissions was discussed earlier. It seems clear that their efforts have neither diminished the size nor power of private organizations.

Efforts of the antitrust division of the Attorney General's office appear ambiguous. The provisions of the Sherman Antitrust Act often have not been rigorously enforced and have not always been supported by the courts when enforcement seemed politically desirable. The most recent example illustrating that regulation is not always desirable to the political party in power is the International Telephone and Telegraph (ITT) case. Vigorous antitrust action against ITT, forcing it to divest itself of the Hartford Fire Insurance Company, allegedly was compromised out of court by the Nixon administration in return for a $400,000 contribution to the 1972 Republican Convention scheduled to be held in San Diego. Although the allegations were not proven, as a result of this controversy, confirmation of Attorney General Richard Kleindienst was held up by the Senate and the convention site moved to Miami Beach.

Finally, some antitrust action seems aimed at size alone, when perhaps private size might serve to strengthen competition.[2] In cases where only a few large companies exist, such as the automotive industry, strengthening the smaller (but still large) company may be desirable. This last point illustrates the dilemma of attempting to control the power and size of public or private institutions. To balance power one must create countervailing power, which centralizes power in fewer and fewer competing organizations. Size begets power and countervailing power requires size.

Organizational size presents dangers in other ways. Citizens and relatively powerless groups may find that they have no meaningful way to redress grievances when dealing with bureaucracies on specific administrative matters. A congressman cannot always intervene effectively and his powerless constituents may not be in a position, through lack of knowledge or inclination, to call on him. The individual must go from door to door, from office to office, in hopes of getting action or having his problem solved. The sheer size of the agency, the number of people involved in each function, and the complexity of the organization combine to make the lot of the individual facing the organization very difficult, indeed. Considerations like these are the basis for the famous antibureaucratic novels by Franz Kafka, *The Trial* and *The Castle*, and for Joseph Heller's *Catch-22*.

The pressures placed on government by large private organizations and the weight of both public and private bureaucracies on individual citizens become dangerous to democratic traditions. A few individuals in each organization, by necessity, wield tremendous power. There is a natural tendency toward oligarchy and the cooptation of new members by the resulting in-group.[3] This group of elites largely dominates organizational decision-making, makes contacts between bureaucracies, and sets the policies under which most of us work. Their power is societal in nature, not merely limited to one bureaucracy—the influence of top management in the Ford Motor Company or the Department of the Navy, for example, is hardly limited to their employees alone.

The increasing trend toward bigness also tends to make it more difficult to maintain organizations (such as unions) small enough for democratic member control and at the same time large enough to exert influence. Thus, in another way, individual social and political control, so highly prized in American culture, is undermined.[4] (But perhaps this control is not as much practiced as prized.) In voluntary associations we also tend to join, pay our dues, and allow some activist or interested group to dominate organizational decision-making, thus depriving ourselves of certain opportunities to participate in governing the organization. Most unions have trouble getting members to attend meetings. In universities many, if not most, faculty members do not care to participate in university affairs. The same tendency can be seen in public and private organizations where specialists prefer to remain aloof from major organizational issues in order to concentrate on their job or technique. While these tendencies may not be inherent in large organizations, their size makes it more difficult to encourage democratic participation and individual control.

The Marxist View of Alienation. This contemporary difficulty in controlling the bureaucracy and in encouraging participation is in some ways analogous to the Marx-Engels view of the alienation of workers (the proletariat) from the means of production in a capitalist society. The question of power was central to them, as it is to many present-day writers who greatly fear the social power of large organizations. Marx, and Lenin after him, regarded the civil bureaucracy, along with the army, as institutions that served as the arm of the ruling bourgeoisie.[5]

Alienation was, strictly speaking, class-based and directed at bourgeoisie domination of the means of production which exploited the worker. In a more specific sense, however, it was also directed at the most obvious evidence of exploitation, the bureaucracy. Man was powerless and dehumanized in the face of the state bureaucracy. Workers lost control of society to the autonomous and oppressive cadre of officials who man the civil and military bureaucracies.[6]

In light of the pervasiveness of bureaucracy, it is interesting to note that Lenin, elaborating upon Marx and Engels, insisted that the power of the state *not* immediately wither away, as the anarchists advocated. The workers must dominate the bureaucracy and direct it against the remnants of the bourgeoisie. Control involves maintaining the technical abilities of the old bureaucracies while dominating it by paying all officials, regardless of rank, the same salary and electing workers to all posts—administrative, judicial, and educational. Eventually the state will wither away, but in the interim before the "higher" phase of communism arises, strict control is necessary.[7]

Even today, the Russian Communist party and state bureaucracies are far from withering away. Lenin later attributed the growth of the bureaucracy to the immaturity of socialism, but concluded that the absorption of bureaucracy into society would come after economic development was achieved. Other Marxists were not so sure. James Burnham, in his celebrated work *The Managerial Revolution*,[8] argues that the development of a bureaucratized, centralized society in Russia, Germany, and other countries indicates that dying capitalism will not be replaced by socialism, but by what he calls managerial society. Marxism must fit the facts of a bureaucratized society. "Managers . . . will be the ruling class in society.

. . . Their preferential treatment in distribution will be allotted to them in terms of status in the political-economic structure. . . ." [9]

Burnham regarded the New Deal as first evidence of the managerial society in America. He characterized the administrative actions and attitudes during the 1930s as follows:

> The firmest representatives of the New Deal are not Roosevelt or the other conspicuous "New Deal politicians" but the younger group of administrators, experts, technicians, bureaucrats who have been finding places throughout the state apparatus. . . . They have no faith in the masses of such a sort as to lead them to believe in the ideal of a free, classless society. At the same time they are, sometimes openly, scornful of capitalists and capitalist ideas. . . .
>
> The managers, in the governmental apparatus and in private enterprise, flourished while the capitalists lamented among themselves about "that man." Congress, with occasional petty rebellions, sank lower and lower as sovereignty shifted from the parliament toward the bureaus and agencies. One after another, the executive bureaus took into their hands the attributes and functions of sovereignty. The bureaus became the de facto "law makers." [10]

These comments have the same thrust as the discussion in the first two chapters about the power role of present federal agencies. Burnham appears completely pessimistic (although he claims to be value-neutral) about hope for "the human condition" in a managed, bureaucratized society. Americans can less afford to be value-neutral.

Organizational Demands for Conformity. The second way in which large organizations create societal problems involves their tendency to dominate the lives of their employees and to exact conformity and passive or apathetic behavior. As far as the development and maintenance of an alert, independent body of citizens is concerned, this threat may be as great as the external power of bureaucracy.

The question of internal organizational demands on individuals is a more commonly treated theme than external power issues. It is highly controversial with conflicting values, generally lacking clear-cut evidence. Many persons believe that size and hierarchy have a tendency to force persons into conformity. There is little empirical data to justify this belief, however. Intuitively, it seems just as appealing to argue that large bureaucracies have enough organizational slack to tolerate the "oddball" and to put up with minor and sometimes major variations from "normal" behavior, while small organizations cannot as easily tolerate these aberrations. If so, the trend favors large bureaucracies, for a loose supervisory pattern is often associated with creativity and innovation—traits ardently sought by organizations and considered very necessary in today's changing world.

Lyman Porter argues this case, relying on some 1,700 questionnaires from executives and managers in large, medium, and small companies. He found that managers in large companies were more likely to use the terms "challenging," "difficult," "intense," "complex," "competitive," and "interesting" than were managers in small companies. They also saw forcefulness and imagination as more necessary while managers of small organizations emphasized caution and tact.

Porter's conclusions were these: (1) large companies offer more challenging jobs to managers, (2) "other-directed" behavior typical of group conformity is demanded more in small companies, while "inner-directed" traits of force and imagination are demanded in large organizations, (3) large company managers generally feel they achieve fulfillment of all their needs to a greater degree than do managers of small companies, and (4) the internal structure of organization work groups, rather than sheer size, may be the source of forces that demand conformity.[11] While persuasive, these findings apply to managers, not to the vast majority of employees.

Melvin Kohn's study of some 3,000 men scattered in bureaucracies over the United States showed a small but consistent tendency for them to be intellectually more flexible, more open to new experience, and more self-directed than men in less bureaucratic organizations. Apparently this is due to higher education levels, greater job protection, and more complex work. This finding may extend Porter's results to a broader, non-management population.[12]

A more polarized view, taken by earlier but better known authors, regards organizational pressures to conform with alarm. These pressures fall most heavily on the key managerial level persons, who must conform by working hard and unquestioningly. They must live and marry in the proper stratum, work at the proper level, and put the corporation or government agency in its proper place—that is, first.

David Riesman and his associates, in a 1950 book entitled *The Lonely Crowd*,[13] developed the thesis that Americans are becoming other-directed rather than inner-directed as were our forefathers who blazed a new nation. Inner-directed persons are those who set their goals through inner, independent direction. These are the pioneers and entrepreneurs driven by the Protestant ethic and by inner forces that operate somewhat as an internal gyroscope. Other-directed persons operate with radar beams to take their behavioral cues from the peer group, the work group, and societal forces in general. Persons with other-directed characteristics tend to dominate organizational life. They are more concerned with adjustment, consumption, leisure, etc., than with accomplishment of a personal internalized goal.

The views of sociologist Riesman are somewhat similar to those of William Whyte, Jr. His polemic against the social ethic, *The Organization Man*,[14] perhaps better than any other book of the 1950s, captured the essence of the fear of organizational demands for conformity upon the executive.

In effect, the book appears to validate Riesman's thesis of other-directedness. The social ethic, as Whyte puts it, is simply the belief that conformity, going along to get along, gregariousness, and acceptance of things as they are, are values legitimized by society. The organization manifests them and in a quiet but incessant manner demands conformance to them. As Whyte says:

By social ethic I mean that contemporary body of thought which makes morally legitimate the pressures of society against the individual. Its major propositions are three: a belief in the group as the source of creativity; a belief in "belongingness" as the ultimate need of the individual; and a belief in the application of science to achieve the belongingness.[15]

This is a not very thinly veiled attack on "human relations" techniques and the social scientists who advocate this approach to management.

Whyte has many examples of the demands of the social ethic, such as interviews of wives to determine their acceptability and personality tests which would exclude those who fail to score high enough on masculinity and authoritarianism scales, and score too high on intellectual interests.

A third influential work concerns authoritarianism as a central aspect of organizational life. Robert Presthus is concerned with the way society, particularly through socialization in its large organizations, uses anxiety reduction and deference to authority to inculcate authoritarian societal values.[16]

He posits three ideal types of organization members: indifferents, ambivalents, and upward mobiles. Indifferents, the vast majority of the work force, care little for the organization and its goals and work only to make a living. Their commitment is to an after-five o'clock lifestyle. The ambivalents are sensitive, highly trained professionals who can neither accept the rigorous demands of power-seeking nor sink to the unconcerned level of the indifferent. The key persons to Presthus' analysis are the "upward mobiles" who readily internalize organizational demands and eagerly mount the organizational staircase. These persons tend to be very authoritarian, scoring very high on the F (Fascism) scale developed earlier by psychologists to measure attitudes.[17] Presthus outlines his views as follows:

. . . the conditions of participation in big organizations place a high value on power, prestige, status, order, predictability, easy acceptance of authority, hard work, punctuality, discipline and conventionality. . . . The significance of the authoritarianism research is that certain individuals have personality needs that include dominance, submissiveness, and rigidity. Our analysis suggests that such individuals have an affinity for big organizations. We also know that values are related to occupational preferences. In a word, to some extent, persons are attracted by vocations that suit their personality.[18]

These fears are supported by Seymour Martin Lipset's research into "working-class authoritarianism," or the tendency of many lower class persons to seek strong leadership, personalize and distort their environment, and scapegoat other groups. These tendencies are encouraged by mass production and the lack of any identifiable connection to the work product. In this case, authoritarianism is associated with the workers as well as the managers.[19] It may even be associated with the earlier mentioned Marxist view of worker alienation.

Riesman's other-directedness, Whyte's social ethic,[20] and Presthus' authoritarianism are all part of the internal threat that bureaucracy allegedly presents to its members. Furthermore, all three authors fear the nature of societal values developing in the present-day United States. Riesman and Whyte clearly indicate that organizations are the bearers of the viruses of conformity, permissiveness, and belongingness. Kohn's and Porter's research, quoted earlier, confronts Whyte and Riesman. It does not directly answer the Presthus charge, however, since the fact that managers and employees are challenged and independent does not mean that the organization does not reward authoritarian behavior.

A middle view is that of Bertram Gross, who argues that while the organization is no monolithic power center endangering democracy (the first basic issue), it does contribute to the dehumanization of man. He points to four characteristics of the relationship between the worker and the organization that effect this dehumanization. The first is fractionalization of work, whereby man becomes merely a cog in the machine unable to see his responsibility for the product. The second is the worker's subordination to the organization, with conformity the price of employer beneficence. Impersonalization leading to alienation as a result of the first two conditions is the third element; the worker, having no control over his environment, undergoes a gradual loss of self-esteem. Finally, frustration and neurosis may develop because of organizational behavior which angers the employee, but is necessary to accomplish work tasks.[21]

Other writers have covered these topics. Victor Thompson, for example, argues that the friction and insecurity in large organizations result in a pathological state he calls "bureaupathic behavior." [22] Amitai Etzioni, on the other hand, notes that while certain personality traits such as achievement orientation and deference of gratification are necessary, large efficient organizations do maintain cultural and social levels.[23]

A few observations may help sum up this brief outline of the alleged dangers of bureaucracies to the American polity and to the organization member himself. First, the real dangers to democracy, if the gloomier views noted are correct, may be in terms of individual psychology rather than in the development of huge and largely uncontrollable corporate giants. The demands of society for docility and submission to authority may be focused through the hierarchies of large bureaucracies much more readily than in smaller primary or secondary groups. Thus, individual will to resist societal demands for homogeneity and conformity is perhaps weakened. The worst elements of mass society are strengthened. The social and psychological effects of large organizations on their members may thus be more dysfunctional for the maintenance of democracy than their potential political influence on the government.

Both threats may reinforce each other. Concentrations of influence and size through corporate mergers and governmental growth may deepen the trends noted earlier. These forces may be exacerbated by the apathy and alienation of organization members caused by the internal bureaucratic process, thus reinforcing both trends. A pessimistic view of the future might predict the degeneration of American political, social, and economic life to routine, almost programmed controversies between organizational giants, both public and private. Some of the younger generation and practitioners of public administration hold similar views, particularly in the case of organizational treatment of more powerless clients such as welfare recipients.

One should be careful here about generalizing. There is relatively little empirical evidence at hand to counter an overdose of normative judgments. Popularization of alleged trends is liable to lead to the wrong questions and irrelevant answers. We do have an organizational society, and the question is how to maintain viable and controllable organizations in an urbanized, industrialized nation of 200 million persons without giving in to dehumanizing forces which increase individual alienation and apathy.

One of the first steps is to understand better the nature of large organizations. No better way to begin could be found than by examining the classic study of bureaucracy by Max Weber.

MAX WEBER AND BUREAUCRATIC THEORY

Max Weber is the most influential figure in the development of bureaucratic theory in modern social science. A German scholar of enormous scope, he completed his major works early in the century. In addition to his famous works on bureaucracy, Weber studied history, the sociology of religion and political sociology, did extensive research into comparative social structures as far apart as Germany, China, and India, and formulated the concept of the "Protestant Ethic." [24]

Types of Authority. Before examining Weber's "ideal type" of bureaucracy, let us first summarize his analysis of societal authority and his outline of the development of bureaucracy. Weber believed that there are three basic forms of authority which undergird social behavior in all cultures: charismatic leadership, traditional domination, and legal rationalism.

Charismatic leadership, or literally "the gift of God," is perhaps the most striking form. The basis of legitimacy for the exercise of authority, or power, comes from the person of the leader himself. He may be a modern demagogue using the mass media, or a berserk tribal war leader. The basis of his leadership is the acts he performs, whether these be vanquishing armies, performing miracles, or leading his people out of slavery. The word "charisma" is now vastly over-used. In the United States it is applied to young, vibrant, political or social trend-setters. Weber used it to describe the type of personal leadership which attracted people to the leader's movement. Modern examples of the charismatic leader might include Adolf Hitler, Martin Luther King, Jr., and Fidel Castro. The important element is that followers defer to authority because of their belief in the leader. Charismatic leadership is intensely personal and thus extraordinarily hard to transmit.

A major problem for the organization once the original charismatic leader is gone is to institutionalize his leadership. The Catholic Church has met this problem by transmitting charisma through ceremonies electing the pope and consecrating bishops rather than by basing divine legitimacy in the pope himself. Charisma, then, is possessed by the church.[25] This devolution of charisma to the institution rather than the individual is rare, however, for true charisma is an almost magical gift of the leader. The classic example is the statement by Christ, "It is written, but I say unto you," demonstrating the personal nature of charisma.

Weber believed that history alternates between periods of charismatic leadership and periods where the routinization of charisma results in legal or traditional domination, the second basic form of authority. Until fairly recently in the Western world, the primary base of authority through the centuries has been traditional domination.

This concept is based on the belief that "it has always been so," on the sanctity of mores and values which have existed since time immemorial.

Time and countless earlier generations lead men to legitimize in their own minds the existence of king, monarch, feudal leader, or tribal chief. Authority rests in the office, which bears the historic traditions legitimizing the occupant's authority and the subject's obedience. Perhaps the purest types of traditional authority are the monarchy and the feudal system.[26]

Feudalism was based on a set of contractual relations between the knight and his vassals who drew their living from his lands. The knight, in effect, operated as a local ruler over his fiefdom. The contracts between him and his vassals, however, were between free men, and operated on a very personal set of relationships which valued the warrior knight and his fighting men highly. This complex set of shared duties, values and relationships formed the base of this type of traditional domination.

Monarchy is a form of traditional authority in which control is passed through blood ties. In most cases, traditional monarchs such as the shahs or kings of some Arabian countries are moving toward a form of parliamentary legitimacy akin to legal rationalism.

There are still absolute monarchs in the world today. Haile Selassie of Ethiopia is one. Even in modern England, the tradition of the Queen asking the victorious party leader to form a government still exists although it is purely ritualistic.

Traditional domination, however, has given way to legal rationalism in all of today's industrialized world, finding its expression in bureaucratic structures. This third form of domination rests on natural law, which justified the enaction of statutory law in keeping with higher values, and on the rationalization of Western society over the centuries. It is associated with the weakening of traditional ties and with demands for rational, rather than personal, justifications for authority. Belief in the legitimacy of laws, if duly enacted, and in the body of rational or legal rules as binding, came slowly after many centuries of traditional domination.

"Ideal Type" of Bureaucracy. To Weber, bureaucracy was the ultimate expression of rational efficiency. His ideal type of bureaucracy distilled the essence of the most bureaucratic structures into a model.

The main characteristics of a full-fledged bureaucracy are as follows:

1. Hierarchy, or a series of graded offices, each superior to the one below it and subordinate to the one above it. This stratum assures control of the organization from the top down.

2. Extensive use of files, in which the activities of the organization are maintained carefully on record to assure predictable and appropriate action in present and future cases.

3. Fixed and specific areas of jurisdiction, which aid specialization and the development of expertise, while eliminating overlapping or duplication.

4. General rules and standards guide the behavior of each office to assure uniform treatment of each case.

5. Impersonality toward client and fellow employee is required to prevent conflict, going from case to case, sympathizing with or abusing a client, and any action which prevents the full play of studied rationality on the part of the official. Weber used the term *sine ira et studio* (without hatred or passion) to describe this behavior pattern.[27]

6. Professionalization of the worker involves the following requirements: that the employee devote full time to his job, that this job be a career vocation, that he normally be appointed for life, that he be highly technically qualified, that he be appointed (not elected), and that he be paid a regular salary and receive a pension.[28] Weber also suggested that the incumbent would have high social status, as did the representatives of the state.

This model, a classic attempt to define the "ideal" bureaucracy, serves a number of purposes for social scientists. As an ideal, it can be used to measure organizations to determine the extent of bureaucratization. Also, cross-cultural and cross-agency comparisons have been made through the use of a bureaucratic common denominator. Basically, the ideal-type construct provided a basis for understanding the structure of modern organizations.

There are a number of limitations to Weber's model, however. First, it is heavily based on the Prussian bureaucratic tradition developed by Bismarck in nineteenth-century Germany, with which Weber was most familiar. France and Germany maintain this tradition, but in other Western nations the model is not as appropriate since they lack one or more of these elements, such as professionalization of the manager class.

Non-Western countries do not fit the model well. Where legal rationality has not pushed aside ages of traditional domination, other forces reduce the play of Weber's model. Professionalization of the worker is nonexistent, while particularistic forces defeat attempts at impersonality. Even in Egypt, a country that centuries ago made the first use of a national bureaucracy, the Weber model is inappropriate, according to recent research.[29] There, increases in levels of professionalization were not associated with increases in hierarchical tendencies, as Weber's model would suggest. While most Westerners find the Weber model helpful, if for not more than a point of departure, it should be used with considerable caution anywhere else.

The construct is perhaps most appropriate in military and paramilitary organizations, and in large capitalistic institutions where work specialization and/or weak unions reduce the impact of human variability. The military forces, police and fire departments, the Catholic Church, and Western governmental, commercial, and industrial enterprises perhaps are most typical. According to Etzioni, the ideal type is less appropriate in hospitals, equalitarian churches, research laboratories, labor unions, schools, and prisons. Here, the relationship of individuals to the organization tends to be ethical in the case of churches, and compulsory in the case of prisons. In the bureaucratic organizations the relation is "calculative" where the individual exchanges his time and suspends his judgment for a salary. Only then, where there is a purely economic tie, does the classic type of bureaucracy apply.[30]

Furthermore, Weber's model is structural and formal rather than behaviorally oriented. One might say it describes the skeleton, bone structure, cranial capacity, and size of the organization, without mentioning the pulse, emotions, attitudes, and environmental adaptability. Weber does not speak of what we now call informal behavior, or the random, individual actions of people as they interact with other people and struggle for recognition, freedom, and power, in pursuing their own individual and group goals. Certainly, the human, emotional and irrational (in contrast to Weber's concept of rational or predictable) side of man contributes equally to any theory of bureaucracy or organization.

Weber's views of bureaucracy have strong implications for political power. Bureaucrats occupy a power position which, when the bureaucracy is fully developed, dwarf the political leader. "The 'political master' finds himself in the position of the 'dilettante' who stands opposite the 'expert,' facing the trained official who stands within the management of administration."[31] Thus, the rational development of bureaucracy not only was the most "efficient" when compared to other organizational forms, but also tends to arrogate political power unto itself. Carl Friedrich comments that Weber's analysis makes it "hard to escape the conclusion that a bureaucracy is the more fully developed the less responsible it is in operation."[32] Probably Weber would not quarrel with this view. He viewed with personal distaste the bureaucratization of the state and the slavish German desire for order, calling it "parcelling out of the soul."[33] Furthermore, he felt that one consequence of a rule by law was the possibility of abdication of leadership responsibility by politicians and the usurpation of policy functions by administrators.[34] As has been noted, at least part of his fears have come true in America.

The crucial variable in Weber's thought is political leadership which can control the administrative branch, for with or without legitimacy, the power of bureaucracy will develop. Only viable political institutions will control the power potential of administrative officials.

While his analysis spanned past centuries, Weber had no way of foreseeing the twentieth century. In his own country, Adolf Hitler's Nazi party dominated the powerful German bureaucracy and bent it to its will. Hitler, although a political dilettante, thoroughly overpowered the bureaucracy by transferring crucial functions to the party bureaucracy, injecting party officials into the career service, and dismissing undesirables.[35] Recent charismatic leaders, particularly in developing nations, have either built up large bureaucracies or else have taken over existing ones. Generally, these charismatic leaders have dominated political life in their countries. However, their bureaucracies, instrumental to date, may dominate future political events or may enter a serious crisis period after the original leader leaves the scene.[36]

Although the leaders of the traditional American public administration school were largely, if not entirely, ignorant of Weber, their views parallelled his analysis of the organization and many social scientists link Weber's work with theirs as part of the formal American tradition.

CONTINUING THE FORMAL TRADITION

The study of American public administration began around the turn of the century. The primary focus for many years was fixed on the formal and legitimized patterns of an organization—charts of an organization's structure, job descriptions, and charters, i.e., the parts of organization life that are subject to standardization, routinization, and predictability.

This tradition, beginning with Woodrow Wilson, was strongly based on beliefs in rationalism, efficiency, and the preeminence of management. It fits nicely with a highly structured Weberian view of bureaucracy, leaving little room for individual or group action. There was little interest in empirical research, other than Frederick Taylor's time and motion study. This was not surprising since data gathering and empirical, rather than *a priori*, theories were not yet commonplace. Their absence, however, led to dogmatic assertions of "principles" which were generally based on intuition and the shrewd observations of practitioners, rather than research and testing.

The formal, or structural, view assumed that men were rational, goal-seeking, and primarily motivated by economic need. If not, why would they work at all? Work, or productive activity, was something that could be taken out of or gotten from men, and for which they could be paid in purely monetary terms.

Efficiency was a second major value. "Economy and efficiency" were the watchwords of the early twentieth century. Students of public administration suggested that once political leaders determined the ends of government, the function of the administration was merely to carry out these goals. Government business was to be reduced to a simple maximization of results or outputs with a minimization of scarce resources. It was then necessary to assume a strict division between politics and administration. Almost universally, it was held that once administration could be freed from the sticky grasp of partisan politics, and politicians allowed to (or forced to) concentrate on policy-making, efficiency could be sought and perhaps even won.

At this point in the history of public administration, the influence of business views and writers was very strong. The questions of management division of labor or staff versus line were largely framed in light of the corporate board room rather than the government agency. This influence, when combined with the view of rational economic man, explains much of the emphasis on management. The chief executive was exalted as the person almost singly responsible for the success or failure of the enterprise. Much of the literature and energy of the formal school dealt with the various formal aspects of his job. He was necessary to counterbalance the worker, who, as a rational person, would shortchange the company or government agency as much as possible by working as little as possible for his salary. Much of management, then, was a game of wits between the top and bottom of the hierarchy—the former to maintain efficiency, the latter to reduce it.

Under such conditions, the chief executive's duties were to select supervisors, expedite production, plan ahead, and maintain the organization. It was somewhat of a corporate giant, "great man of management" era. The need to impute charisma to each top-level executive was felt strongly.

Exaltation of the chief executive was not found entirely in the business sector. The Progressive movement in the early 1900s had as one of its major tenets the strengthening of the government's chief executive. The movement was a powerful social force aimed at increasing citizen control over government policy-making and also rationalizing government structure. The Progressives advocated a national budget system, the short ballot, recall of elected officials, and the city manager form of government. They believed in efficiency, but also in strong, effective, visible government, as a base for democratic decision-making by the people. To achieve these ends required strengthening the government's chief executive at all levels and holding him responsible for the performance of his administration. The Progressive demand for a strong, responsible executive combined neatly with the business model of organization. A formal tradition devel-

oped which included a strong centralized management viewpoint, emphasized efficiency as an end as well as a means, and assumed men were
driven by economic rationality. Thus, it was taken for granted that changes
in structure and work assignments could be transmitted down through the
hierarchy and put into practice with few problems once the principles of
management were mastered.

Scientific Management. Perhaps more than any other approach, scientific
management embodied these beliefs in management, efficiency, and rationality, combined with an unusual commitment to production research
through time and motion studies. Frederick Taylor, the founder of scientific management, believed that there was "one best way" to do each and
every job, and that sufficient research would determine this. His detailed
studies of work processes popularized time and motion studies, and led the
way for distinguished followers, such as Louis Brandeis and others, to advocate a widened ideal of scientific management as the way to combine social well-being and industrial production.[37]

Taylor himself was more interested in specific industrial applications.
His thoroughness is indicated by a study of workers which he controlled
carefully for size, fatigue, and other human factors. He concluded, for example, that the most effective coal shoveler should take about twenty-one
pounds with each shovelful to maximize output and endurance.[38] The results of these detailed studies, however, had impact far beyond their immediate findings. The philosophy Taylor propounded sought to bring about a
mental revolution in the minds of both worker and management, for it assumed that there was no conflict between the interests of labor and the
profits of management, and thus labor-management relations could proceed on the basis of mutual cooperation. How? Primarily by assuming that
the worker was a rational, calculative person who, if paid on a piece rate,
would produce at the highest possible level to maximize his earnings. Management, on the other hand, would spare no efforts in its attempts to iso-
late and remove all impediments to his performance, keep his machines in
perfect working condition, and make the necessary materials immediately
available. Removal of most employee discretion was therefore necessary
and desirable to both parties, since substitution of standardized tools and
procedures for rule-of-thumb methods would impart maximum efficiency
and predictability to the system.

Scientific management had four basic principles. The first was the development of a science, which primarily involved standardized tools and procedures. Secondly, scientific selection and training of workers was necessary. Third, the trained workers and the science had to be brought

together. Finally, management had to assume numerous large responsibilities in order to make this more complex system work. The development of the science proceeded on the "one best way" to do each task, based on detailed time and motion studies. Conversely, only the best workers would be selected and trained, those who held the promise of becoming first-class workers. It was necessary to pay them on a piece rate basis and to demand that they earn large sums, or be dismissed.

An unstated, but important part of scientific management was Taylor's objection to "soldiering," or loafing as it would be called now. He considered this due both to the workers' mistaken belief that higher productivity meant unemployment, and to defects in management since the bosses did not know precisely what a full day's work involved. From this view evolved, in effect, the whole of scientific management as a scheme to overcome these difficulties. Taylor's stopwatch and aversion to soldiering brought him into conflict with labor unions, who feared a "speed-up," followed by a drop in pay. This agitation led to strikes and in 1911 after House committee hearings, Congress enacted a rider to the appropriation bill which prohibited the use of government funds for time studies and stopwatches. This rider was reenacted until World War II.[39]

Scientific management had been defeated by American democracy. It was, however, a cornerstone of the formal tradition in administrative thought, and Taylor's time and motion studies are a hallmark of the "machine model." The formal school is often called the "machine model," since assumption of human nonvariability made it possible for man to be fitted, almost as an appendage, to the design of the machine. Scientific management was, however, by no means the only part of the structural school. Another important part of the school, perhaps of even more significance for public administration, involved the principles of organization and management. The early leaders in public administration believed that management was a science. Thus, certain principles of action could be determined by study and could then be taught to future leaders of business and government.

The "Principles" of Administration. Again, leadership in the development of public-administration thought came from business, in this case from two General Motors' executives, James Mooney and Alan Reiley.[40] Their theories, of course, were not "principles" by any means, if one defines principle as a universal rule, such as the law of gravity. Later students argued that they were not even effective "guides" to administrative action because they were mechanical and nonempirical. Their arguments, however, were popularly known as principles and still are so called, even though their strongest supporters claimed that they were only guides to organization practice, based on observation and experience.

Mooney and Reiley in the book *Onward Industry* outlined four general principles.[41] The first and most inclusive rule was the "coordinative principle," generally known as unity of command. It was based on the need to coordinate all activity through the organization by centering authority at increasingly higher levels in the hierarchy, ending with the chief executive.

The second principle is "scalar," or use of the hierarchy. It relies on a vertical division of labor and of authority, and differs in this respect from the third principle, that of specialization, or the "functional principle." This principle deals with the differences of authority necessitated by the responsibilities carried out by each subgroup—for example, the difference between artillery officers and the infantry officers, contrasted to the scalar authority of a colonel over all majors. Finally the principle of "staff and line" is outlined, indicating that the line, or operating personnel, represent authority and that the staff, or advisory services such as personnel and accounting, represent ideas and advice.

Mooney and Reiley consider the Catholic Church the archetypical example of these organizational principles in history with the military second. The pope illustrates the classic coordinating function of unity of command, aided by strong doctrine and morale. The scalar chain from the pope through the bishops to the parish priest is very short, made possible by the unifying doctrine of the Church. The principles of staff and line and of specialization are found perhaps best typified in the military.

Such was the Mooney and Reiley model, at least in outline. The development of principles of administration and organization had an important effect on the study of public administration since much of the formal tradition consisted of announcing principles similar to or derived from those of Mooney and Reiley. In addition, the practice or habit of deriving *a priori* or purely theoretical rules and applying them to organizational matters was largely a result of a similar practice in business theory.

Some of the principles on which public administration relied heavily in guiding administrative decisions are worth mentioning at this point—not only because they were central in the 1930s and early 1940s, but because they are still in use by many scholars. One of them concerns span of control, asserting that one man can supervise only a certain number of persons before his ability to coordinate and direct them suffers. There seems to be no agreement on number, although most writers argue for five to nine subordinates for a top managerial position and about fifteen for operatives.[42] Although the span of control is a commonly held belief by many practitioners, there are few controlled experiments to verify it.[43] One result of applying these principles is the creation of additional numbers of hierarchical levels whenever a person's span is limited. The organizational pyramid becomes much steeper, with fewer subordinates at each level but larger numbers of levels. This may or may not be effective, depending on the organization.

There has been some impetus in the other direction. The decentralization movement has caused many organizations to flatten their organizations by developing impossibly wide spans to prevent over-supervision. Such is the case of the Bank of America in California, where one vice president supervises all of the hundreds of local branches. The same effect may occur in government where demands for access by interests through their administrative counterparts result in large spans of control.

Another principle involves the concept of specialization, or departmentalization. Luther Gulick's classic essay outlines the four alternative ways of grouping work as follows:

1. The place where the service is rendered. Examples of areal services are federal regions, county extension agency, or district police offices.

2. The major purpose of the service, such as fighting fires, directing flight patterns, or providing drinking water.

3. The major process being used, such as accounting in the Finance Department or engineering in the Public Works Department.

4. The persons or things dealt with. The clientele of the Bureau of Indian Affairs is the American Indian population, the farmers of America are the persons the Department of Agriculture deals with.[44]

The preferred way is by purpose, to maximize citizen understanding of the service and to simplify programs generally. A fire department might have accounting and personnel departments (process), and in large cities would have fire stations over the entire city (place), thus combining some of the alternatives listed. A major difficulty is that these principles do not specify which option is best in the specific case, and thus the classification is essentially descriptive. It gives no guides for the typical case, or the case where opposing options, such as place or purpose, can be chosen.

Gulick, in the same article, enunciated the seven functions of the manager in the made-up word POSDCORD. These functions were Planning, Organizing, Staffing, Developing, Coordinating, Reporting, and Directing. These were originally intended as only a descriptive outline of the executive job. They became hardened into so-called principles which not only purported to envelop the entire world of the administrator, but to explain much of organizational behavior as well. Organizational life was seen from the perspective of the manager, whose responsibility was to activate and direct people in an authoritarian manner, using these principles to accomplish designated tasks.

Public Administration Model. Principles of management led to proposals with impact far beyond the organization chart. Progressive reformers combined with business and conservative interests to advocate a number of structural changes embodying many of these principles. Their proposals, referred to as the Public Administration Model or the Administrative Reorganization Program, are briefly outlined as an example of the embodiment of structural principles. The outline of the Public Administration Model included, with particular emphasis on state governments, the following concepts:[45]

1. Organization by Major Function. Departments are to be grouped into broad categories such as finance, public welfare, or public works.

2. Reduced Span of Control. The total number of departments ought not to exceed twelve or fifteen.

3. Unity of Command Under the Governor. The governor should appoint and remove each major department head, who should have terms no longer than his. These department heads should constitute a cabinet to officially advise the governor on matters of administration and budgeting. There should be no competing elected officials to diffuse responsibility.

4. Boards are undesirable as administrative agencies. They tend to diffuse responsibility and contribute to administrative inefficiency. Single executives should be used, with boards and commissions used for advisory purposes.

5. Staff services attached to the governor, such as budgeting, personnel, and purchasing, are essential for control of operating agencies. Indirect control through these staff agencies is superior to direct line supervision. The budget is by far the most important of these controls and an executive budget with full formulation and execution powers should be developed in the governor's office.

6. Distinction between policy and administration. This rule is not as clear as the first five since it conflicts with the attempt to develop a strong administrative leader in the governor or president. It was a bit clearer when the city manager form of local government was developed, since this local executive could, theoretically, stay out of politics. Essentially, to combat the corruption of earlier times, reformers sought to develop a strong executive to insulate administrative officials from outside pressures from citizens and legislators. By making him strong, of course, it was possible for him also to interfere with administrators, but his public visibility presumably made this unlikely.

These concepts can be seen in constitutional convention proposals and in miscellaneous reform attempts to increase the governor's term of office, eliminate boards and commissions with administrative duties and with terms overlapping the governor's, reduce the number of elected officials such as school superintendents, and develop departments of finance and administration. A recent example is Alaska, which elects only the governor and, on the same ticket, a secretary of state who serves as lieutenant governor. While most states are far from following this pattern, the general trend is in this direction. This is due less, perhaps, to public awareness of the advantages of structural efficiency than it is to demands for political visibility. It involves a quest for executive leadership with the interest in "efficiency" or structure essentially a byproduct.[46]

The Public Administration Model is a good illustration of the formal tradition. The reform proposals were rational, coherent and, to many people, convincing. They concerned the structural or formal part of governmental organization, with coordination through a strong executive, and an emphasis on principles. These principles, whether alternate ways to divide work or preferred organizational patterns to maximize executive leadership, became the primary criterion for administrative or political action in reorganizations or other changes. Deviations from this mold were generally frowned upon by public administration scholars.

The belief in principles got out of hand at times. Earl Latham refers to the hieratics, or sacred writings, of the formalists, and implies that administration was in reality a minor branch of theology with a belief in first principles and first causes.[47] Certainly, the questions of power, of interest, and of program concerns were brushed aside, if they were considered at all. The focus of the first three chapters on politics was exorcised by waving the wand which divided the world into two parts—politics and administration.

NOTES

1. The terms "large organization" and "bureaucracy" are being used interchangeably here.
2. For a discussion of the concept of countervailing power see John K. Galbraith, *American Capitalism*, rev. ed. (Houghton Mifflin, 1956).
3. Robert Presthus, *The Organizational Society* (Knopf, 1962), pp. 39–52.
4. Peter Blau, *Bureaucracy in Modern Society* (Random House, 1955), pp. 100–118 has an excellent summary of the conflicts between bureaucracy and democracy, upon which I have relied rather heavily.
5. V. I. Lenin, *State and Revolution* (International Publishers, 1932), *passim*.
6. Nicos Mouzelis, *Organization and Bureaucracy* (Aldine, 1968), pp. 8–11, 32–35; and Isaiah Berlin, *Karl Marx* (Time Inc., 1963), pp. 112–16.
7. Lenin, pp. 27, 37, 53, 64, 75–90.
8. James Burnham, *The Managerial Revolution* (Indiana University Press, 1960). Originally published in 1939.
9. Burnham, pp. 72, 80.
10. Burnham, pp. 254, 255, 256.
11. Lyman Porter, "Where Is the Organization Man?" *Harvard Business Review* 41 (November–December 1963), pp. 53–61.
12. Melvin Kohn, "Bureaucratic Man: A Portrait and an Interpretation," *American Sociological Review* 36 (June 1971), pp. 461–74.
13. David Riesman, *The Lonely Crowd* (Yale University Press, 1950).
14. William H. Whyte, Jr., *The Organization Man* (Simon & Schuster, 1956).
15. Whyte, p. 7.
16. Presthus, *The Organizational Society*.
17. T. W. Adorno et al., *The Authoritarian Personality* (Harper and Brothers, 1950).
18. Presthus, pp. 126–27.
19. Seymour Martin Lipset, *Political Man* (Doubleday Anchor, 1960).
20. Whyte, p. 12. Whyte insists that he does not equate the social ethic with conformity, but nonetheless I find this term the most appropriate shorthand for his argument.
21. Bertram Gross, *The Managing of Organizations*, 2 vols. (Free Press, 1964), p. 74.
22. Victor Thompson, *Modern Organization* (Knopf, 1961).
23. Amitai Etzioni, *Modern Organizations* (Prentice-Hall, 1964), p. 2.
24. The most often cited work is H. H. Gerth and C. Wright Mills, *From Max Weber* (Oxford University Press, 1946). I have also heavily consulted Reinhard Bendix, *Max Weber, an Intellectual Portrait* (Doubleday Anchor, 1960).
25. Bendix, p. 311.

26. See, for example, T. F. Tout, "The Emergence of a Bureaucracy" in Robert Merton et al., eds., *Reader in Bureaucracy* (Free Press, 1952).
27. Max Weber, "The Essentials of Bureaucratic Behavior: An Ideal-Type Construction" in Merton, p. 27.
28. Most of this outline is from Gerth and Mills, pp. 196–203.
29. See Morroe Berger, "Bureaucracy East and West" in *Administrative Science Quarterly* 2 (March 1957), pp. 518–29.
30. Amitai Etzioni, *A Comparative Study of Complex Organizations* (Free Press, 1961).
31. Gerth and Mills, p. 232.
32. Carl Friedrich, "Some Observations on Weber's Analysis of Bureaucracy" in Merton, p. 31.
33. Bendix, p. 464.
34. Bendix, p. 486.
35. Frederic Burin, "Bureaucracy and National Socialism: A Reconsideration of Weberian Bureaucracy" in Merton, pp. 33–47.
36. For a discussion of this and related themes see Joseph LaPalombara, ed., *Bureaucracy and Political Development* (Princeton University Press, 1963), particularly the introductory essays by the editor.
37. Albert Lepawsky, ed., *Administration* (Knopf, 1949), pp. 116–26.
38. Frederick Taylor, *The Principles of Scientific Management* (Harper and Brothers, 1947), pp. 5–7, 65–66.
39. Lepawsky, p. 121.
40. The discussion of Mooney and Reiley is largely from John Pfiffner and Frank Sherwood, *Administrative Organization* (Prentice-Hall, 1960), pp. 59–63.
41. James Mooney and Alan Reiley, *Onward Industry* (Harper and Brothers, 1939). Reprinted with few changes under the sole authorship of Mooney as *The Principles of Organization* (Harper and Brothers, 1947).
42. Alton Baker and Ralph Davis, *Ratio of Staff to Line Employees and Stages of Differentiation of Staff Functions* (Bureau of Business Research, Ohio State University, Research Monograph 72, 1954), p. 31.
43. The classic theoretical argument for span of control is by V. A. Graicunas, "Relationship and Organization" in L. Gulick and L. Urwick, eds., *Papers on the Science of Administration* (Public Administration Service, 1937), pp. 183–87.
44. Luther Gulick, "Notes on the Theory of Organization," in Gulick and Urwick, pp. 1–46.
45. This outline is primarily from Pfiffner and Sherwood, pp. 64–5, and A. E. Buck, *Administration Consolidation in State Governments* (National Municipal League, 1928), pp. 5–6.
46. Herbert Kaufman, *Politics and Policies in State and Local Governments* (Prentice-Hall, 1964), chapter 2.
47. Earl Latham, "Hierarchy and Hieratics," *Employment Forum* (April, 1947), pp. 1–6.

5

COMPLEX ORGANIZATIONS AND CONTEMPORARY VIEWS

THE INFORMAL TRADITION

Hawthorne Study. The formal management tradition paid attention to the individual worker as a rational, economic being. The informal tradition was more concerned with man as a social being, who had "non-rational" and non-economic needs demanding satisfaction on the job. Most of these needs were met by group interaction, argued the founders of the human relations school. They based their conclusions on research by sociologists, psychologists, and other behavioral scientists. The most important study was the Hawthorne experiment (1927–1932) conducted at the Western Electric Company plant near Chicago. Originally designed to measure the effects of fatigue on production, the study resulted in five years of controlled experimentation in worker output under varying conditions. Much of the research was conducted by the prestigious Harvard Business School, lending substance to the findings.

The studies began after engineers were unable to explain the lack of relationship between productivity and increased illumination. Under the controlled experiment, a segregated test room containing six operatives was set up to assemble relays. Production of each person was checked before beginning the test. For several years, twelve different sets of working conditions were studied, including such variations as no rest breaks, rest breaks, shortening and lengthening work days, and finally, a return to the original situation with no breaks, lunches, or any of the added benefits. Production increased or remained constant with *every* change, and was highest during the final test, when conditions were returned to original levels. The investigators concluded that the improvement in production was caused by improvements in workers' attitudes toward their work and employer. This occurred through the psychological "lift" caused by group interaction and from being the center of attention.

Another experiment at the Hawthorne plant involved observation of a group of fourteen laborers who worked in a separate room, wiring telephone switchboards (banks). The workers were paid individual hourly rates based on their average output, plus a bonus for average group output with an allowance for work stoppage beyond their control. This was clearly in line with scientific management theory, and it was assumed that the men would work as hard as possible to maximize earnings, and that they would cooperate for additional income. They did not, preferring the group norm of a "proper day's work," about two banks. Pressure to conform was very strong. Overproducers were labeled "speed kings" or "rate busters" while underproducers were called "chiselers." Workers believed that increased production would result in pay cuts or layoffs (this was during the Depression), while decreased production would be unfair to the company and raise management questions. Although both these beliefs were invalid, they controlled production. Management, for its part, continued to believe that two banks a day was a reasonable total for a hard-working man.

Based on these and other studies, the following conclusions were reached:

1. Social norms, rather than physiological capacity, establish the level of production.

2. Non-economic rewards and sanctions, largely related to group pressures, significantly affect worker behavior and limit economic incentive plans.

3. Often, workers react not as individuals but as members of a group.[1]

The Hawthorne experiments ushered in the human relations era, although the findings were not widely publicized until the late 1930s. The emphasis on human behavior and its practical application through human relations in supervision did not achieve maximum effect until after World War II.

Other Studies. Other studies supported the Hawthorne findings on human variability and group norms. One involved English coal miners. The original coal-mining system involved small groups of from two to eight men working as highly autonomous teams, selected by team captains for compatibility. Members developed long-term commitments to, and personal friendships with, each other. However, technological change resulted in the introduction of mechanical equipment for cutting and removing coal. The new method changed small groups to large groups of forty to fifty men under a supervisor, with the men spread out and divided into three shifts. No longer a single unit, the group was now differentiated by common tasks such as loading the coal or blasting the coal from the mine face. Emotional strains between and within subgroups of the new larger groups developed, while the spreading out of the men reduced supervisory effectiveness. The more rigid sequence of the new system added to these strains. Finally the dangers of the work situation, *without* opportunities to release tensions through the earlier small group emotional ties, led to reduced output. A norm of low productivity developed as the only psychological way to cope with the various difficulties. Finally, the new system had to be redesigned, since it had disrupted the social organization of the workers to the extent that it was not workable.[2]

A study by Whyte provides support for some of these findings. His work concluded, through extensive observation, interviews, and background studies of high and low producers, that

1. Relatively few production workers are motivated by money alone. Perhaps only 10 percent will ignore group norms to pursue incentive plans.

2. When incentive plans do work, it is not due to economic reasons, but because of some of the following reasons: workers perceive it as a game and work hard to win; workers want to please the supervisor; or fast work is less boring than slow work.

3. "Ratebusters" tend to be most individualistic of all workers. They come from homes where economic individualism is prized (farm families) and have weaker social needs. "Restricters" who conform to group needs are from urban working class homes, place a higher value on cooperation, and tend to join outside social clubs more often.[3]

The first two findings clearly demonstrate the inadequacy of a view of man as an economic rationalist, while the latter suggests the variability of men and the necessity for looking beyond the physical conditions of the work into the motives of men for explanations of productivity.

In interpreting the Hawthorne experiments, most industrial sociologists stress the increased status workers gained and the shared sense of participation from being within a primary work group. Marxists and neo-Marxists stress the alienation of worker from his work due to lack of power. Their explanation of the increased production is that workers gained power over their work situation since the observer was nondirective and relied on the workers for cooperation to make the experiment a success. If the Hawthorne experiment is interpreted as an increase in worker power and corresponding decrease in alienation, "real participation" leads to an increase in production.[4]

C. Wright Mills attacked industrial sociologists for their refusal to consider power questions and their tendency to play into management's hands by providing behavioral data to better manipulate workers. Management's goal is a cheerful and willing worker (manipulated pseudo morale) who does not participate (has no power), but believes he does by mistaking group cohesion and status for participation.[5] Many non-Marxist sociologists largely agree. Etzioni notes that the human relations school underemphasizes the inherent conflict between workers and the organization in an industrial setting.[6]

The Marxist view has not been influential, however. Most industrial practice has viewed the Hawthorne experiments and the human relations approach as involving simple participation.

A specific example of a company which has attempted to put into effect some of the findings is Non-Linear System, Inc., a small electronics firm. Emphasizing job enlargement, work patterns were reorganized into small, self-paced teams who have responsibility for assembling whole instruments, rather than individual parts. Emphasis on reducing economic pressures and supervisory practices that imply distrust of workers, combined with higher motivation of work groups, has led to a 30 percent increase in productivity and considerable growth of the company.[7]

Much human relations research has been directed at leadership, seeking the most effective patterns in an era where the feelings and attitudes of employees were considered important for the first time. A leader in these studies was Kurt Lewin's Group Dynamics school, begun in the 1930s at the University of Iowa. There, one famous study of children making masks indicated that authoritarian leaders, who remained aloof from the group, were less effective in maintaining the quality of work than democratic leaders, who offered suggestions and encouragement and participated with the group. While higher production was achieved under authoritarian leaders, the quality of group life was much higher under democratic leadership, as was the ability to produce in the absence of a leader. Authoritarian leaders tended to be associated with more aggressive behavior among some members and also with the development of apathetic behavior among other group members. Laissez-faire leaders, who answered questions when asked and did little else, scored lowest both on production and on group satisfaction, and considerable frustration developed in their groups.[8]

Although these results were only laboratory tests with children, there have been attempts to broaden their findings. L. Coch and J. R. French found that democratic industrial leadership, in terms of group member participation in planning work changes, resulted in improved production and reduced grievances.[9] Other studies have indicated that a task leader is not sufficient, and that a group requires a "socio-emotional" or informal leader, to maintain its viability and to satisfy members' needs. Rarely does

one person fill both leadership roles.[10] Fred Fiedler found that effective
groups, whether in team sports or business, have a leader who perceives
greater differences among members. It is not clear if the leader then rejects
poorer members or if this finding merely reflects greater perception of personal variances on his part.[11]

Chester Barnard, former president of the New Jersey Bell Telephone
Company, made the persuasive and influential argument that authority is
not the possession of the manager, or leader, but of the followers. The extent to which they accept his leadership, or their "zone of acceptance," determines the boundaries of his authority, which varies with the organization and with the situation.[12] Routine orders by a sergeant are followed in
the barracks, but not necessarily under combat conditions.

With a large array of research findings and the support of business leaders such as Chester Barnard, the human relations movement became the
new orthodoxy in management thinking, both public and private. It largely
replaced the older formal tradition. It became popular, indeed, fashion-
able, to train supervisors in human relations. Every organization developed
training courses to help managers and supervisors handle employee problems. Books on human relations became popular. College courses, graduate
and undergraduate alike, tried to explain how and why it was important to
understand the human and social side of organizational life. This wave
reached its peak in the 1950s.

But the movement was no more impervious to continuing research than
the formal tradition had been. New findings developed which seemed to
shake some of the human relations findings. It was becoming apparent that
the relationship between man, his work, and the organization was far too
complex to submit to any one particular view.

Traditionalists believed that man was a rational, economic animal who
worked for money. They believed that the most efficient worker was happiest, since he could make the most money, while human relations views
held that the happiest worker, through group interaction, was the most
efficient. A most significant attitude of these schools was that both assumed
the absence of conflict between man and his organization, once artificial
impediments were removed. While the traditionalists were guilty of using
a priori assumptions and unfounded principles to posit their economic
man, the human relationists were also somewhat unsophisticated. Their experiments led them to believe in the value of group support, happiness of
the worker, and humane leadership and supervision as an article of faith.
In one sense, they too ignored the variability of man and overlooked power
relationships.

SELF-ACTUALIZING AND COMPLEX MAN

The most important research to challenge the findings of the human relationists dealt with man's relation to work. The foundations were laid by Abraham Maslow, who posited a hierarchy of human needs, in which a person moved upward as each lower set of needs was satisfied. The hierarchy begins with physiological needs such as food, water, and survival, followed by safety needs usually met by minimum job security. Above these very basic needs come social needs, including acceptance and friendship. The next step of the hierarchy involves ego satisfaction and independence needs, achieved by self-esteem through knowledge, achievement, and recognition. At the peak of the hierarchy, self-actualization is met by self-fulfillment and using one's creative capacities to the highest level. Since a satisfied need is no longer a motivator, men continue to strive for higher needs as each lower one is met.[13]

Basing his conceptual scheme on this research, Frederick Herzberg studied the motivations of engineers, accountants, and some nonprofessional persons. He concluded that work itself, plus related factors such as recognition and autonomy, is the key to job satisfaction. Pay, discipline, working conditions, or company policy primarily result in dissatisfaction. Deficiencies in these latter factors will produce unhappiness with the company, but by themselves do not develop a happy or satisfied employee. Only the intrinsic nature of work itself will, because only commitment to a job which seems vital and rewarding allows a worker to achieve self-actualization.[14] This argument, well accepted now, struck at the heart of the human relations belief that good working conditions and effective supervision were crucial to job success. Herzberg argues that most employers are emphasizing dissatisfiers, which can only ameliorate attitudes toward the employer or agency, and not emphasizing the need for self-actualization through work. Pensions, vacations, and even pay will not motivate employees—only interesting work will, since it allows them to use their creative energies. Herzberg's research complements that of Chris Argyris in its emphasis on the psychological need of workers to associate with their work. Argyris, a noted social psychologist in the area of human behavior in organizations, stresses that the human personality system strives toward self-actualization, through goal-directed action manifested on the job by drives toward meaningful work. If these drives are blocked, the employees may "turn off" and become passive. Another common worker response is to create meaning and interest in his work by attempting to outwit the job and the company, or to band together in groups dysfunctional for the work situation.[15]

The research of Argyris and Herzberg strongly suggests that man is a work-centered animal, striving to achieve and to self-actualize. One difficulty with the motivational, or self-actualizing, model of organizational behavior is that in many cases there simply isn't enough work that can be made meaningful. Assembly lines often do not lend themselves to job enlargement or meaningful work, and the low morale and supervisory problems that crop up there are largely the result of not having meaningful work. But paying this social cost is, in most cases, cheaper than assembling a car by small group or individual work. Many organizational members can only hope for a "fair day's pay for a fair day's work." They will, of necessity, work at less meaningful jobs to earn livelihoods enabling them to self-actualize on their time off. Argyris argues that this is a waste of human resources. He is probably right, but it is difficult to see an easy way out. Hopefully, as society continues to demand services which require high skills and training, more and more workers will hold professional positions in which they can at least hope to achieve job motivation. For the foreseeable future, many jobs will continue to be "dead-end" and the problem of motivation will remain, perhaps to be met partly by professionalizing work and partly by reductions in the work week.

However, even the self-actualization view is partial, fitting only a portion of the work force. Research suggests that all persons do not respond the same way to work and to organizational life. Man is too complex for this and not all workers, even executives, want to or are able to self-actualize. Nor do they want to join groups, it seems. Robert Dubin found that only about 9 percent of workers preferred the job-centered informal group life in his study of the central life interests of industrial workers.[16] Some workers even prefer to work for higher wages rather than to have higher achieving jobs—one study indicated that a 30 percent salary differential led steel workers to exchange nonrepetitive skilled jobs for the assembly line.[17] At the managerial level, sales and personnel managers tend to have strong social needs while production managers have the desire to work with mechanical things.[18]

Whyte's study, noted earlier, indicated that workers varied sufficiently in motivational factors for "ratebusters" to exist, despite group norms. Clearly, neither economic, social, nor work achievement views of motivation are complex enough to do justice to man's variability. There may never be another school of organizational behavior which claims to explain all of worker motivation. Perhaps this is best—after all, who would wish to reduce man to a routinized, predictable animal, shorn of mystery and uniqueness?

It might be worth considering here the implications which each of the schools of organizational behavior has for organizational management.[19] The traditional school places the burden for organizational performance almost entirely on management. Employees are expected to do no more than the control and incentive system requires, and are regarded as having at best only an economic incentive to produce. Consequently, they must be constantly directed and closely supervised. When production drops, the answer is found in the pay plan or the organizational structure.

The human relations approach places responsibility on the manager for concern about employee well-being and morale, for developing group incentives, and for developing employee commitment to the organization by humane and personalized treatment of workers. If this is not accomplished, workers will join work groups dysfunctional to the organization. If it is done, it is possible for a psychological contact to be reached between the employee and the organization, rather than a mere calculative arrangement in which a man sells work for money. Thus, some sort of a moral integration between worker and organization becomes possible.

Self-actualizing man calls for a managerial strategy somewhat similar to social man's, but primary emphasis is for the manager to design work in a challenging way. If employees find meaning primarily in their work, the nature of the job commands primary managerial attention. Humane treatment and awareness of social needs are still important, but secondary. The basis of motivation, and therefore the psychological contract itself, changes from something the organization gives (money or happiness) to something intrinsic in the job. This approach is perhaps the most difficult for management, for it calls for reduction in the manager's prerogatives and in the scope of power over employees he has under different views of worker motivation.

The view of man as an animal too complex to categorize simply calls for management to "hang loose." A diagnostic and flexible approach to the relations between worker, job, and organization must be adopted. Recognizing that men vary among themselves and that no one strategy can be uniformly applied, the manager must be prepared to adopt different strategies for individuals and groups, as the situation changes. Furthermore, he should learn to value human differences, and learn to vary his own attitudes and behaviors. One common difficulty is that executives will adopt an "up-to-date" strategy of social or self-actualizing man, and apply it uniformly to all employees. This again ignores the variability of human nature.

MODERN ORGANIZATION THEORY

The major thrust of organizational analysis is changing. It is moving toward empirical management science, systems analysis, general organizational theories, and analysis of the interaction of the organization with the environment. The primary difference between the new and old schools lies in the areas of mood and manner. In mood, strong commitment to logical positivism prevails, led by the work of Herbert Simon.[20] A deliberate attempt to separate facts and values is made, resulting in a rather detached view of organization proceedings. The researcher concerns himself with verifiable facts, eschewing value judgments. This approach contrasts with the more normative views of earlier writers, who made much less pretense about, and hence devoted less effort to, eliminating values from empirical research. They were also less reluctant to promote or even advocate their findings. This is not the mood of present-day research.

Modern organizational analysis is also different from past work in terms of methodology. Use is made of quantitative data, computer simulations, aggregate data, and modern statistical analysis largely unknown to earlier researchers. Carefully worded questionnaires and interviews are common, compared to earlier research conclusions based on participant observation or analysis based on experience. Improved tools are available, and they are increasingly being used. Since methodology is rarely neutral, findings differ widely, even when apparently about the same subject.

Modern organization theory also differs from prior theories in complexity. Because of its attempt to account for behavior and structure in organizations as disparate as General Motors, the University of Florida, and the Sierra Club, the school has, of necessity, become involved in complex abstractions. Universals of function, structure, and behavior must be isolated and woven into a conceptual scheme.

A major result of this search for universals is the treatment of organizations as complex open systems in constant interaction with their environment. This approach is based on some of the concepts and approaches of general systems theory, developed from physics and biology.

Systems Theory. General systems is, briefly, a theory or set of theories which seeks to explain physical, mechanical, and social phenomena in terms of their similarities as *organized things* made up of interacting components. The human nervous system, for example, has many similarities with large complex organizations. It sends and receives information, adapts to changing environmental situations, and remains in equilibrium with its subsystems. All of these requirements are also true of an organization.[21]

A number of new approaches to organizational phenomena have developed which are more or less directly related to systems theory.[22] Cybernetics (from the Greek word for steering) is a new discipline based on the principle of feedback or circular causal loops which provide the basis for goal-seeking and self-regulating behavior. The thermostat is the best-known physical example of this concept.

Information theory introduces the concept of information as a quantity which can be measured in physical terms as negative entropy, and for which transmission principles can be developed. Entropy is a term from the second law of thermodynamics, which posits that all forms of organization move toward a state of randomness or chaos, and lose their individuality. The reverse of this process is negative entropy. Information theory thus posits that the process can be restrained by introducing information into the system.

Game theory analyzes mathematically the formal competition between antagonists for rewards, gains, and losses.

Decision theory similarly analyzes rational competition within human organizations based on examination of a given problem, its alternative solutions and the likely outcomes.

The most elaborate explanation of the organization as an open system, from a social psychological interpretation of systems theory, is that of Daniel Katz and Robert Kahn. They note a number of elements of open systems. The organizational analogy is implicit, if not explicit.[23]

1. Importation of energy from the external environment. This includes material as well as psychic and information sources of energy. Attention to the way the organization draws support from the environment is crucial to understanding organizational behavior.

2. Transformation of this energy into a new form. This is where the organization takes environmental input and changes it into the output. The transformation can be through an assembly line, a medical checkup process, or the human body changing starch and sugar into heat and action.

3. Exportation of the new form, as an output, into the environment. The export can be a product, a service, or a car's mileage. Some of the export can be waste products as part of the transformation process, such as the vehicular exhaust or perhaps the evidence of organizational inefficiency.

4. Systems are cycles of events and activities, not buildings and people. While many organizations, for example, seem bounded by physical barriers and their membership, their real existence is in the cycles of events which involve obtaining, transforming, and exporting energy. The transformation process, not buildings or persons, characterizes the system.

5. Organizations must acquire negative entropy (information) to survive. Open systems can acquire or import more entropy than they expend and thus defeat the

tendencies toward entropy. Acquisition of information is considered the equivalent of negative entropy, as noted earlier.

6. Organizations receive feedback through information input, coding this information so that information signals of use to the organization are imported. Sales information or other cues from congressmen, clients, or customers are all examples of this feedback concept, which operates as an information loop testing the extent to which the organism or organization achieves its goal. A simple form of feedback is a burned finger on the stove; a complex example is a computer printout showing inventory levels.

7. Open systems maintain themselves in a steady state called homeostasis. This is a dynamic equilibrium which changes and adapts to the environment while maintaining a constant relationship to the import transformation and exportation functions. In complex living forms and in complex organizations, this equilibrium is accompanied by growth and adaptation and includes a number of important factors. One is a balance between inducements to and contributions of all organization members. Too low inducements result in decreased contributions or employees leaving the system.[24] Internal equilibrium is closely related to external equilibrium, for new employees must come from the outside environment. Another element is ultrastability, the capacity of the organizational system to persist despite structural changes. Organizations learn, change, and modify their behavior, but persist.[25] Their existence as cycles of events and activities rather than sets of people or buildings allows the organization to persist even if modified drastically. This organizational equilibrium is multiple, as all subsystems must maintain their separate equilibriums. Overemphasis, for example, of the production subsystem at the expense of the member needs subsystem will destroy or weaken the latter. Workers then become apathetic or may engage in organizationally dysfunctional acts. However, it is impossible to satisfy all subsystems at all times. "Organizations are continually churning internally as subsystems struggle for equilibrium against their reciprocally disturbing influences." [26]

8. Open systems move in the direction of elaboration and differentiation, replacing simple, or diffused, functions with specialized ones. This is simply an organizational analogue of the process described later in Chapter 7 as bureaucratic development and specialization.

To illustrate the Katz and Kahn analysis in more concrete form, Figure 5-1 depicts a model of an administrative agency, its inputs and outputs, and general relationship to the environment. Briefly, the agency converts or transforms inputs into outputs. It copes with changes in environmental factors by sensing these changes through inputs, modifying its internal processes, and using the feedback loop to modify or change inputs by providing new outputs. Feedback on organizational effectiveness to the organization comes via inputs and to the environment from the agency via changed outputs.

There are two types of inputs. Demands are for (1) services or goods by interest groups, constituents, and the general public, and (2) agency behav-

FIGURE 5-1

A Systems Model of an Administrative Agency

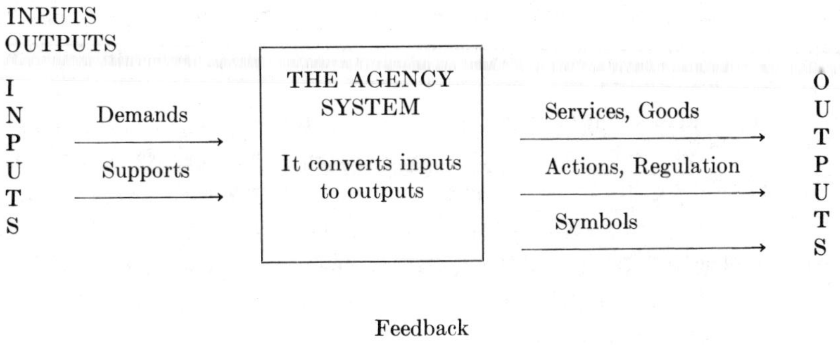

INPUTS
OUTPUTS

I		THE AGENCY		O
N	Demands	SYSTEM	Services, Goods	U
P	———→		———→	T
U	Supports	It converts inputs	Actions, Regulation	P
T	———→	to outputs	———→	U
S			Symbols	T
			———→	S

Feedback

SOURCE: David Easton, *A Framework for Political Analysis* (Prentice-Hall, 1965), p. 112. Copyright © 1965 and adapted with permission by Prentice-Hall, Inc., Englewood Cliffs, New Jersey.

ior or attitudes by the same parties, and also from control groups such as Congress and the president. Supports are: (1) congressional appropriations, (2) pronouncements by interest groups, control groups, or the mass media, (3) obeying rules and laws by constituents and the public, and (4) commitments by groups and individuals to organizational goals.

There are three types of outputs. Services and goods are tangible or intangible specific benefits to groups or individuals. Regulations and actions are specific regulatory activities of certain groups or individuals. Symbols generally include imagery maintained by general pronouncements or mere agency existence.

The conversion process, in converting inputs to outputs, has to maintain equilibrium by balancing total demand and support levels against possible outputs. Internal-external equilibrium involves (1) member inducements to remain in the system versus appropriate member contributions (hiring and retaining staff), and (2) outside versus inside program and group commitments. An agency makes commitments and promises to groups inside the organization and interests outside, as well as having commitments and responsibilities outside to control groups (Congress, Office of Management and Budgeting) and professional standard-setting control groups.

Internal equilibrium requires balancing (1) production demands versus individual organizational member needs, (2) maintenance of organization "slack" for reserve periods against production demands, and (3) some mutually acceptable balance of rewards among hierarchical levels.

Alternative Analyses. Although systems theory is now the broadest model used to conceptualize organizations, its very comprehensiveness causes it to treat specific cases in very general and abstract ways. Partly for this reason, not all modern organization scholars rely on it. Many focus on one or another basic element of organizations, trying to use this element as a tool for generalizing about all complex organizations. One of these elements is organizational goals, or the basic purposes for organizational creation and activity, and for the commitment of members.[27] Another approach is the study of leadership concentrating on the effect of varying leadership patterns and the socio-psychological interaction between the leader, his followers, and the organization.[28]

A third approach is technology. Robert Blauner studied the relationship of various levels of technology and worker satisfaction.[29] Joan Woodward studied 100 industrial firms in Great Britain to see how technological differences affected organizational form. Simplest technologies involved unit and small batch production; more complex ones included mass production and large batches, such as on assembly lines; and the most complex included process production such as chemical plants or the production of gases and liquids. There was a high correlation between complex technologies and the levels of management, and also a negative relationship between complex technology and the manager-supervisor ratio. Thus the organization pyramid was steeper in complex technologies, but narrower because the span of control was smaller.[30]

Organizational Change. Another approach is that of organizational change. Jerald Hage and Michael Aiken are concerned with change because of its ubiquity and pervasiveness in modern organizations.[31] Why are some organizations quick to change and innovate while others resist change? Seven characteristics were selected for analysis, and have been related to change in the form of hypotheses, as follows:

The greater the	Complexity	the *higher* the rate of
	Job satisfaction	program change.
The greater the	Centralization	the *lower* the
	Volume of production	rate of program
	(versus quality)	change.
	Formalization	
	Emphasis on efficiency	
	Stratification	

Complexity is the level of knowledge and expertise in an organization, while job satisfaction is the level of morale. Centralization increases when decision-making is restricted to a few persons. Formalization is the codification and formal specification of jobs. Organizations with production emphasis change little because they tend to be successful and have little nood to adjuot. Emphasis on efficiency militates against change because of the unknown and additional costs. Stratification refers to differences in the distribution of rewards for jobs in the organization.

These predictive variables operate within two general styles of organizational change, the dynamic and the static. In static change, the organization and its environment have reached a more or less stable equilibrium, and the change that occurs is through emphasis on those characteristics noted to lower rates of change (centralization, increased production, etc.). In dynamic change, the unit and its environment are in an unstable equilibrium. The following factors arc usually present: rapid growth of knowledge, internal complexity, expansion through diversification, and the instability of the environment for specific products or outputs of the unit over a long period of time.[32]

Louis Gawthrop analyzes the forces of change as involving the need to adapt to the environment and the need for integration of the organization. The latter is adaptation to the internal environment. These forces generally are met by two response options. First is the responsive reaction, which resolves demands within the existing structures, and which is labeled consolidation. Anticipatory change is usually characterized by innovation, which resolves change demands by internal search and development. The most dynamic organizations are those that emphasize anticipatory responses whenever possible. They persistently seek change, driven by the internal demands of their professional and technical members.[33] This type of response corresponds closely to the dynamic style mentioned by Hage and Aiken.

Edgar Schein, a psychologist, speaks of the adaptive-coping cycle.

1. Sensing a change in the internal or external environment.

2. Importing the relevant information about the change into those parts of the organization which can act upon it.

3. Changing production or conversion processes inside the organization according to the information.

4. Stabilizing internal changes while reducing or managing undesired by-products (undesired changes in other subsystems due to the new change).

5. Exporting new products, services, and so on, more in keeping with the changed environmental demands.

6. Obtaining feedback on the success of the change by further sensing the environment and the integration of the internal environment.[34]

Illustrative of this process would be a large public works department in a city government, which begins to sense contractor dissatisfaction with driveway inspection practices. Perhaps the department requires 24-hours notice for an inspection. The director obtains cues (step 1) from the city manager (or directly from the contractors) that dissatisfaction is being transmitted to the council, and then meets with the inspection division to determine what changes may be necessary (step 2). A solution, the assignment of one inspector for short-time "emergency" calls, is determined (step 3). Repercussions from other departments who do not wish to see a precedent of "special service" are allayed by clarifying the "one-time" nature of the position (step 4). The new inspector arrangement is tried (step 5) and the director later checks with the manager and the inspection division checks with contractors to obtain feedback on the reception to the change (step 6).

Summary. There is no royal road to understanding modern organization. Perhaps all that unites the different approaches is awareness of the complexities of large social systems and dissatisfaction with the inadequacies of past research. Yet, even in the 1970s some students and managers analyze or discuss organizations with the assumptions and tools of earlier times, having learned little since Frederick Taylor or the Hawthorne studies.

Even among the modernists, there are a vast number of approaches, generally related to disciplinary attitudes toward social phenomena. General systems theorists have the broadest concepts, finding their research base in the natural sciences, particularly biology, and in mathematics. Schein, Katz, and Kahn are psychologists and place their emphasis on the capacity of individual organisms to adapt to change. Hage and Aiken are sociologists whose view more readily encompasses groups or total institutions. Economists tend to study decision-making and the rationality of organizations and their members, while business schools reflect an approach which is a blend of economics, mathematics, and the structural relationships typical of earlier years. Political scientists are eclectic, using a variety of approaches including analyses of power within the organization and the politics of the environmental impact.

Modern organizational theory is evolving rapidly and it is not likely that we will see again a universally accepted set of assumptions upon which to base analysis. The field as a whole is richer for this.

NOTES

1. The complete record of the Hawthorne studies may be found in F. J. Roethlisberger and William Dickson, *Management and the Worker* (Wiley, 1964). The conclusions noted here are from the summary in Amitai Etzioni, *Modern Organizations* (Prentice-Hall, 1964), pp. 34–35.
2. E. L. Trist and K. W. Bamforth, "Some Social and Psychological Consequences of the Longwall Method of Coal-Getting" in *Human Relations* 4 (February 1951), pp. 1–38. The above summary is from Edgar Schein, *Organization Psychology*, 2nd ed. (Prentice-Hall, 1970), pp. 35–37.
3. William F. Whyte, *Money and Motivation: An Analysis of Incentives in Industry* (Harper, 1955) as summarized in Schein, p. 62.
4. Paul Blumberg, *Industrial Democracy* (Schocken, 1968), Chapters 2 and 3.
5. Blumberg. See also his comments on the triviality of the human relations findings in *The Contributions of Sociology to Studies of Industrial Relations*, Proceedings of First Annual Meeting, Industrial Relations Research Association, vol. 2, 1948, pp. 199–222.
6. Etzioni, p. 44.
7. Arthur Kuriloff, "An Experiment in Management—Putting Theory Y to the Test," *Personnel* 40 (Nov.–Dec. 1963), pp. 8–17.
8. R. Lippitt and R. K. White, "An Experimental Study of Leadership and Group Life" in G. E. Swanson, T. M. Newcomb, and E. L. Hartley, eds., *Readings in Social Psychology* (Holt, 1952), pp. 40–55.
9. L. Coch and J. R. French, "Overcoming Resistance to Change" in Swanson, pp. 474–90.
10. R. F. Bales, "Task Roles and Social Roles in Problem Solving Groups" in Eleanor Maccoby, T. M. Newcomb and E. L. Hartley, eds., *Readings in Social Psychology*, 3rd ed. (Holt, Rinehart and Winston, 1958).
11. Fred Fiedler, *Leader Attitudes and Group Effectiveness* (University of Illinois Press, 1958).
12. Chester Barnard, *The Functions of the Executive* (Harvard University Press, 1938).
13. Abraham Maslow, *Motivation and Personality* (Harper and Row, 1954).
14. Frederick Herzberg, Bernard Mausner, and Barbara Synderman, *The Motivation to Work* (Wiley, 1959).
15. Chris Argyris, *Integrating the Individual and the Organization* (Wiley, 1964).
16. Robert Dubin, "Industrial Worker Worlds: A Study of the 'Central Life Interests' of Industrial Workers," *Social Problems* 4 (May 1956), pp. 136–40.
17. C. R. Walker and R. H. Guest, *The Man on the Assembly Line* (Harvard University Press, 1952), p. 91. The latter two footnotes are outlined in Etzioni, pp. 46–49.

18. V. H. Vroom, *Motivation in Management* (American Foundation for Management Research, 1964), summarized in Schein, pp. 61–62.
19. This section is largely based on Schein, pp. 48–63.
20. Herbert Simon, *Administrative Behavior*, 2nd ed. (Free Press, 1957).
21. Ludwig van Bertalanffy is the best known name in this field. Much of this discussion is taken from his article in *Yearbook of the Society for General Systems Research*, vol. VII, 1962, pp. 1–20. Reprinted as "General System Theory—A Critical Review" in Joseph Litterer, ed., *Organizations: Systems, Control and Adaptation*, vol. II (Wiley, 1969), pp. 7–30.
22. Bertalanffy, *Yearbook of the Society for General Systems Research*, pp. 4–5.
23. Daniel Katz and Robert Kahn, *The Social Psychology of Organizations* (Wiley, 1966), chapter 2. In some cases I have elaborated on their elements, drawing primarily on Litterer.
24. James March and Herbert Simon, *Organizations* (Wiley, 1959), pp. 84–88.
25. Mervyn Cadwallader, "The Cybernetic Analysis of Change in Complex Social Organizations" in *American Journal of Sociology* 65 (September 1959), pp. 154–57.
26. Litterer, p. 19.
27. Etzioni, pp. 5–20. See also chapter 2.
28. Philip Selznick, *Leadership in Administration* (Harper and Row, 1957); and Robert Guest, *Organizational Change: The Effects of Successful Leadership* (Dorsey and Irwin, 1962).
29. Robert Blauner, *Alienation and Freedom* (University of Chicago Press, 1969).
30. Joan Woodward, *Industrial Organization: Theory and Practice* (Oxford University Press, 1965).
31. Jerald Hage and Michael Aiken, *Social Change in Complex Organizations* (Random House, 1970). Other sources are Edgar Schein, and Louis Gawthrop, *Bureaucratic Behavior in the Executive Branch* (Free Press, 1969). An interest in change is not limited to academic studies, as shown by the recent best-seller by Alvin Toffler, *Future Shock* (Random House, 1970).
32. Robert Biller discusses dynamic change as turbulence. He goes on to define public organizations as those that are undergoing turbulence. Robert Biller, "Adaptation Capacity and Organizational Development" in Frank Marini, ed., *Toward a New Public Administration* (Chandler, 1971).
33. Gawthrop, p. 182.
34. Schein, p. 99.

6

POLITICAL AND CAREER EXECUTIVES

Only a small percentage of public employees fall into the managerial or executive category. Most are blue collar workers, clerks, technicians, or specialists. In 1972 there were only 11,000 executive and professional persons in the federal government at or above the GS-16 grades, in both political and career positions. This is a minuscule part of the total civilian employment. Yet these persons have the major responsibility for the conduct of the agencies for which they work. They set, revise, and implement major policies of the agencies—in short, they manage the federal government's business. The statement "the agency opposed this program" means simply that key executives opposed the program. To speak of bureaucratic politics means primarily the aggregate administrative and political life of these executives.

Who are these persons? Where are they found? What is their job and their background? What is their relationship to bureaucratic life? This chapter will attempt to answer these questions.

POLITICAL LEADERS

Federal political executives, as the term is normally used, are cabinet departmental secretaries, undersecretaries, assistant secretaries, general counsels, administrators, and deputy administrators of agencies, regulatory commissions, and boards.[1] Career executives are to be treated separately in this chapter, even though this may appear to suggest a major difference in function and a lesser concern with policy and political life. Such is not true, as will be seen. Political leaders occupy the top posts, careerists usually hold the next highest positions. While there is often little effective difference in behavior between the two groups, executives are appointed by the victorious administration and hold the major positions of political responsibility. They are expected to chart the agency future and direct the work of careerists in carrying out agency programs.

While backgrounds of the top political leaders vary somewhat between agencies and from administration to administration, certain broad trends emerge. A study of more than 1,000 political appointees between 1933 and 1965 shows patterns which did not vary greatly among the administrations of Roosevelt, Truman, Eisenhower, Kennedy, and Johnson.[2]

A typical federal political executive comes from Washington, D.C., or a large eastern town, is Protestant, is likely to have gone to an exclusive private secondary school and a prestigious university, is 48 years old, was in business or law, and will serve twenty-eight months in his position.

Washington is the home of one-quarter of all federal executives, primarily because many have served in lower ranking jobs before appointment. In general, all areas of the country are represented in the remaining three-quarters of appointments, with the Midwest and Great Plains states having a somewhat smaller proportion than their population warrants. Considerably greater dispersion is revealed when the totals are broken down by agency. For example, the Department of Interior draws largely from states west of the Mississippi River, while the Department of Agriculture draws from the prosperous farm areas of the Midwest.

Most political executives come from large cities such as New York, with only 11 percent of them coming from cities with populations under 25,000 (which contained 60 percent of the population in 1950). This cosmopolitan orientation persisted through all administrations, although the Eisenhower administration more than the others patronized small towns as well as favored larger cities other than Washington and New York.

Many executives (44 percent) chose not to reveal information about their religions, but those who did were 77 percent Protestant, 19 percent Catholic, and 4 percent Jewish. While the proportion of Catholics may seem small when we realize that Catholics comprise 36 percent of total church membership in the United States, it is still double the 1950 share of Catholic business executives.

Federal political executives are extremely well educated. Table 6-1 indicates that 93 percent have completed college. This is the highest figure of any group in the table.

Over 40 percent have law degrees and nearly 20 percent have master's degrees in some field. Many attended exclusive prep schools and "selective" colleges, particularly in the Ivy League.

Average age at appointment was 48, varying from 46 during the Truman administration to 51 during Eisenhower's terms. Considerable variations exist, with 17 percent of all appointments involving men in their thirties and 12 percent in their sixties. General counsels and deputy administrators were the positions to which younger men were most often appointed.

TABLE 6-1

Percentage of Federal Political Executives with
College Degrees, Compared to Other Groups

Federal political executives	93
U.S. Senators	83
Career federal executives	83
California state government executives	75
Big business executives	74
U.S. adult white population over 25	8

SOURCE: David Stanley, Dean Mann, and Jameson Doig, *Men Who Govern* (Brookings, 1964), p. 18.

Richard Murphy was 31 when President Kennedy appointed him assistant postmaster general, while Kennedy also appointed Averell Harriman assistant secretary of state at age 70.

Not all appointees were of the president's party. Between 10 and 24 percent were of the opposition party or were independents. Roosevelt appointed the most members of his own party, 89 percent Democrats, while Eisenhower appointed the most independents, 20 percent.

Businessmen tend to dominate occupational backgrounds for most positions except general counsels who were, of course, lawyers, and regulatory commissioners who also tended to be lawyers. As expected, Eisenhower made the most use of businessmen in his appointments, although he did not select as many from the largest corporations as Kennedy, Johnson, and Truman. Career executives ("Appointive federal" in Table 6-2) were selected in 22 percent of the cases, most often to the position of assistant secretary or deputy administrator. Their appointment was most frequent in the Department of State, where senior foreign service officers were often rotated through assistant secretaryships.

Most political executives do not retain their positions for long periods of time. The average for all positions is only twenty-eight months, with cabinet secretaries averaging forty months. Marion Folsom, a former secretary of Health, Education and Welfare, testified before the Senate Subcommittee on National Policy Machinery:

It is difficult to get able people down here. By the time [political executives] get trained, they leave. I know it would be very difficult to run a business on that basis.[3]

TABLE 6–2

Federal Political Executive Occupations
Before Appointment

Occupation	Percentage of Appointments
Business	24
Law	26
Education	7
Other	8
Total Private	65
Elective public service	4
Appointive federal	22
Appointive nonfederal	9
Total Government	35
Total	100

SOURCE: David Stanley, Dean Mann and Jameson Doig, *Men Who Manage* (Brookings, 1964), p. 34.

This "in and out" practice of supplying political leadership is detrimental to any continuity of policy. It is often impossible for political appointees to direct career subordinates. The careerist is then forced to assume a political role to make up for political executive weaknesses. If this does not occur, policy direction over careerists' work is reduced, and the agency is less subject to overall administration priorities.

Approximately six months are required for a new political appointee to find his footing in the Washington environment. It takes another six months to begin operating at near optimal levels. Given an average of twenty-eight months, this means that effective performance may be limited to about a year and a half.

One out of five executives stayed in his position a year or less, while only one out of eleven stayed as long as five years.[4] Compared to many other equivalent positions, this is a very short term. For example, New York City mayoral appointments from 1933 to 1958 show longer tenure for political appointees (see Table 6-3).

However, the short tenure of federal executives is not as debilitating as it may seem. Many of the appointees served in federal positions prior to the ones they left—from 1933 to 1961 nearly 150 individuals held more than one federal executive appointment in the administrations of Roosevelt

TABLE 6-3

New York City Mayoral Appointments
and Their Tenure

Mayor	Total Appointees	Length of Service (months)
O'Brien	47	57.5
LaGuardia	115	54.7
O'Dwyer	81	36.2
Impellitteri	51	51.4
Wagner	60	50.5

SOURCE: Theodore Lowi, *At the Pleasure of the Mayor* (Free Press, 1964), p. 131.

through Eisenhower, and nearly forty held three or more. Many of these were promotions or reappointments within the same department or agency. In addition, about 75 percent of the men appointed had some previous experience in government at the state, local, or federal level.[5] This includes, as Table 6-2 showed, the 22 percent of federal careerists who were elevated to political positions.

Short tenure is due to a number of reasons. Until late in the 1960s salaries were abysmally low in comparison with private incomes for executives and lawyers. Before 1949, cabinet secretaries were earning only $15,000 and lower positions correspondingly less. Since then there have been increases which, by 1970, seemed to make the financial hardship less of a major question.

The question of job expectations is a bit more significant. Washington positions, even when avidly sought, are generally seen as short-term appointments. They are accepted to cap a political avocation, to take a career break, or, more often, as a duty which must be rendered to the party, candidate, or nation. Although this may be changing, an executive rarely receives a tangible reward from his law firm or company for serving his country. He may even lose his place on the promotion ladder.

Finally, short terms have some positive advantages. They make possible inter- and intra-agency mobility and provide a cover for shuffling out men who could not perform. They also make easier various modifications in the overall set of commitments to various interests which every administration must make. Continuity, although important, is only one consideration.

The selection of political executives is an important matter to every incoming administration. The process of selecting them varies considerably, however.[6] Eisenhower plunged into the selection process immediately after his election, using a small group of trusted advisers and a list of some 5,000 possible candidates developed by a management company. By December, 1952, cabinet selections were made. Balanced among factions and interests, it included two New York lawyers, prominent businessmen, several politicos, one woman, one labor leader, and two westerners. It was composed of persons who supported Eisenhower before the 1952 GOP convention and several independents, with little solace for the unlucky Taft wing of the party. Eisenhower delegated to the cabinet appointee authority to select his own subordinates and rarely intervened. This determination to delegate authority, perhaps formed by his military experience, was not shared by other presidents.

John Kennedy and his advisers articulated two criteria when searching out talent—service to the party and proven competence. One group of talent seekers was designated for each criterion, although the divisions did not hold up. The less formal Kennedy approach resulted in a longer lag in appointing his cabinet. The first member was appointed on December 1, the same date on which Eisenhower had announced his entire cabinet. Once a cabinet officer was appointed, Kennedy and his aides allowed him to select his own subordinates only when a balancing of interests was not required or where Kennedy had no strong policy preferences. For example, the first appointment Kennedy made was Governor Mennen Williams to the position of assistant secretary of state for African affairs. Dean Rusk was later appointed secretary of state. That same day Chester Bowles was appointed undersecretary of state and it became known that Adlai Stevenson had been offered the position of ambassador to the United Nations. Table 6-4 indicates graphically the varying approaches of these two presidents.

Under Eisenhower, the individual secretary and his associates were the primary participants in twenty-seven of forty-seven appointments. Kennedy, keeping more control at the White House level, allowed the secretary and his associates primary participation in only seven of twenty-four appointments. Kennedy's White House staff worked with the secretary in ten of twenty-four appointments. Eisenhower's staff was primarily involved in only eleven of forty-seven appointments, compared to thirteen of twenty-four under Kennedy.

The department head or secretary, in selecting his assistants, generally weighed three factors, specific expertise, general experience, and political considerations including service to the party. The latter factor was not the

TABLE 6–4

Participants in Recruitment for Assistant Secretaries
in Eisenhower and Kennedy Administrations

Chief Participants	Eisenhower	Kennedy
President–White House Staff	2	3
Secretary–Friends and Associates	27	7
Secretary–White House Staff	9	10
Secretary–Congress	5	3
Secretary–Interest Groups	1	1
Secretary–Party Officials	3	0
Total	47	24

SOURCE: Dean Mann and Jameson Doig, *The Assistant Secretaries* (Brookings, 1965), p. 88.

crucial one in most appointments. General experience was more important in selecting persons for later appointments during an administration, while specific expertise was perhaps an important factor in appointments to assistant secretary positions associated with a specific function such as assistant secretary of state for a certain region.

So much for the political appointees themselves. What is their job? Basically, it entails providing political and administrative leadership to federal agencies and taking responsibility for an administration's conduct of office. Advancing alternative programs while in office and implementing them if enacted by Congress or administratively adopted is another way to provide leadership. A further function is agency supervision, directing their career subordinates in the paths of righteousness, as defined by the new administration. This latter function suffers greatly because of the demands on political executives to react to short-term emergencies, congressional inquiries, and minor and temporary exigencies of office. In addition, they serve short terms and tend to leave details to their subordinates.

It is very doubtful if many political executives succeed in making a significant impact on their agencies in terms of changing behavior or redirecting agency goals. There are notable exceptions, such as Secretary of Defense Robert McNamara (1961–1968) whose planning-programming-budgeting system of decision-making has significantly changed organizational practices in many agencies (see also Chapter 7). Generally, however, political executives rarely have a major effect. Career executives, if they choose, can usually outwait their political leaders.

Marver Bernstein summarizes the views of a number of top level political executives on this matter as follows:

In a civil service system that makes employees relatively secure and in an unstable environment that makes political executives relatively insecure, the obstacles confronting the executive seeking to maximize his influence on his organization are formidable and frustrating. They can be overcome only by executives who understand the governmental environment and who combine a capacity for popular leadership with a capacity for management of large-scale complex enterprises.[7]

Understanding the governmental environment and possessing a capacity for large-scale management are criteria which few, if any, persons can be expected to meet, particularly when political factors must also be considered. Again, the short terms of office held by many political executives work against the business or noncareer man being able to understand the governmental environment. Many signs point to the increasing use of career officials in political positions as the most likely way to satisfy the needs Bernstein mentions.

Even men with these abilities find it difficult to be as effective as they would like. Most executives spend a great deal of time on the Hill (with Congress). Assistant Secretary B, supervising a cluster of bureaus and offices in a large department, reports, ". . . The distribution of my job depends upon Congress. If the department is subject to legislative pressure, I have to give that business top priority. During the last investigation that concerned me, I spent about 90 percent of my time testifying before committees or else getting ready for the next day's appearance."[8] Another official, an Eisenhower appointee, said, "You're bumping into Congress all the time. This is particularly true when the Congress and the executive branch are controlled by different parties."[9]

Preoccupation with Congress is inevitable since political executives work in an overtly political milieu. It is a mixed blessing, having both favorable and unfavorable aspects. Good congressional relations can be a base for leverage over other actors in the executive branch and thus strengthen the executive's hand. Business executives, however, find it galling to drop everything for a congressional hearing or even an individual congressional call. The proportion of time devoted to Congress cannot be programmed or scheduled. Day-to-day pressures drive out the ability to do any long-range planning. This responsibility is usually delegated to careerists, if it is done at all.

These day-to-day pressures include, for many executives, a 70-hour work week, with phones jangling from morning to evening, and briefcases loaded with work after that. From an Interior Department secretary: "I worked from 9:00 a.m. to 8:00 p.m. nearly every day and a large part of Saturdays and Sundays as well. . . ." [10] This is an almost universal complaint.

Another pressure is the difficulty of working in a "goldfish bowl" where every action is subject to public second-guessing. Washington is both the most sophisticated and the most provincial town in the United States, and news circulates rapidly. The heavy concentration of reporters for the mass media explains much of this. A reputation can be made and unmade in a few short days, and the necessity of protecting one's position from attack is always present.

A major element in the life of political executives is the necessity both to compete and to cooperate publicly with other agencies. The necessity for executive branch teamwork conflicts with the value of departmental pluralism and the need for the executive to advance his agency's program. The effective executive carries water on both shoulders. Often a representative of one agency will be called to testify before a congressional committee on one side of an issue, and his counterpart in another department will present the opposite view. On occasion, divergent economic views will be presented to industry boards and committees. Discipline within the executive branch, in the view of many executives who value teamwork, is often shattered by this tradition. These disputes are hard for political executives to manage, while careerists are often rather unconcerned about the lack of integration in government. [11]

With these distractions, it is small wonder that most political executives prefer to leave technical matters to careerists. Unfortunately, policy questions are full of technical issues. Withdrawing tax exemptions from the Sierra Club for its lobbying actions and deciding whether to accept Boeing's or Lockheed's bid to build the TFX fighter can be defined as technical matters. Both, particularly the latter, became hot political issues. Most political executives, even if they do not leave these types of questions entirely to subordinates, often let career technicians frame the alternatives. This is unfortunate, for it is in these "technical" matters that a political executive can make a significant impact on his department. McNamara's impact was due largely to his refusal to accept the way the military framed technical decisions. [12] The political executive who comes into his department with some previous competence in the subject matter area can begin to ask technical questions earlier. To a large degree, his effectiveness depends upon his ability to ask the right questions at an early stage and to continue to ask them. [13]

Only very general statements can be made in summarizing the effectiveness of political executives. The three major works on the subject tend to come to the same conclusion.[14] Generally, there is little difference between private occupations and effectiveness, based on ratings by highly placed political officials and senior career officials. Law, business, and other professions all produced about the same proportion of successful executives. However, those businessmen who came from banking and finance were rated higher than those from manufacturing.

The major difference in effectiveness is between those having government experience in the executive branch and those having none. Another difference is in tenure—those who served less than two years were rated lower. Executives with prior experience had significantly higher ratings, and fewer in the "poor" ratings. Those with no experience in the executive branch, whether from private life or from Congress, were rated lower. Congressional experience was apparently the least helpful. The two branches of government apparently demand separate orientations.

These results gave support to the increased use of careerists or at least "in-and-outers" who move from public to private and back.

CAREERISTS

As noted earlier, there is very little difference in social characteristics or political function between the highest ranking federal careerists and political executives. Both are concerned with top level management and policy questions, and any line between policy and administration quickly becomes academic. Any distinction between the two is blurred even further by the increasing tendency to use careerists for political positions. This trend started many years ago, but seems to have accelerated under the Kennedy administration.

Careerists do not normally define their jobs as political positions but it is easy to drift into such a position.

If the political executive cannot answer the questions, Congress calls in the fellow who can, the careerist. If the careerist turns up a few years later with a new head of the department who is an appointee of the opposite political party, the same Congressman may now regard the careerist as a politician who cannot be trusted. . . .[15]

This is not a drawback as far as all careerists are concerned since a job without policy implications does not appeal to vigorous executives. One comment made a number of years ago was:

You would not be able to recruit top executives for a strictly nonpolitical job. That kind of job is without flavor. It is not the kind of job that a man with spunk would live with, and he couldn't even if he wanted to.[16]

The interest of careerists in policy-making jobs is understandable, even as it is regarded by congressmen and persons outside the bureaucracy with deep distrust. There is a tension between the need for long-time merit system stability, with its inevitable drift of careerists into policy positions, and the need for policy innovation and enthusiasm for new ideas. This tension was dramatically revealed in the early years of the Eisenhower administration. After twenty years in the wilderness, Republicans were darkly suspicious of the competence and loyalty of higher grade federal executives, particularly since many of them had been "blanketed in" by Roosevelt's executive order, never taking competitive tests. In addition, the victorious party had to find some means of rewarding at least a few loyal supporters and had to assure that new programs would not be sabotaged by incumbent careerists. In view of these concerns, Eisenhower in March, 1953 created a new Schedule C composed of policy positions which were not already exempted by law but which were deemed necessary for the new administration to manage the government effectively. Schedule C eventually included some bureau chiefs and assistant chiefs of bureaus, information officers, general counsels, and special aides to political officers. Even though the schedule aroused a storm of protest from civil service reform groups, a year after it was created only 700 positions had been identified, of which 50 percent saw incumbents appointed, 27 percent being filled by other federal employees, and only 23 percent by persons outside the government! Even Republican partisans complained about the lag in placing "loyal Republicans of proven merit" in jobs.[17]

Looking back twenty years later, the dispute seems to be a tempest in a teapot. Now the problem seems to be finding enough new blood to assure that change will take place, not displacing a few career officials. Even so, the account does illustrate the continuing tension between stability and innovation. Then and now it is very difficult to establish any line between career and political positions which remains meaningful over time. Even designating certain positions as political is inadequate, as duties change rapidly. Republican advocacy of Schedule C was only partially due to the need for political patronage. It was concerned also with program advocacy and loyalty.

There have been some attempts to bridge the gap between political and career executives by institutionalizing a corps of career policy-makers. These attempts have been hampered by a disinclination to recognize that careerists make policy.

The second Hoover Commission, in making a number of sweeping rec-ommendations, suggested that a Senior Civil Service be created, to estab-lish the highest civil servants as an elite cadre of highly qualified adminis-trators. They could move from agency to agency, retaining their personal rank as they moved, to meet varying management and program needs. They were to be strictly neutral, having nothing to do with "politics," but highly qualified as instrumental tools in the hands of political executives. This plan was never adopted. It received a mixed reaction from academics and political leaders. A form of the plan was adopted by executive order in 1957 but the career executive board was terminated in 1959 when Con-gress denied it funds.[18] The plan was highly unpopular with career execu-tives who strongly resisted it. The idea of an elite corps is offensive to many Americans, both inside and outside government, as well as being counter to the strong specialization of the various agencies and their relationship to specific interest groups.

Even so, many of the original Senior Civil Service recommendations have been adopted. Executive development training, higher pay schedules, and a placement roster were installed before the 1967 Executive Assign-ment System. This latter system included an automated inventory of all federal executives in grades GS-15 through GS-18. Agency openings had lists of executives from other agencies automatically certified for selection to high level jobs. Agencies still preferred their own employees, however, and the system did not result in large numbers of placements.

A number of problems still exist. Manpower planning is virtually non-existent, the feeling persists among political executives that the bureauc-racy is simply not responsive enough to the demands of a new administra-tion, and agency heads do not want to appoint "unknown quantities" to permanent positions. As a result of these and similar considerations, Presi-dent Nixon asked Congress for authority to create a new Federal Execu-tive Service (FES).[19]

The FES is to include some 11,000 "supergrade" positions in most major cabinet departments and large agencies. Both career and noncareer posi-tions will be included, with a quarter of the positions being noncareer. Agencies will have greater leeway to set salary levels and assign positions without external control by the Civil Service Commission. They will select their career executives subject only to approval of the candidate by a qual-ifications board. Noncareer executives serve at the pleasure of the agency head, and careerists are to be given a renewable three-year contract. Ca-reer executives may return to a GS-15 rank upon completion of a nonre-newed contract. After termination of a contract the careerist is guaranteed at least a two-year appointment at the GS-15 level (just below supergrade levels) or retirement, if he is eligible.

If the FES package is successful, the three-year contract will force agency heads to weed out "dead wood" periodically and will encourage them to use more careerists in policy positions in a better mix with political executives. From the careerists' view, better manpower planning (if the FES or anything else can guarantee it) will give aspiring young executives a better idea of their future in an agency.

At least one state, California, adopted a somewhat similar program in 1967. It calls for assignment of career executives to policy positions with nonpunitive removal and reassignment to their regular civil service positions. It has not as yet been heavily used.[20]

Only large and relatively professional jurisdictions are now "ripe" for some kind of a senior career officer program. Those which are, such as the larger states, some major cities, and the federal government, are most likely to use such a program as a means of tapping senior careerists for political management and policy positions, as a way of meeting the twin needs of expertise and political responsibility.

The two best known types of careerists are the federal supergrade executive and the city manager. Although these jobs are quite different, in unique ways they blend administrative expertise and political judgment. First to be considered are federal careerists.

The Federal Careerist. It is now generally agreed that high level federal officials are deeply immersed in policy questions and that they no longer deal with management questions separate from political questions. There has not been complete agreement on how to reconcile the imperatives of expertness and democratic control. The Nixon proposal mentioned here is one attempt to balance them.

Another view, perhaps held by a majority of academics, is that the dangers of bureaucratic power are diluted because of its representative nature. The classic argument is that of Norton Long, who argued that the federal bureaucracy is more representative than Congress.[21] The federal bureaucracy represents more fully the American people in their variety of skills, classes, races, economic interests, and religions, than does Congress, which overrepresents the dominant interests in society, such as upper-class Protestant churches, men, whites, and certain occupations such as the law. Long also believes that the bureaucracy is more likely to reexamine positions on major issues and to consider alternatives to a specific goal than are the specialized committees of Congress. Finally, he argues that the bureaucracy is much more likely to maintain a consistent ethical position in regard for due process than are the congressional committees, which are subject to the dramatic changes in public opinion that sweep over America. McCarthyism and Communist witch hunts are less likely to mark administrative due process, partly because it is more protected and less visible than congressional action.

Careerists may, indeed, be more representative of all segments of the American public than Congress. They still are not typical Americans, as a short statistical profile will show. A composite senior careerist was, in 1971, a 53-year-old man, with twenty-six years of federal service.[22] Only 3 percent were from minority groups; 58 percent had advanced degrees while only 9 percent had less than a bachelor's degree. Federal careerists clearly stand out in educational attainment from the general public. In terms of college majors, 24 percent were from engineering, 22 percent law, 14 percent social sciences, and 13 percent physical sciences.[23] Most of these senior careerists worked in the field in which their training was taken, with those in general administration more likely to have studied law than any other subject.

TABLE 6–5

Occupations of Fathers of Civilian and
Military Federal Executives, 1959

Father's Occupation	Civilian	Military
Laborer	21%	14%
White collar worker	9	9
Business executive	15	20
Business owner	20	19
Professional	19	18
Farmer (including owner or manager)	15	10
Uniformed service	*	9
Other	*	1
Total	100%	100%

* Less than 1%

SOURCE: W. Lloyd Warner et al., *The American Federal Executive* (Yale University Press, 1963), pp. 29, 323.

Most federal executives come from middle- or upper-class parents. In this respect they do not perfectly reflect occupations in the United States (see Table 6-5). There is a good deal of generational mobility, however, since 36 percent of civilian and 24 percent of military executives come from working-class (laborer and farmer) parents. Military executives tend to come from slightly more highly placed positions. Civilian executives reflect the proportions of occupations in the United States somewhat more closely.

Career advancement is normally through one agency, although this has changed in recent years. The major group of federal executives, comprising more than three-fifths of the total population, can be termed "non-mobile." Of this group, 73 percent have worked in only one agency since reaching GS-13. These tend to be the program managers in technical positions. All members of the other major group of "generalists," totalling almost one-fifth of the executive population, have worked in at least two agencies, with 56 percent having worked in four agencies. These latter tend to be staff planners and persons in management support. Generalization is difficult, but certainly the larger group is short of broad experience in a variety of agencies. They compare unfavorably to the mobility of city managers. If flexibility and breadth are determined by a wide variety of administrative experiences, questions are raised by this "non-mobile" career pattern.

Many factors determine breadth of experience, including range of positions and geographic mobility. Most top level executives in America have experience primarily in only one agency or organization, whether military, corporate, or financial. Even within one agency, however, the range of management responsibilities may vary sufficiently for intra-agency transfers to develop broad perspectives.

Federal executives generally find considerable fulfillment in their work, naming challenge and scope of work, as well as a sense of accomplishment, as their principal career satisfactions. At the bottom of their gratification is job security, mentioned by only 6 percent (only the top five satisfactions were listed). Dissatisfiers included primarily a "government complexity" factor which lumped together red tape, required clearances, and excessive rules. Table 6-6 gives some of the findings.

A 1971 survey generally verified these findings. The United States Civil Service Commission recorded the views of all federal executives on the Executive Inventory regarding reasons they entered the service. Table 6-7 indicates that challenging assignments was the reason most often given, with next emphasis on occupational expectations. This probably reflects the fact that more and more occupations are largely found in the federal service. Part of the satisfaction found by federal executives in their work is no doubt related to the enormous variation in job content from agency to agency or even from assignment to assignment. One job may involve tech-

TABLE 6-6

Principal Career Satisfactions and Dissatisfactions
of Past and Present Federal Career Officials

Principal Satisfactions

Challenge, scope, variety of work	42%
Sense of accomplishments	41
Public service, sense of mission	36
Working with good associates	27
Pride in making a contribution	25

Principal Dissatisfactions

Government complexity—cumbersome procedures, paperwork, multiple clearances	45%
Timid or inadequate supervision	18
Inadequate pay levels	13
None	11

SOURCE: David Stanley, *The Higher Civil Service* (Brookings, 1964), p. 61.

TABLE 6-7

Principal Reasons of Top Career Executives for
Entering the Federal Service

Motivating Factors

Challenging assignments	29%
Chosen occupation	25
Best offer	14
Public service	12
All others	20
Total	100%

SOURCE: United States Civil Service Commission, *Executive Manpower in the Federal Service* (Washington, D.C., 1972), p. 22.

nical duties in the field, another financial management in Washington, a third legislative liaison with Congress. The same person may hold all three.

One top careerist's experience was as follows:

One job was a managerial one in a large field activity. Here virtually 95 percent of the job was internal management of an industrial research plant. In my second job I served as a senior assistant to a political executive almost exclusively on a staff basis. Here the assignments dealt mainly with the internal management of a huge department. In the third job, my time breaks down very differently.

I would say that about 50 percent of my time is devoted to the internal management of the agency. This half of my time breaks down into three general areas. The first is the program area. . . . The second is personnel. . . . The third is financial management.

About a quarter of my time is devoted to customer service within the executive branch. . . . Probably no more than 5 percent of my working day is devoted to congressional matters. . . . The balance, about 20 percent, is devoted to work with outside groups. . . .[24]

Some executives spend as much as 75 percent of their time on external matters involving Congress and other outside interests, while others have relatively little outside contact and perform primarily management functions. Others are primarily staff to the political executives, generally at the assistant secretary level.

City Managers. Perhaps the quintessential careerist position is that of the city manager. Subject to dismissal at any time by the city council, he is expected to administer simultaneously the affairs of the city without regard to politics and to advise the council on policy issues. Councils frequently regard him as a hired hand, but demand his recommendation on volatile political issues. Conversely, many managers attempt to convert broad policy issues into administrative or technical questions in order to maximize their own influence over the policy area. Some cities are extraordinarily politicized, while others operate at a humdrum level.

The council-manager plan sprang out of the reform tradition at the turn of the century. The Progressive movement, as noted earlier, had as a central theme the exaltation of executive leadership and more democratic control of public officials. Although built originally on a business manager model, the manager plan fitted well into these themes, and spread rapidly from Staunton, Virginia, in 1908 to some 2,100 cities and counties by 1970.

The first manager was an engineer, hired to bring a technical, no-nonsense, businesslike viewpoint to hopelessly muddled civic affairs mismanaged by amateurs. The efficiency orientation was largely responsible for the initial popularity of the plan and most early managers were originally engineers. Their job was conceived in rather narrow terms as fixing streets and installing accounting systems. At this time, the major theme in administrative life was a rigid dichotomy between politics and administration, with the manager not to venture into policy questions and the council not to interfere with the professional manager and his "technical" prerogatives.

Under these conditions it is unlikely that the plan would have continued to flourish since the line between policy and administration was becoming more and more artificial. It was also apparent that more dynamic approaches to policy-making in municipalities were required. The plan developed because the Progressive reform tradition made the manager directly and visibly responsible to the elected council—emphasizing democratic control—and gave him significant powers (at least in the cities with full manager powers)—thus emphasizing executive leadership. Had the manager been a political cipher, the plan would have faltered.

As time went on, managers developed a sense of professional community which resulted in the formation of the International City Managers Association (ICMA) and the promulgation of a code of ethics. This professionalization resulted in a dual responsibility—to the city council as the representative of the citizenry and to the ICMA's Code of Ethics for guidance on professional behavior. Generally, proper professional behavior came to mean control over all personnel transactions including hiring and firing; control over formulation of the city budget; non-interference by the council in administrative matters; and, where no city clerk was elected, control over the council agenda at least for manager items. Deference to democratic norms was maintained by vesting absolute control over the manager's tenure in the hands of the council. Managers take pride in both sets of responsibilities. They insist on their administrative prerogatives in hiring and firing, and preparing the budget (although not at the risk of unnecessarily ruffling council feathers); while complaining that "my job is on the line every Council meeting," they carefully take pains to reduce conflict situations that might actually risk it. Managers behave precisely as most career public executives would behave in similar situations where they are deeply involved in the policy process.

The career of a manager normally encompasses a number of cities, going from smaller to larger or from simple to more complex ones, with his salary and responsibility increasing commensurately. Not all managers spend all their working lives as managers. Many work either in other governmental positions, such as department heads and federal or state employees, or as consultants. Varied career patterns among jobs and governmental levels in urban affairs have become more common in recent years. Most managers, however, begin their careers with an administrative position in one city and work their way up to a manager's job. Many new managers have college training and a master's degree in public administration. Table 6-8 indicates that in 1971 more than two-thirds of all managers had college degrees. This is not far from the educational levels of federal executives, and far above the level of municipal and state department heads. Tenure in any city averages only about three to five years, as managers move up or are removed from their posts. Managers, as a group, are heavily Protestant, male, and white. The average manager is under 40 years of age.

TABLE 6-8

Social Data on United States
City Managers in 1971

Average Age	38 yrs.
Under 30	26%
Religion	
Protestant	48%
Catholic	13%
Jewish	3%
College Graduates	69%
Advanced Degree	27%
Major Course Work	
Liberal Arts	39%
Engineering	33%
Public or Business Administration	26%
Salary	
Median, all cities	$18,000
Median, cities over 50,000	$23,000

SOURCE: International City Managers Association, *The Modern City Manager: A 1971 Profile* (Washington, D.C., 1972).

The job of the city manager falls into three categories: internal management, external relations, and councilmanic relationships. These are not watertight compartments and effectiveness in any area helps the manager in the others. A manager who is seen as a no-nonsense, top level administrator is on the way to developing a reputation which may increase his leverage with the council at budget time. Conversely, ineffectiveness in contacts with citizens or the business community may have a detrimental effect on his influence over department heads who are long-time community residents. The internal management job is not far different from that of other public executives, at least in broad parameters. The manager coordinates the work of department heads, settles disputes between them, tries to operate the city efficiently by reducing or eliminating unnecessary costs, supervises subordinates who work with city commissions, and watches monthly expenditures of department heads. In very small cities he actually may do some or all of the staff work himself, such as supervising personnel training and recruiting, establishing and monitoring the accounting system, and acting as the civil defense director. These jobs require a good deal of detailed knowledge about city government, but probably no more than the corresponding knowledge about Washington life and agency programs required of a federal career executive.

Relations with the city council are a crucial part of the manager's job. He acts as their policy adviser, as their staff aide, and as the executive head of the city. These roles overlap and sometimes conflict. For example, on an annexation proposal the manager may have to act as policy adviser to the council regarding future precedents if the annexation is approved. As staff aide he will negotiate any agreements with property owners being annexed. As executive head of the city he may have reservations about the financial wisdom of the annexation.

In one or more of these roles, some managers dominate their councils, setting the municipal policy agenda, proposing alternatives and recommending a solution. The council is limited to ratifying the proposal or turning it down. At the other extreme, some managers appear not to be a significant factor in policy formulation. They may wish to take no more visible role than to list alternatives for council discussion and action, or to provide information on alternatives mentioned by councilmen or civic groups. These managers usually see themselves as administrative rather than policy leaders. Most managers fall between these two extremes and their participation in policy matters tends to vary with the issue. Some may take a more active role in issue areas where they have specialized competence, such as planning or zoning if they have experience there. Another consideration involves the level of conflict generated by the issue. If he is unwary, very heated controversies may involve the manager in more open political positions than might be desirable, since the manager must adopt a nonpolitical, "low profile" stance.

External relations are the part of the manager's job which require him to interact with the general public and civic or business groups. The manager often is the most visible member of city government. Councilmen are part-time officials and even they may not be well known publicly. But the manager is the full-time person responsible for "running the city" and, if the citizenry may forget this, the press does not. The manager represents the city to many people, and is expected to explain, if not justify, a wide range of issues from "why wasn't my garbage picked up?" to "why doesn't the city have an urban renewal program?" The manager, projecting a business-like, professional image, often places the politicians on the council in an unfavorable light. This impression often places the manager in political competition with the council, although most managers try to avoid this situation.

In relation to earlier discussion of administrative power, the manager can be seen as a person who both seeks power or influence over policy, and who is sought out by power. If the manager does not take a position it is likely that one side or another of the particular dispute will attempt to enlist his aid by widening the scope of the dispute to include an expert or technical opinion. A Machiavellian view is that managers are successful to the extent that they can "convert political issues to technical matters." This implies an inevitable and necessary search for power. A more balanced view is that since the ICMA Code of Ethics now recognizes that he is a "community leader," it is inevitable that he take some position on major civic issues, if he does not overstep the bounds of propriety (these are not defined and vary from city to city and manager to manager). In such cases, managers will likely base, or at least justify, their position on technical or administrative grounds. A case in point is a new manager of Palm Springs, California, who was faced with council and civic indecision over means of financing a municipal golf course that was operating shakily. He strongly recommended financing its purchase by a general obligation bond issue, rather than a purchase arrangement, since the interest rates are much lower. This recommendation was made in the face of councilmanic and civic leader fear that the public would not support a bond issue. It passed by 94 percent. A policy decision? Surely, for the proposal involved an important political issue and a solution opposed by many civic leaders. A technical issue? Surely, for interest rates and financing arrangements are best settled by financial experts. Of course, it was both, and the manager could not have avoided the matter for long.

A study by Ronald Loveridge of most managers in the San Francisco Bay area divided them into two broad categories corresponding to the previously mentioned activists and nonactivists in council policy-making. Each category was further divided into two types based on interview responses and attitudinal questionnaires. These four types were political leader, political executive, administrative director, and administrative technician.[25] Each falls into one of two basic policy orientations, political or administrative. The political leader has views similar to these:

. . . The most important things are to bring to the attention of the city council the problems and needs of the community, to propose solutions to these problems, to keep the council informed on city operations, and to provide effective leadership for the administrative staff. . . . A city manager is obligated to bring his expertise, experience, and ability to the council. He should actively take part in policy recommendations. . . .[26]

A political executive tends to share these views, but is more cautious about the implications of appearing too visible in the community.

The real distinction is what you should not do publicly in contrast to what you must do privately. A city manager should be more than a council adviser. He should urge and recommend policy. . . . Of course, a city manager's activity depends on the caliber of the council. Especially if it is poor, the city manager should lead from behind the scenes. But he should not lead publicly.[27]

Administrative directors, generally, share positive views of the manager's responsibility for policy-making, but prefer situations where it is unnecessary. "The manager, like it or not, is involved in policy. . . . I do not see a city manager as the leader of the community. It seems to me that he should be in the background and work through the council. It is best if the council carries the ball." [28] Administrative technicians tend to regard themselves as staff persons, somewhat in the administrative area of the classic politics-administration dichotomy. They carry out policy, honestly and efficiently. "The most important things are: Policy decisions to the council, administrative decisions to the city manager. Just that simple. . . ." [29]

These policy orientations involve complex roles to be played, which are not randomly distributed among managers. Political types have the professional credentials of the management profession, generally college social science backgrounds plus graduate work in public administration. Political types tend to have planned careers, starting at the university levels. Conversely, administrative types have greatly varied educational backgrounds and a tendency to have accidental careers, such as a department head who was asked to become manager by the council.

Administrative types are less likely to attend professional conferences and to have weaker views on whether or not city management is a profession. Since the professional code posits the manager as a community leader, weaker ties will normally be associated with a more restricted view of the manager's leadership roles. Administrative types also tend to hold a more limited concept of what proper government activities are than their political colleagues.

Environmental forces within the community also affect policy orientations. Small cities usually have administrative types. Social controls are stronger there and less innovation is required (or tolerated). Cities with a restricted view of city services and a "low tax" view also tend to have administrative type managers, largely for the same reasons. However, when cities are divided into those with high family income versus those with low family income (blue collar, working class), Loveridge found that political types were associated with low income cities and administrative types with higher class suburbs. Lower class cities seem to elect councilmen who require more advice and policy direction from the manager. Conversely, high status cities elect professional people with greater social awareness and political competence. High status city residents also tend to hold an expectation that friends and neighbors will rule and that the manager is largely instrumental.

Political Activity. Since top level careerists are so deeply immersed in policy questions, some fear the specter of a cadre of bureaucrats controlling policy through technical expertise and also intervening directly in campaigns for candidates favorable to their program. Those so concerned seek statutorily to prevent this. They also, with many others, wish to protect employees from political pressures exerted by the party in power in the form of forced contributions or election-day poll work. The desire both to separate policy and administration and to protect workers is seen in the federal Hatch Act, which largely forbids employees to engage in partisan political activities, such as holding party office. The act applies to state activities where federal grants are used. Many states, as well as many larger cities, also have "little Hatch Acts" which place similar prohibitions on their employees.

Federal prohibitions have been largely successful, although the Hatch Act, passed in 1937, has been challenged in court as being so restrictive that it deprives federal employees of their constitutional rights to participate in political activities. Frequently, at the state level, and most certainly in many other countries, careerists freely take part in political activity.

An outstanding example of non-neutral bureaucracy is found in Japan where political activism has been a historic tradition. In recent years, a political link has been developed among the bureaucrats, the ruling political party, and outside interests. Between 1954 and 1961 about one-third of the cabinet ministers were former bureaucrats and one-third of the upper legislative chamber in 1959 were former bureaucrats.[30]

France is another country where careerists have been active politically, frequently serving as cabinet ministers.[31] France and Japan are classed as democracies, although they do not have neutral bureaucracies in the sense of the American tradition. There is little comparative evidence that careerist political activity endangers established democratic politics.

A study of careerists in ten American states asked for self-reports of five kinds of partisan political behaviors: voting, trying to influence the vote of others, giving money, attending a political rally, and working for a party or candidate. State executives participate in partisan politics to a high degree: 98 percent report voting in the 1968 presidential election; more than half tried to influence the vote of others; more than 40 percent gave money; 36 percent attended a political rally; and one in five worked for a party or candidate. These rates of activity are far higher than the electorate in general and also higher than comparable federal executives or high level businessmen and professionals employed privately.[32] Table 6-9 shows the comparison.

The very high rates of participation by state executives are even more significant when over half of them are restricted by federal and/or state law from engaging in one or more of the reported behaviors. Legal prohibitions tended to reduce activity, but not eliminate it.

In the case of the federal executives, there is a slight tendency for those in lower grades (GS-13 and 14) to participate more actively, but the small number prevents drawing any conclusions.

Fred Grupp and Allan Richards did find that participation is related to three personal characteristics. State executives are more likely to participate if (1) their original motivation for entering public service was "service-oriented" rather than for less altruistic reasons; if (2) they perceived that the election of a new governor would result in "significant turnover" among career executives; and if (3) they rated their future job prospects higher than their current positions.[33] A combination of altruism, perceived self-interests, and upward mobility seems to be related to political activity.

Administrative Functions of the Top Level Executives. Decisions on the extent of their engagement in partisan political behavior face most careerists at some time in their careers. It is not, however, a major issue in the determination of agency or bureau policy. The real participation of careerists in public policy involves the way in which agency programs are formed, carried out, defended, and changed. Appointed agency heads become most effective and most involved in policy matters as they manage to

TABLE 6-9

Comparison of Partisan Political Participation
Between State, Federal, and Private Executives

Type of Executive		Partisan Activity			
	Vote	Try to Influence	Give Money	Attend Rally	Work for Candidate
Private					
N = 83	86%	40%	19%	13%	8%
Federal					
GS-13 and above	87	32	26	29	8
GS-14 and above	83	80	25	38	8
GS-15 and above	79	26	16	32	11
N = 38					
State					
N = 1870	98	52	44	36	19

SOURCE: Fred Grupp, Jr. and Allan Richards, "Partisan Political Activity Among American State Executives," a paper presented to the American Political Science Association in Chicago, September 1971. Table 1, p. 9.

shape the means and ends of the agencies they serve. This applies to all top level careerists who work near the chief executive at all governmental levels.

Despite the policy content of top level administrative positions, traditional views of the chief executive's job have changed little since Mooney and Reiley (Chapter 4). In this view, the manager coordinates different groups, directs subordinates, supervises their work, and maintains a close check on the profit and loss statement (or in government, the rate of program accomplishment). The "great man" view is important—charisma is attributed to the leader through hierarchical levels and upward communications. He "commands" rather than leads since his position of authority enables him in most cases to easily direct and control the behavior of his subordinates. Former presidential aide Jack Valenti once publicly stated that he "slept better knowing Lyndon Johnson is my President." This apparently sincere hero worship is an extreme example of imputing charisma to the leader, and it occurred despite LBJ's reputation for abusing subordinates.

The made-up word "POSDCORB" describes the traditional executive's duties well. He *plans, organizes, staffs* his organization with subordinates, *directs* them, *coordinates* the various parts, *reports* to a higher level, and *budgets* available resources in an efficient manner.

Today, as a modified traditional view goes, the manager carries a softer stick and wears a velvet glove over his iron fist. He consults with his key subordinates on major issues and may even delegate certain matters to them for final determination. He now has to deal with strong labor unions or employee groups and must be more flexible. Having learned from the Hawthorne studies how to manipulate people, he often does it in such an effective way that he is honestly admired by most of his subordinates. A vintage definition of management applies here: management is accomplishing organizational aims through people. A certain tough-mindedness is required. After all, people may be expendable if they fail to meet organizational needs. The executive, as the key person, has to keep organizational needs uppermost at all times.

This view of the manager's job might be appropriate, even today, in a closed organizational system, where interaction with the environment is not required. When the only requirement is maintaining the organization at a steady pace without much environmental pressure, traditional means may work. In many firms and even some public organizations POSDCORB still describes the manager's job.

Traditional views do not account for the political nature of organizations. The manager in an open organizational system must place much, if not most, of his attention on the world outside the organization. The social and political environment impinges directly upon and often determines the nature of the manager's job. His real job can be divided into three parts, all of them interrelated. Organizational maintenance involves most of the traditional management duties, of which coordination is perhaps the most important. Organizational representation involves the job of public spokesman for the agency. Organizational definition involves the complex job of delineating organizational purpose.

Organizational Maintenance. Organizational maintenance is the job that encompasses most managers' time and effort, although it is the most routine of the three functions. Since organizations are open systems, the maintenance function is to maintain some sort of internal equilibrium. Disequilibrium tendencies arise from such events as the drive of specialists to pursue separate and divergent ends, thus splintering the organization. To an accountant, for example, organizations exist to maintain ledger systems, while doctors often conceive of a hospital primarily as a place for medical interns and residents to gain experience. These splintering tendencies are matched, at the static end of the continuum, by tendencies toward continued low level, mediocre performance of organizational functions. The challenge to organizational maintenance is to prod and inspire where necessary and on occasion to modify the reward-punishment system in order to improve performance. Generally, coordination is the art of inducing or manipulating people to perform their tasks in line with overall organizational needs and to accomplish these tasks in harmony with other organizational members. This function is sufficiently difficult so as to occupy the vast majority of most executives' time. Often it prevents adequate attention to the broader executive responsibilities. This is what has been described as "Gresham's law of planning"—routine duties drive out long-range organizational planning.[34]

Organizational Representation. Organizations are personalized. The Federal Bureau of Investigation and J. Edgar Hoover were literally one and the same. Many city managers are personally identified with virtually all of the administrative acts of their city. Robert Hutchins represented for many years the essence of the University of Chicago's academic thrust. Robert McNamara was the "new look" in the Pentagon from 1961 to 1968.

Whatever the executive says is usually taken as an authoritative statement of organizational policy. It could hardly be otherwise, since he defends the agency before legislative committees, gives speeches to clientele groups as well as to the general public, and holds press conferences. Organizational members take their cues about internal policies from his speeches. Indeed, the target of his words may not be the public but the organization itself. Leon Sigal writes:

Officials at all levels depend to some extent upon their immediate superiors for career advancement. Giving the boss what he wants, or at least avoiding the appearance of insubordination, is a bureaucratic way of life. Because of his constitutional authority, if not his power, the President is the one official whose preferences matter most to bureaucrats. He often finds it efficient to tell the press what he wants to ensure that all officials find out quickly and to tell them openly through press releases and press conferences.[35]

The very same process operates at lower levels although officials ranking below the president have a more difficult time obtaining formal press conferences.

The public executive ideally should be articulate and convincing in his public appearances and statements, conveying clearly departmental objectives and plans. The key is clarity rather than rhetoric—Mayor Daley in

Chicago is not considered a polished public speaker, but listeners rarely miss his point. The job of organizational representation places a heavy burden on many executives, in some cases requiring up to or more than half their time. There is a close relationship between this job and the next function, defining the organization's purpose. Only by environmental feedback can the top executive be sure how the legislative body, clientele groups, and the general public react to the agency. Others in the organization also sample the environment, but the major responsibility for broadly evaluating views outside the organization and responding to them rests with top level executives.

Defining Organizational Purpose. Strictly speaking, executives do not define objectives, for that is the responsibility of the legislature or the president. One federal official comments, "By and large, the objectives of agencies are spelled out in law and practice prior to the appointment of executives, who have to spend a good deal of their time finding out what these objectives are. . . ." [36] Another noted, "Instead of defining the objectives of his agency, he must make certain that the agency conforms to the policy of the administration." [37]

The legislature and the president, however, can only give broad guidelines to which the agency itself must give flesh and sinew. A strong executive may be able to transform agency goals and objectives from routine nonessentials to bold programs which command wide attention. Sargent Shriver provided this kind of leadership for the Peace Corps.

Whether or not an agency will be activist and aggressive in carrying out its initial objectives is only partly a function of congressional and interest group influence. Much depends on agency leadership. An activist leadership will be constantly sampling and monitoring the environment to determine whether changes in emphasis are necessary and/or possible. The ability of top level executives to carry weight with other actors on the political scene is also of significance here. It was claimed that the federal government's decision in 1971 to instigate a court suit against Black Jack, Missouri, for obstructing the construction of low-income housing by restrictive zoning represented a victory for HUD Secretary Romney over the counsel of more conservative members of the Nixon administration. Acts such as this shape the image of an agency and do much to set its objectives. Most agencies have a sufficiently broad charter for wide interpretations of desirable and necessary goals. Often, what is required is administrative leadership rather than legislative sanction.

Philip Selznick refers to this general process as "institutionalization." It involves infusing the organization with value beyond efficiency or other routine criteria. Whenever groups and individuals become attached to an organization as a way of life and as a symbolic representation of shared values, institutionalization takes place. The organization, to the committed person, then becomes a valued source of satisfaction in itself.[38]

Institutionalization can take place much more readily when there is leeway for personal and group interaction and correspondingly less agreement about specific organizational goals. The key element here, then, is the quality of organizational leadership. Selznick regards the primary function of leadership as "infusing with value," or as institution building. Organizational maintenance by itself is not leadership, for leadership here cannot necessarily be associated with those in high places. Even organizational representation can be considered as "command" rather than leadership. In Selznick's view, leadership is the process of changing an organization to an institution. The leader's job is the development and maintenance of values and maintaining the institution's integrity.[39]

The Tennessee Valley Authority, the Marine Corps, and the FBI are institutions rather than expendable instruments for a given purpose. Leadership was required to attain the present status, and is required to maintain it. At a heroic level, this is the job of defining the organization's purpose.

NOTES

1. This is the definition used by David Stanley, Dean Mann, and Jameson Doig, *Men Who Govern* (Brookings, 1964).
2. Stanley et al. Unless otherwise indicated, most of this section relies on this study.
3. Dean Mann and Jameson Doig, *The Assistant Secretaries* (Brookings, 1965), p. 227.
4. Stanley et al., p. 59.
5. Mann and Doig, p. 229–30.
6. The following section is largely from Mann and Doig, pp. 68–86, 86–93.
7. Marver Bernstein, *The Job of the Federal Executive* (Brookings, 1958), p. 15.
8. *Ibid.*, p. 17.
9. Mann and Doig, p. 202.
10. *Ibid.*, p. 205.
11. Bernstein, p. 30.
12. Robert Art, *The TFX Decision* (Little, Brown, 1969).
13. Bernstein, pp. 24–25.
14. Stanley et al., Mann and Doig, and Bernstein. The actual detailed generalizations are from Mann and Doig, pp. 446–48, and are corroborated in the other works at various places.
15. Bernstein, p. 43.
16. *Ibid.*, p. 43.
17. This account is from Felix Nigro, *Public Personnel Administration* (Henry Holt, 1959), pp. 7–15.
18. Lloyd Musolf, "Separate Career Executive Systems—Egalitarianism and Neutrality" in *Public Administrative Review* 30 (July/August 1971), p. 416.
19. This account is largely from Musolf, p. 417. A complete report of the president's statement and the Civil Service Commission summary is contained in the "Documentation" section of the March/April 1971 issue of the *Public Administrative Review*. See also the exchange between George Graham and Roger Jones in "Currents and Soundings," *Public Administration Review* 31 (July/August 1971), pp. 451–54.
20. Musolf.
21. Norton Long, "Bureaucracy and Constitutionalism" in *American Political Science Review* 46 (September 1952), pp. 808–19.
22. U. S. Civil Service Commission, *Executive Manpower in the Federal Service* (Washington, D.C., 1972), p. 14. Unless noted, all further data is from this source. In some cases I have computed figures from their reported totals.
23. David Stanley, *The Higher Civil Service* (Brookings, 1964), p. 4 and *passim*. (This data is from an earlier period than the 1971 Civil Service Report).
24. Bernstein, pp. 50–51.

25. Ronald Loveridge, *City Managers in Legislative Politics* (Bobbs-Merrill, 1970).

26. *Ibid.*, p. 54.

27. *Ibid.*, p. 55.

28. *Ibid.*, p. 56.

29. *Ibid.*

30. Ferrel Heady, *Public Administration: A Comparative Perspective* (Prentice-Hall, 1966), pp. 51–52.

31. Henry Ehrmann, *France* (Little, Brown, 1968), pp. 255–71.

32. Fred Grupp, Jr., and Allan Richards, "Partisan Political Activity Among American State Executives," a paper presented to the American Political Science Association in Chicago, September 1971.

33. *Ibid.*, p. 38.

34. See Bernstein, p. 13.

35. Leon Sigal, "Bureaucratic Objectives and Tactical Use of the Press: Why Bureaucrats Leak," a paper presented to the American Political Science Association in Chicago, September 1971, p. 8.

36. Bernstein, p. 13.

37. *Ibid.*, p. 14.

38. Philip Selznick, *Leadership in Administration* (Harper and Row, 1957), p. 17.

39. *Ibid.*, p. 139.

7

POLICY- AND DECISION-MAKING
IN PUBLIC AGENCIES

This chapter deals with policy-making in the United States, primarily at the federal level. We will approach it in the following manner: first, policy-making in the United States will be briefly contrasted to that in the Soviet Union, thus indicating the parameters of the process; second, the process of incremental decision-making in the United States will be discussed; and third, the Program-Planning-Budgeting system (PPB) at the federal level will be analyzed as an alternative, "rational" decision-making and policy-making scheme to incrementalism. Finally, the chapter will mention some of the ways that the federal, state, and local levels have upgraded their policy-making process in recent years.

POLICY-MAKING—AN OVERVIEW AND COMPARISON

The policy-making process can be divided into four phases for purposes of analysis: initiation, persuasion, decision, and execution. In the United States, a "bubble-up" system of initiation occurs where groups, interests, agencies, and individuals inside and outside government propose a wide range of policies to the top political leadership (president, Congress, or agency heads). Rarely does the top leadership actually initiate proposals. Rather, it adopts a somewhat judicial or legalistic approach to proposals coming from below, judging one against another and hearing each party out. This is largely due to political values which regard the ends of government to be a response to the felt needs of society. Under this belief, groups and interests within that society should initiate proposals based on their needs and desires. This contrasts with the Soviet system (and, Samuel Huntington and Zbigniew Brzezinski note, most European countries) where the top political leadership normally initiates policy.[1] This situation might be expected where the role of party leadership is actively to assure ideological continuity.

Persuasion is the way to build support for a new or changed policy. In the United States, persuasion is consensus building, a competitive process among a great variety of groups. Normally consensus precedes decision-making in the United States, while in the Soviet Union the party leadership usually makes a decision, then attempts to mobilize support for it. In the United States, consensus building is most common on domestic issues. The decision-making process on foreign affairs is generally contained within the executive branch, proceeding hierarchically to the president, who is preeminent in foreign affairs. Often he makes decisions himself, consulting a few aides and experts. The lesser requirement for consensus on foreign affairs is similar to the USSR practice, where policies can be initiated and decided among only a few men in the Presidium or Central Committee.

The decision process either approves or vetoes a proposal authoritatively. As noted, in the United States decisions follow the building of a consensus, a process in which many policies fail or are modified beyond recognition. Many interests are "veto groups" that may stop a proposal even if they cannot get their own policy approved. In the USSR, decisions are routinely ratified by the legislature after being settled by the party. Mobilization of support is designed to secure implementation of and public information about the proposal, not to obtain consent for it. In the Soviet Union, a "correct" policy is one that Marxist-Leninist ideology supports, and the central party leadership authoritatively interprets Marx and Lenin. Internal Presidium struggles among a few men determine the result. In America, a "correct" decision is one that attracts wide support. Since there is no guiding ideology to be invoked (democracy, freedom, and the liberal tradition are too vague to be used definitively), the only way to indicate correctness is to obtain the consent of a wide range of institutions, groups, interests, and key individuals.

The execution of a policy in the United States may not be closely linked to the other three phases of policy-making, and autonomous agencies may have a free hand in implementing it. The president cannot oversee all programs and, in addition, has limited authority in some areas such as regulation of industry. Under these circumstances, there is relatively less control over the execution of policy than in the Soviet Union where the party faithful carefully oversee policy management. In the USSR, the four phases of policy determination are closely linked. Although all elements of the economic system are centrally controlled there, however, major problems of coordination and control of policies result.

Two further questions highlight any analysis of comparative policy-making.[2] First, does the process make possible clear-cut choices between alternatives? Secondly, does it facilitate major innovations in policy? In America, policy-making is hopelessly muddled and tends to frustrate choice between policy alternatives, as will be discussed in the next two sections of this chapter. It is not quite so clear whether practice in the Soviet Union is as incremental as in the United States. If it is, one is led to consider the possibility that decision-making in any society with a complex set of political structures is incremental. Huntington and Brzezinski conclude, "On the whole, it can probably be said that Soviet history offers more examples of clear-cut selection, both domestically and in foreign policy." [3] They suggest that the difference is considerable, but that the USSR may converge in this respect with United States practice as political resources increase and more interests favor than resist changes.

Both the Soviet and American systems innovate when necessary, but the processes are quite different. Innovations are proposed constantly in the United States, with modest piecemeal changes occurring continually. Once an innovation is made it is rarely reversed. In the USSR, innovation has frequently occurred in the form of major, unpredictable shifts of power at the top of the party leadership. Policy changes usually occur more slowly, partly because of the leadership's dislike of "idea men." When change is clearly necessary, however, it can proceed more quickly and more comprehensively than in the United States; innovation usually comes in response to a crisis. In power struggles, policy reversals are often highly visible. It can thus be said that in the Soviet Union, major innovation is more possible; in the United States, modest innovation is more likely.

INCREMENTAL DECISION-MAKING

Decision-making and Rationality. So far two policy-making systems have been contrasted. Broadly speaking, they are both "rational." This is not the case when the individual decision-maker is considered. Administrative man falls far short of rationality in his decision-making. He cannot absorb and relate the large amounts of data necessary to assess the relation of a program to a set of goals. At times, he may not even know the goals. He also has trouble in assessing the future and in predicting how proposals will work under uncertain circumstances.

Because of this, errors inevitably develop in the process of policy-making, and less than optimal policy outcomes occur. The classic decision-making scheme of philosophic/economic man fails either because of the nature of the circumstances or because man cannot apply it properly. This failure raises a number of questions. Why cannot man be more rational? What implications for the conduct of public business do policy-making errors have? Finally, are there institutional arrangements for correcting mistakes of individual decision-makers?

Herbert Simon indicates that men "satisfice" (find a decision that satisfies them and suffices for the question at hand) because they do not have the wit to maximize.[4] This suggests that suboptimal decisions are normally made. There are a number of reasons for this. First, all the information may not be available. New programs for the elimination of drug addiction and reducing highway deaths may be presented by HEW and the Department of Transportation to the Office of Management and Budget. Only enough money for one program is available. Which should the president support? It is necessary to know the initial and long-range cost of each, the relative cost-benefits of each (lives saved per dollars spent), the likelihood that Congress will support either or only one, whether one or both agencies are able to administer still another program, the effect of the program upon the recipients, and the types of incentives (reward versus punishment) most likely to succeed in obtaining client compliance. The proposing agency may have tentatively studied some of these issues but the president and his staff must puzzle out most of these questions for themselves.

Time may not always be available for a decision. The answer may be called for in short order—such as in the 1963 Cuban missile crisis.[5] Often, issues surface slowly, but after a point, events call for rapid decisions to be made and implemented—in spite of the fact that no basis for these decisions may exist. Such appears to be the case in the ill-fated Bay of Pigs invasion. Time constraints are not only important in foreign policy matters. The pressures in preparing a domestic legislative program put tremendous demands upon gaining information in a very short time. Often decisions must be made upon the hunches and guesses of the individual decision-maker.

Above and beyond the limitations of time and knowledge, human decision-makers are plagued by their own biases and values. Ideologies or cultural patterns form one limitation. Most federal executives do not seriously consider nationalizing the steel industry (though Presidents Truman and Kennedy surely gave it a passing thought), just as their Soviet counterparts do not consider substituting private enterprise for state ownership on any large scale. Broad values prevent any decision-maker from toying with these ideas. Subnational political cultures impose the same limitations. The village manager of a small city may decide not to recommend a municipal health program because the city will have to hire a doctor from another city and he believes that his council will not approve any program using "outsiders."

Muddling Through. The classic decision-making model calls for an impressive display of cerebral talent on the part of the individual decision-maker.

He is to establish his ends, study all the alternatives, and then dispassionately select the most appropriate means toward his ends. The process simply does not work this way. Rather, the decision-maker "muddles through." In a famous article, Charles Lindblom has argued that the process of muddling through is "superior to any of the decision-making methods available for complex problems in many circumstances, certainly superior to a futile attempt at superhuman comprehensiveness." [6] Lindblom compares the rational comprehensive (root) method of decision-making with the muddling through (branch) system. The root method starts anew each time while the branch method continually builds from the current situation. The root method, which is virtually the same as the classic decision-making scheme, begins with clarifying and ascertaining values and ends prior to considering options and alternatives. The branch method of muddling through, used by most if not all administrators and decision-makers, does not try to separate values (ends) from analysis of the options because "one doesn't know what he wants until he knows what he can get." [7] Since one can neither rank values precisely nor keep them constant over time, he chooses among ends and means (specific policies) at one and the same time.

The root method calls for policy-making based on a search for the appropriate means to maximize determined ends. Actually, as in the branch method, they are not separate.

The root method argues that a good policy is one that best selects means to match ends. According to the branch method, a good policy is one that achieves consensus among actors in the decision process. These actors need not agree on means and ends. A city manager, for example, may advocate a proposed annexation to control zoning along a major highway, while a key councilman may support the annexation to make the city "bigger and better." The annexation is thus a good policy though neither advocate shares the same values.

The root method calls for comprehensive analysis of *all* relevant factors. The branch method denies that analysis can be complete—it overlooks major possible outcomes and important potentialities and often neglects important values.

This apparent irrationality of the branch method is due to the fact that, unlike the root method which relies on theory and a large body of knowledge, it relies only on limited successive comparisons. The decision-maker need only know if the likely consequences of a policy differ from well-known alternatives, and by approximately how much. It requires merely the analysis of a small number of roughly similar alternatives. Theory is not relied on, because it requires bringing knowledge to problems—and a body of knowledge is generally not available on social issues. Therefore, comparative analysis of alternatives replaces it.

Lindblom explains how the above "muddling through" system of individual decision-making has been institutionalized, and how the system smooths out its own worst aspects.[8] As noted earlier in the United States-Soviet Union example, the decision-maker relies first on ideology to greatly reduce all possible alternatives. Generally, the more ideological the system, the greater the number of alternatives outlawed by definition, and thus the faster potential decisions can be made. Looser ideological systems act more slowly but are more likely to consider a greater number of alternatives and thus be more "rational," in the sense of the classical tradition of decision-making.

There are many other strategies or dodges which act as shortcuts to rationality. "Satisficing," rather than maximizing, requires only that a policy satisfies the decision-maker and suffices his need, not that the "best" policy be found. "Next change" and "seriality" assume that policies are sequential, will frequently be reviewed, and can be modified easily upon review. Frequent review may be easier than a one-time expensive study of all alternatives. These strategies assume that no policy is ever final and is always subject to revision. Policies may be chosen that maximize feedback in the policy period, rather than a "one best solution" which cannot be definitely evaluated.

"Remediality" is employed when policy-makers do not know precisely what will work but do know what does not or has not worked. Progress can thus be made by eliminating poor practices or policies without having to ascertain what is "good." City planners require side and front yard property line setbacks for residential areas, not because these setbacks automatically guarantee that the area will remain blight-free, but because previously their absence has been associated with rapidly declining neighborhoods. Planners thus try to anticipate and remedy problems that have occurred in the past, even though they are not sure what is good for the future.

"Bottlenecks" are problems that arise during the operation of a plan. While the best possible policy may have no bottlenecks, one that "satisfices" may have a few. It is easier to adopt a policy which assumes that some minor problems will arise which can be dealt with when they occur, than it is to attempt to develop a more comprehensive master plan at the outset.

"Incrementalism" assumes that plans change only at the margin. The decision-maker's attention can then be concentrated on familiar experience and on reducing the number of alternatives and factors he has to understand.

Incrementalism. Clearly all these strategies are interrelated. They provide institutional methods of improving rationality in policy-making. An important consequence of adopting them is that they tend to favor programs that require frequent but minor changes, thus discriminating against far-reaching policies that demand long-term commitments of the decision-maker and/or the agency. The method of "muddling through," or of successive limited comparisons, is often referred to as the incremental system of making policy. Most policies in the United States develop in this way, with exceptions such as the post-Sputnik federal program of aid to colleges.

The present system of incremental policy-making in the United States has many supporters. Most high and middle level bureaucrats at all levels of government, particularly in the federal establishment, are "incrementalists" since their interests are generally perceived to lie with the present decision-making system. Perhaps the most noted "incrementalist" among academic ranks is Aaron Wildavsky.[9] His arguments for an incremental system come from his study of federal budget processes, but they have considerably wider ramifications. Arguing for the present budgetary system and against a program budget, he makes the following points. First, incrementalism tends to increase agreement among participants: it is not necessary that they agree on ends or values, only on a specific dollar amount. The worth of a program is not debated, only its cost, since it is assumed that the incremental system will not eliminate programs in any drastic manner. Indeed, since only dollars are at stake, it is possible to decrease conflict by making side payments to non-winners. In return for supporting a smaller appropriation for military operations, for example, a congressman may be able to have a military base in his district. This process is widely described as political log-rolling, although its usage is not restricted to legislative chambers. It can also be looked upon as a means of restraining or of decreasing conflict, not an insignificant social value in American life.

Incrementalism also increases the ease of making complex social calculations. Few persons understand government programs well and relatively few can then demand a certain level of funding as absolutely necessary vis-à-vis alternate levels. Calculations are made upon relative evaluations of the strength and merits of alternative programs which other groups and/or agencies push forward. The legislative or administrative decision-maker depends on an institutionalized system of vocal and visible interests, each advancing his own program as far as he can. Pluralism becomes the key to budgetary decision-making and a means of decreasing abstract calculations of the worth of a program. Weighing support for and opposition to a program or appropriation becomes the calculus of consent.

Wildavsky's arguments are similar to Lindblom's in his advocation of the branch system of decision-making. Both place incrementalism in a broad institutionalized system of political decision-making. Wildavsky suggests that alleviation of conflict is perhaps the major advantage of incrementalism. To a certain degree this is correct. Two basic questions have not been met, however. The first is whether an incremental approach does not too quickly abandon attempts at careful evaluation of competing programs on an economic cost-benefit basis, thus allowing difficult questions regarding the nature and values of a program to be determined by purely political considerations. This question will be discussed shortly.

The second matter involves the assumption that interest group pluralism is a satisfactory basis for assuring that all points of view will be considered during the continuing series of decisions that make up an incremental system. Large agricultural interests are considered, but are sharecroppers? Large producers and suppliers are considered, but are consumers? Historically, black interests have been overlooked. Perhaps competition is good only for those that can compete, particularly since no one is protecting weak or dispersed interests. E. E. Schattschneider noted that "the flaw in the pluralist heaven is that the heavenly chorus sings with a strong upper-class accent. Perhaps 90 percent of the people cannot get into the pressure system." [10] To the extent that groups are not organized or represented in administrative agencies and in congressional committee memberships, they will stay outside the system as spectator interests. This, of course, is not a strong argument against an incremental system, for even if a more comprehensive "program" view were to be adopted, it is not clear that powerless groups would be considered.

THE NEW "RATIONALITY"—PPB

Planning-Programming-Budgeting systems have been described by phrases as widely varying as "a revolution in federal budgeting and decision-making" to "merely what we have been doing all along." While some agencies previously may have been doing the kinds of analysis called for by PPB, the dramatic effect of the PPB system marks it as a significant innovation in federal budgeting. State and local governments are now adopting PPB language, if not the actual analysis, and thus a new budgeting system is spreading over all government levels.

What is PPB? *Planning* stands for a greater emphasis on selecting ends for governmental action and for analyzing means to reach them. Existing agency programs are not necessarily related to attainment of broad social goals—careful analysis is needed to relate the effectiveness of the program (means) to the social value (end).

Programming refers to a strong effort to redirect budgeting attention away from specific line item expenditures such as salaries and travel to broader program packages such as cancer research or police traffic control. These programs become the basis for cost-benefit or cost-effectiveness analysis in order to sharpen the choice between them.

Budgeting refers simply to the inclusion of planning and programming in the budget process rather than having them considered separately from the means by which money is allocated. Choice without resource allocation is meaningless.

PPB Goals. The PPB system is most closely associated with Robert McNamara, secretary of defense from 1961 to 1968. Enormous attention was paid to the cost and effectiveness of the existing weapon systems and new proposals. Not only were these systems expensive, but they involved major questions of national strategic interest. Decisions on the size of the United States Army depended on considerations about the need to fight one, one-and-a-half, or two land wars at the same time, or on whether the future of international conflict involved small, guerrilla-type insurrections or nuclear conflict. These decisions depended, of course, on high level calculations of American vis-à-vis Russian and other national interests. While these calculations could not, of course, be quantified, they were brought into stark reality by a budgeting system that insisted on specific goals to justify programs (in this case, strategic considerations to determine weapon systems or army size), thereby linking the budgeting system to broader strategic questions.

PPB appears to have six basic goals which, as a unit, maximize the kinds of analysis discussed here:

1. Careful examination and identification of the goals and objectives in each major area of government activity.

2. Analysis of the output of a given program in terms of these objectives.

3. Cost measurement over a number of years, including all social costs as well as the actual outlays. If a highway project requires relocating persons from the route, for example, all the costs to these relocatees (such as for driving farther to work) should be counted whether or not the government will reimburse all of them.

4. Formulation of objectives and programs beyond the year of budget submission.

5. Analysis of alternatives to find the most effective means of reaching program objectives and achieving these objectives for the least cost.

6. Establishing these analytic procedures as a systematic part of program review.[11]

Even a brief glance at these six goals will stamp them as elements of a system quite different from the present incremental system. Items 1, 4, and 5 are very close to classic decision-making process. The PPB system as a whole places heavy emphasis on the possibility of human rationality and on institutionalizing procedures in the budget process which will increase the likelihood of rational decisions being made. The other goals generally call for the institutionalization of rationality within the budget process by measuring costs over a number of years, analyzing outputs of programs, and making the analytical procedures a systematic part of the program review. Agencies are to analyze programs carefully after determining their objectives (actually, even PPB devotees admit that, as Lindblom suggests, program and objectives cannot be separated) and apply a critical eye to their successes and failures. All future costs are to be considered to avoid understating the smaller first year "start up" costs of new programs and to make the calculation of costs include social costs to all parties (such as cost of water pollution).

Program Evaluation. The key to PPB is in its emphasis on program evaluation. Not only are all programs to be scrutinized and analyzed, they are (at least in theory) to be arrayed against all other competing programs on a cost-benefit or cost-effectiveness basis. A program is to be selected by a search among alternatives as an effective means toward objective organizational or social goals. How different this is from the incremental system which searches among readily available options only long enough to find a satisficing solution! This gap between practices and ideal is, of course, why PPB program analyses have not been widely implemented and perhaps why they may never be.

Programs are to be evaluated by cost-benefit analysis much as the benefits and construction costs of dams are calculated by the Corps of Engineers. When this is not possible, cost-effectiveness techniques are used to compute total costs and compare the effectiveness of competing program alternatives. The example shown in Table 7-1 rates all proposed motor vehicle injury reduction programs on the cost-effectiveness basis of cost per death averted. Even where estimated costs and effectiveness cannot be specifically compared, PPB demands that objectives be clarified and specific programs carefully scrutinized. Even at this "softer," qualitative level of analysis, the emphasis on programs could result in what Wildavsky predicted—increased conflict over a prize program and less ability to fund smaller programs as side payments (these small "pet" programs supported by a key decision-maker may be inefficient and thus cost-benefited out). Only time will tell. Most PPB proponents stoutly deny that PPB seeks to replace the present system of political bargaining. It will, they say, merely sharpen the debate by supplying more detailed information on policy options.[12]

Another reason PPB and program analysis have become widespread throughout the federal government and in some state and local governments is that the volume of proposed social programs has exceeded the capacity of the concerned agencies to evaluate them in the conventional way. The costliness of these new proposals, even without the success of PPB in the Defense Department, would probably have required some additional analysis.

TABLE 7-1

Motor Vehicle Injury Control Alternatives, 1968–1972*

Program	PHS[2] Cost[3] ($ million)	Savings[2] ($ million)	Benefit Cost Ratio	Deaths Averted	Cost Per Death Averted
Seat Belt Use	$ 2.0	$2,728	1,351.4*	22,930	$ 87
Restraint Devices	.6	681	1,117.1	5,811	100
Pedestrian Injury	1.1	153	144.3	1,650	600
Motorcyclist Helmets	7.4	413	55.6	2,398	3,000
Reduce Driver Drinking	28.5	613	21.5	5,340	5,300
Improve Driver License	6.1	23	3.8	442	13,800
Emergency Medical Services	721.5[1]	1,726	2.4	16,000	45,000
Driver Skills	750.5	1,287	1.7	8,515	88,000

* Numbers have been rounded to a single decimal point from three decimal points; therefore, ratios may not be exact result of dividing column 1 into column 2 as they appear here.
[1] Includes $300 million state matching funds
[2] Public Health Service
[3] Discounted

SOURCE: Elizabeth Drew, "HEW Grapples with PPBS," *The Public Interest* (Summer 1967), p. 16. Reprinted with permission of the author and Basic Books, Inc.

Table 7-1 shows how eight alternatives to reduce motor vehicle injuries were reviewed.[13] Driver licensing involved a medical screening program.

Reducing driver drinking was a program to educate people not to drink before driving. Seat belt usage programs were to encourage people to "buckle up." Most of the other programs were designed to encourage individuals to protect themselves more effectively: cyclists, for example, were urged to use motorcycle helmets, and "accident prone" pedestrians to cross streets more carefully. A national driver training program was to be established, while medical services were to upgrade community emergency care with federal grants. Since this latter program had social benefits beyond preventing motor vehicle injuries, it was supported along with high cost-effectiveness programs such as seat belt usage.

The savings figure included dollars for medical care that would not be spent and indirect savings such as earnings not lost by death or disablement. Divided by the Public Health Service (PHS) costs, this gives the benefit-cost ratio. Another factor is the cost per death averted which merely divides deaths averted (an estimate) by the PHS cost. This does not take into account the costs associated with deaths, as shown in the savings column.

These findings are limited by lack of knowledge of the true effectiveness of programs of trying to educate and persuade people to use seat belts or motorcycle helmets. It may be that negotiations with automobile companies to standardize safety installations, such as seat belts which must be fastened before the ignition can be turned on, may be a better alternative than educational programs. In this case, PPB caused competing programs to be evaluated on a careful cost-effectiveness basis, resulting in a much greater likelihood that "rational" decisions will be made.

The effect of PPB is not merely limited to providing a technique for comparing programs. If it were, there would be relatively little value in discussing it for the tools of cost-benefit analysis have been available for many years. PPB has a more significant effect on the budget and decision-making process than this. Broadly speaking, it centralizes power, changes the way outcomes are weighed, and changes the views of participants in the process.

Changing Outcomes. Thinking in terms of program packages often changes the outcomes of the budget process. An army may be viewed differently if it represents only one program package (conventional warfare) in the Department of Defense, or if a number of programs include army units. In the former case, the army must defend to the death the package lest one program change wipe out its existence. In the case of reducing motor vehicle injuries, if certain programs seem potentially effective enough, there might be pressures to eliminate other programs to finance accident prevention more heavily. Emphasis on cost-effectiveness means that programs which can be quantified may be preferred over non-quantifiable programs. PPB advocates deny this, but the possibility exists.

Emphasis on programs or performance began well before PPB. The program movement began early in the 1950s with the advent of the performance budget. Performance was stressed by listing the specific services which budget line items supported. In addition to salaries and travel expenses, the budget would also list such performance data as the number of miles of street swept or acres of forest land replanted. When possible these performance indices were translated into per unit costs. The performance budget thus centered attention on the end result of government activity.

The PPB movement, also by stressing programs, moved attention of the budget participants to the ends of government action rather than on the process of justifying and defending budget proposals. In this respect PPB is profoundly reformist, rejecting the political bargaining approach. Group pluralism in the process becomes less important because programs are generally evaluated in terms of their effectiveness for the larger public by technicians with less respect for the balance of interests. Political bargaining will always be important, but there will be considerably greater emphasis on economic rather than political efficiency, at least in the initial analyses.

Centralizing Power. To date, PPB systems have had the effect of centralizing power in the budgetary process. This was clearly the case in the Department of Defense under McNamara, who used program evaluation and cost-benefit analysis as tools to draw decision-making power away from the services toward civilian control. Most previous secretaries had been limited to endorsing or denying requests.[14] McNamara established specific requirements for analysis and also designated the program categories. He thus succeeded to a large degree both in changing the orientations of the services (or at least the language and form of budget presentations) *and* in seizing power from them. The shifts in program categories which occurred in the department under McNamara are shown in Table 7-2, where the PPB system has eliminated service groupings in favor of broader program groupings.

This is a clear-cut case of an attempt to compare programs rather than organizations and to reduce interservice competition for a larger share of the defense budget. Table 7-3 shows the 1970 budget for the Department of Defense and its program distribution.

The Office of Management and Budgeting in the White House Office—by requiring that budgets be prepared on a program basis, by specifying

TABLE 7-2

Organizational versus Program Allocations in the Armed Services

Old Budget System	Planning-Programming-Budgeting System
Navy	*Strategic Forces*
Polaris	Polaris
Marine Corps	ICBMs
Carrier task forces	Long-range bombers
Air Force	*General Purpose Forces*
ICBMs	Marine Corps
Tactical aircraft	Armored divisions
Air defense aircraft	Tactical aircraft
Long-range bombers	Carrier task forces
Army	*Continental Defense Forces*
Air defense missiles	Air defense aircraft
Armored divisions	Air defense missiles

SOURCE: Murray Weidenbaum, "Program Budgeting—Applying Economic Analysis to Government Expenditure Decisions," *Business and Government Review* 7 (July–August 1966), p. 22–31.

TABLE 7-3

Program Distribution of 1970 Department of Defense Budget
(Millions of dollars)

Program Category	1970 Estimate
Strategic Forces	$ 9,087.4
General Purpose Forces	29,856.3
Intelligence and Communications	5,832.4
Airlift and Sealift	1,889.2
Guard and Reserve Forces	2,848.6
Research and Development	5,500.3
Central Supply and Maintenance	8,848.8
Training, Medical, and Other General Personnel Activity	9,967.8
Administration and Assorted Activities	1,407.3
Support to Other Nations	2,408.8
Retired Pay	2,735.0
Total of Above Programs	$80,381.8
Financing Adjustments	144.3
Total Budget, Department of Defense	$80,237.5

SOURCE: Special Analysis R., *United States Budget*, Part 4, "Analytic Program Structure" (Washington, D.C., 1970), p. 259.

the format and the types of analysis, and by mastering program review—has further strengthened the president at the expense of the agencies. Since he needs expert advice, it has also strengthened the OMB. In those agencies doing careful program analysis, PPB systems have centralized power and influence, normally at the level of the secretary or deputy secretary. Knowledge is power and those who understand PPB systems gain power.

A similar accretion of power to those who control budget categories occurred under a traditional budget system in New York City: ". . . an almost incredibly detailed 'line item' budget, which the Budget Director has in fact prepared and [of] which only he and his staff are masters . . ." is a potent factor in increasing that official's influence over budgetary decisions.[15] The ability to define the categories upon which the budget is settled is a major element of power, regardless of the actual form. In New York, a program budget system might increase the power of the mayor over budgetary decisions.

Changing Views. Congress has not yet given its blessing to PPB systems. It still requires budget submission on a line item system and still prefers to make decisions on an incremental basis, as do most public officials. Given this reluctance, the question is: to what degree, if any, will PPB change the present decision-making system? Most devotees see PPB as an aid to political decision-making rather than a replacement. It is a bit unfair to categorize them as "apolitical technocrats," as do some defenders of the bargaining process. Rather, they are searching for ways to improve the present system. Advocates such as Charles Schultze see PPB as standing midway between the present bargaining system and a zero base budgeting system which would call for every agency program to be reviewed once a year.[16] A realistic hope for program analysis is to provide more and better information to decision-makers so that they bargain with more realistic programs and with better awareness of the alternatives associated with a program. Lindblom argues that this is what analysis now is used for. In political bargaining, information and policy analysis is used as a weapon to convince some that "a policy he desires can serve the values of another policy-maker to whom the persuasion is directed." [17] Thus, a vast public works program giving jobs to many hard-core unemployed may appeal to another decision-maker who favors dams and roads but does not care about unemployment. If both parties are aware of the alternative, outcomes, and cost of the program, it is likely (concludes Lindblom) that better policies will emerge from the political bargaining process. As noted, Wildavsky argues that more information will result in more conflict.

PPB and Social Reform. Program analysis is likely, in the context of the late 1960s and early 1970s, to have considerable impact on the content, as well as the process, of public policy-making. In recent years a general public commitment to social reform has produced heavy demands for federal, state, and local programs dealing with major societal problems. Under these circumstances program analysis may focus policy-making on specific proposals for alleviating many of the social ills that beset America, rather than merely comparing two "value neutral" alternatives.[18] Table 7-1 (page 168) suggests this possibility as the article about reducing motor vehicle injuries was written by a journalist, supported by a foundation, and intended for a wider audience than public officials. With a commitment by significant elements of American society (mass media, professions, federal bureaucracies, universities, youth) to social progress in ending poverty, pollution, and other social ills, the mere existence of defined alternatives may result in demands for action which would not have arisen previously.[19]

There always have been zealots inside and outside organizations who thought that money to this or that agency would solve most of the country's ills. Once alternatives are dramatized, the resulting demand by reformers is likely to be much stronger than any past year's enthusiasm which had to be whipped up for turgid statements such as "higher levels of appropriations for the Department of Health and Education." This effect is precisely what some earlier advocates of performance and program budgeting sought—at least those who had program responsibilities. They argued that a budget should portray the end results of government action. For example, in 1970 a program category in the budget for Housing and Urban Development was "assuring decent housing for all Americans." [20] It is thus possible that PPB advocates may create demand, not merely compel choice.

MAJOR IMPROVEMENTS IN
THE FEDERAL POLICY-MAKING PROCESS

PPB systems are only the most recent attempt to improve the federal policy-making process. Upgrading the policy process has been a major concern of public administration scholars, administrative officials, and political leaders since the nation was created.

This interest has not gone under the name of improving policy-making. In earlier days this would have implied far too much executive branch activism and would have conflicted with the prevailing view that the bureaucracy (early-day reformers would not have liked the term "bureaucracy," either) should be a quiet, neutral tool. Even so, early movements to democratize, to make more efficient, and to reform the federal government were historical analogues to contemporary attempts to rationalize the policy-making process. Two major events have been strengthening the chief executive and upgrading the individual federal executive.

Strengthening the Chief Executive. Many of the major administrative events of the present century have resulted in strengthening the president. As the ripples of change spread, the same effect gradually reached state and local chief executives. These events appear to be of much less importance than political landmarks such as social security or civil rights acts, but their impact on the policy-making process has been very significant.

The 1921 Budget and Accounting Act created a federal budget system centralizing in the Treasury Department authority to present to the Congress one fiscal plan which, when adopted, could be centrally administered. Designed only to create a system of expenditure control where none had previously existed, it provided the basis for all future budgetary process improvements.[21]

The 1939 Brownlow Committee report laid the groundwork for subsequent presidential control of the policy process and institutionalization of the White House staff. It recommended that the Bureau of the Budget be placed under the president, removing it from Treasury responsibility. This completed the centralization process; budget authority had moved from the agencies to the Treasury to the president. The Brownlow Committee also recommended that the president should be given many more key personal assistants (with a "passion for anonymity") to enable him to control executive agencies. It was also suggested that he should have additional staff agencies to strengthen his managerial effectiveness. This attempt to institutionalize the presidency met with some strong opposition by Congress and some students of government, but most of the recommendations were adopted.

Institutionalizing the presidency has resulted in the steady growth of the White House staff from a few personal Roosevelt aides in the late 1930s to a very large number in the present Nixon administration. The Office of Management and Budget has more than 500 employees, Henry Kissinger's staff numbers perhaps 100, and there are many others. These groups of highly qualified specialists improve the rationality of agency policy-making by enabling the president to coordinate and evaluate a wider range of executive branch programs. Indeed, the process has become so successful that relatively minor issues can be now elevated to presidential preview. It is reported that John Kennedy personally selected the names of nuclear submarines. This change defeats one traditional principle of public administration—limiting the chief executive's span of control so that he can concentrate on major issues. It may also sap the vitality of lower units.[22]

Nevertheless, the White House continues to expand from administration to administration. It provides the president an alternative source of expertise, and he need rely less and less on the agencies. In the case of Henry Kissinger's staff, it seems obvious that the State Department is too slow and cumbersome to give the president the instantaneous information he desires. A further advantage to the alternative bureaucracy is that Kissinger and his staff are much more loyal to Nixon than the State Department ever can be to any president. Furthermore, this staff cannot be called before Congress to answer embarrassing questions.

Reorganizations have also tended to strengthen the chief executive. Some have emphasized abstract concepts of "efficiency and economy" while others have been aimed specifically at increasing executive ability to coordinate divergent programs. Still others have tried to strengthen the executive through reducing his span of control, enabling him to concentrate on the most important policy questions. The well-known First and Second Hoover Commissions in 1949 and 1955 made a vast number of recommendations aimed at increasing efficiency and economy in the executive branch. The effect, particularly associated with the earlier Commission report, was to strengthen the president specifically and, to a lesser degree, agency heads.

Personnel Upgrading. Another major pattern which has resulted in improved agency and system policy-making is upgrading the individual federal executive. The continuing efforts to increase the competence and effectiveness of the federal executive have not had the conscious aim of improving policy-making. They did result in strengthening and professionalizing the members of federal bureaucracies, thus propelling their agencies into the policy-making sphere armed with greater internal competence.

One major step in this direction was the creation of a federal civil service system whose analogues are now becoming more and more common at the state and local level. It should be emphasized that civil service protection has protected key technical and professional persons as well as rank and file employees. Thus, civil service protection has helped the policy process by allowing key careerists to concentrate on technical matters which contribute to agency expertise.

A major impetus to upgrading the individual employee was the Government Employees Training Act in 1958. Here, specific recognition was made of the need to train and retain federal employees. Before this time,

Congress had regarded training as largely unnecessary, believing that government employees should possess required skills before being hired. There are now a large number of training opportunities available to the individual employee, particularly in metropolitan areas. Usually operated by the Civil Service Commission (although agencies sometimes develop their own courses), training programs include such subjects as PPB analysis, management development, supervisory training, secretarial skills. The emphasis of the entire federal training program is on individual development and the creation or expansion of personal skills that the individual can use in his job.

While each federal agency is required to develop an overall training plan, this has not led to an emphasis on organizational development courses at the expense of training for individual skills. Organizational development puts primary emphasis on the ongoing organization, stressing improved relationships among organizational members, the removal of barriers to communication, and a higher level of interpersonal trust. Much of what is called "sensitivity training" is similar to organizational development when taken as part of a group training program.[23] Group training has not proven very popular at the federal level. Political executives often do not wish to rely heavily on trust relationships with subordinates. Security requirements work against group training, as does the high degree of career mobility.[24]

Thus, the contribution to improved policy-making made by training is by increasing individual employees' capacities, rather than by binding them into stronger, more cohesive organizations. Agencies will be stronger for the development of their members' skills, but perhaps no more able as an organization to affect the policy process than before. This training could further fragment and weaken the policy-making process by strengthening organizational subspecialities.

For many years low salaries combined with the low prestige of public service dissuaded the best qualified persons from entering government employment. Low pay was a detrimental factor in recruiting and retaining top political executives, as discussed in Chapter 5, but it was equally a problem at the career level.

A study of public attitudes toward public employment and top level federal executives in the early 1960s showed that the generally employed public, along with most of the educational and occupational groups, considered top federal executives superior to their private counterparts in honesty and in their interest in serving the public. However, interviewees generally considered federal executives lower in ability and in the drive to get ahead, and often held them in lower regard.[25]

Public attitudes change, particularly during periods such as the turbulent 1960s. There are reasons to believe that public service now ranks as high in prestige as business employment among college students, and possibly as highly as business among key occupational and professional groups. This may be due partly to the fact that some occupations are found primarily in government, as opposed to the private sector. Additionally, the advent of the welfare-social service state and the awareness of an unfinished social agenda have improved the relative prestige of governmental service. This may be only a temporary or relative improvement.

The advent of a service economy may result in a major shift in employment patterns. Personal preferences for smaller service organizations employing highly skilled technicians and professionals could come at the expense of traditional public and private employers. People may want to "do their own thing" outside of organizations. This is, of course, only an impression obtained from the general dissatisfaction of college students and many professionals with large organizations in general. As far as government is concerned, large numbers of qualified applicants are now looking for entry level positions, as well as some higher level positions. A weak national economy is responsible for much of this. The key positions are, however, at higher grades. Recruitment, training, and promotion for these top level career positions is a more complex question which a temporary economic recession will not resolve.

Indeed, prestige and salary are highly interrelated matters. Federal salaries have increased dramatically in recent years. Effective in 1968, a middle level manager (GS-14) with ten years of federal service in grade would receive $27,000. This level is by no means unusual for college graduates to reach. At higher levels, the supergrades (GS-16 through 18), with no experience, begin at almost $28,000 and can go up to $36,000. This seems high enough to attract well qualified persons from outside the service. These salary increases were enacted to make federal employment more comparable to private employment. Even so, it seems unlikely that they would have been approved by Congress unless there had been some change in public attitudes toward government service in recent years. Pay scales are both a cause and effect of the prestige of public employment, but improved salary levels tend, over time, to have a very positive effect on the policy-making process.

NOTES

1. This section relies primarily on Zbigniew Brzezinski and Samuel Huntington, *Political Power: USA/USSR* (Viking, 1963), chapter 4.
2. Huntington and Brzezinski mention a third element, the extent to which policy-making integrates policies in different areas of subject matter.
3. *Ibid.*, p. 225.
4. James March and Herbert Simon, *Organizations* (Wiley, 1959), pp. 140–41.
5. See Robert Kennedy, *Thirteen Days* (Norton, 1969). Also Graham Allison, "Conceptual Models and the Cuban Missile Crisis" in *American Political Science Review* 63 (September 1969), pp. 689–718.
6. Charles Lindblom, "The Science of Muddling Through" in *Public Administration Review* 19 (Spring 1959), p. 87.
7. Aaron Wildavsky, *The Politics of the Budgetary Process* (Little, Brown, 1964).
8. Charles Lindblom, *The Policy-Making Process* (Prentice-Hall, 1968), chapter 4.
9. Wildavsky has written extensively on this matter. Most of the discussion is from his *Politics of the Budgetary Process*. Another important article is "The Political Economy of Efficiency: Cost-Benefit Analysis, Systems Analysis, and Program Budgeting" in *Public Administration Review* 26 (December 1966), pp. 292–310. Also see Charles Lindblom and David Braybooke, *A Strategy of Decision* (Free Press, 1968) and Lindblom, *The Intelligence of Democracy* (Macmillan, 1965).
10. E. E. Schattschneider, *The Semi-Sovereign People* (Holt, Rinehart and Winston, 1960), pp. 40–41.
11. These six goals are from Charles Schultze, *The Politics and Economics of Public Spending* (Brookings, 1968), chapter 2. Schultze was the director of the Budget Bureau under President Johnson when the PPB system was adopted virtually service-wide by a presidential directive. While not all analysts or students would select precisely these six goals, they are generally those central to the PPB system. I have elaborated several of them without changing the basic goals. The student of PPB should consult a number of other works: Clay Whitehead, "Uses and Abuses of Systems Analysis" (Rand Corporation, paper P-3863, 1967) is an excellent overview; also see Charles Hitch and Roland McKean, *The Economics of Defense in the Nuclear Age* (Harvard University Press, 1960); Allen Schick, "The Road to PPBS: The Stages of Budget Reform," *Public Administration Review* 26 (December 1966); and David Novick, ed., *Program Budgeting: Program Analysis and the Federal Budget* (Harvard University Press, 1965).
12. William Capron, "The Impact of Analysis on Bargaining in Government," a paper presented to the American Political Science Association in New York City, September 1966. Schultze specifically makes the same point.

13. The following discussion is from Elizabeth Drew, "HEW Grapples with PPBS" in *The Public Interest* 8 (Summer 1967), p. 9–29.

14. See the difficulties of the Navy and of Navy Secretary Fred North in meeting McNamara's demands for rigorous analysis in Whitehead.

15. Wildavsky, *The Politics of the Budgetary Process*, p. 140. The quote is from Wallace Sayre and Herbert Kaufman, *Governing New York City* (Norton, 1960), pp. 368–69.

16. Schultze, p. 81.

17. Lindblom, *The Policy-Making Process*, p. 33.

18. Perhaps the best statement of a new view of politics in America and its relationship to PPB is Allen Schick, "Systems Politics and Systems Budgeting" in *Public Administration Review* 29 (March/April), pp. 137–52.

19. Daniel Moynihan once referred to this process, at an earlier and happier time, as the "professionalization of reform." This referred to a change in the political system which initiates "reform," or new and/or modified social programs from within; and which relies on the professions, social scientists, and academics for interpretation of social data determining the need for "reform." The key point is that social needs and programs to meet them are now being largely determined by federal technocrats rather than by the normal process of interest group demands. Moynihan has now recanted; see his *Maximum Feasible Misunderstanding* (Free Press, 1970). No one is now as optimistic as in the halcyon days of Great Society legislative triumphs. Even so, there is more than a grain of truth in the "professionalization of reform" argument. We are likely to see this process again in the "post-industrial," or technocratic, society whenever that era arrives.

20. Special Analysis, 1970 Budget of the United States.

21. Schick, "The Stages of Budget Reform."

22. See Paul Appleby, *Policy and Administration* (University of Alabama Press, 1949).

23. See John Rehfuss, "Training, Organizational Development and the Future Organization," *Public Personnel Review* 32 (April 1971), pp. 118–22 for a further discussion of the implications of individual training contrasted to group or organizational development.

24. Robert Golembiewski, "Organization Development in Public Agencies: Perspectives on Theory and Practice" in *Public Administration Review* 29 (July/August 1969), pp. 367–79.

25. Franklin Kilpatrick, Milton Cummings, Jr. and Kent Jennings, *The Image of the Federal Service* (Brookings, 1964). This work involved a cross-section of the employee population outside the federal government. About 5,000 persons were sampled. To a large degree, the findings were consistent with earlier studies, although the public is a bit more favorable toward the federal service. See also Leonard White, *The Prestige Value of Public Employment in Chicago* (University of Chicago Press, 1929) and Morris Janowitz, Deil Wright, and William Delaney, *Public Administration and the Public* (University of Michigan Institute of Public Administration, 1958).

8

BUREAUCRACIES IN
WORLDWIDE PERSPECTIVE

American public administration has always been ethnocentric. Ever since Woodrow Wilson wrote his famous essay in 1887, arguing for a science of administration free from alien philosophies, American public administration largely has been limited to influences from within the United States. Only occasionally were longing glances made at the British or other Western European civil services, when reformers sought a model for a stronger, more effective federal bureaucracy.

Changes in this restricted view have been occurring in recent years. In 1947, Robert Dahl, in a celebrated essay, argued that public administration could hardly be considered a science until it took a comparative view of bureaucratic and administrative phenomena.[1] It is possible, he noted, that there could be an American public administration, a British public administration, and a French public administration, but this would be better determined by empirical studies than by implicit assumptions.

In the 1950s students of comparative government and politics began to pay more attention to the problems of developing nations. A major question revolved around the development, improvement, and control of the national bureaucracy. The success of a new nation in developing and modernizing itself is often determined by the effectiveness of its national bureaucracy in affecting the life of the citizen and helping thus to create a sense of "nationness." Whether or not a country wishes to modernize or Westernize is not important; a strong, national bureaucracy is crucial in maintaining the traditional pattern of behavior. If development is to occur, new national governments will have to rely on centralized direction of the economy. There is, therefore, a strong pressure to place any source of national expertise at the state's service. The role of both civilian and military bureaucracies in these new nations, therefore, was, and is, of crucial importance. Many students of politics thus began to compare bureaucracies or at least to pay more attention to national bureaucracies as a crucial part of the political and nation-building process.[2]

Study of the administrative problems of other countries leads to cumulative knowledge which can be applied to the American scene. It is unlikely that there are laws or principles to be discovered. However, most social scientists would gladly settle for insights which make possible broad generalizations. These in turn lead to the tentative construction of hypotheses or of models which eventually will predict, with some limited validity, bureaucratic and administrative behavior.

The next section considers political regimes and national bureaucracies in various countries. After this, some major conceptual schemes for comparative analysis will be outlined, and finally, one of them will be used to study bureaucratic behavior in France and the Philippines. This chapter will not attempt to build hypotheses or models, but the two case studies will attempt to relate bureaucratic behavior in France and the Philippines to the particular social and political culture of each nation. The next step in theory building would be to develop generalizations from these two nations to a range of similar nations. For example, France is a developed nation with severe class divisions and a very strong national bureaucracy. Do countries with similar class cleavages also have powerful bureaucracies, or only those that are developed? And most importantly, why?

Before going further, however, some definitions are necessary since terminology is not entirely consistent in this area. Comparative politics is the study of different political systems and the attempt to develop hypotheses and generalizations. In this chapter national bureaucracies are to be compared to each other. The two bureaucracies in the case studies will be analyzed in terms of their relationship to the social structure of the larger society, their relationship to the political system, and their meaning for American bureaucracy.

"Comparative administration" normally refers to the activities of national bureaucracies, but since it seems to imply a division between politics and administration which I do not accept, the term will not be used. A final term is "development administration." Generally, this refers to the attempts of national leaders to move their people toward higher levels of economic and political development. Development administration aims at increasing living standards and integrating citizens into a sense of "nationness." This is a major function of the bureaucracy in most developing nations.

REGIME ANALYSIS

The ranges in levels of development are matched by the variations in types of political regimes and in the demands placed on national bureaucracies.

Ferrel Heady contrasts the higher civil bureaucracies in a variety of political systems.[3] Political participation and policy-making are the focus, since the study is limited to higher bureaucrats and managerial elites.

The following questions are discussed:

1. What are the major operating characteristics of the bureaucracy representing its composition, hierarchical arrangements, pattern of specialization, and behavioral patterns?

2. To what degree does the bureaucracy become multi-functional, helping make public policy decisions as well as execute them?

3. What are the principal means and their effectiveness for exerting control over the bureaucracy by outside forces?

Heady then applies these questions to political regimes in developing counties and the likelihood of controlling bureaucracies and assessing their power positions. His analysis has several broad categories of political regimes: traditional-autocratic, bureaucratic elite, polyarchal competitive, dominant-party semicompetitive and mobilization, and Communist totalitarian. Traditional-autocratic systems are traditional ruling systems and generally seek change slowly if at all. They use the bureaucracy, both civil and military, as their instrument. The operation of these administrative systems is generally ineffective since traditional characteristics hamper its operation and government penetration into the nation is difficult due to ancient customs and patterns. Iran is cited by Heady as the archetype of this kind of regime, with many countries in the Near East and Africa falling into the category.

Bureaucratic elite sytems exist in countries such as Thailand or Burma where power is found in the hands of career government officials. Traditional elites have been replaced, with modernizing goals articulated by the new leadership, if not accepted by the people. Generally a political party system or political participation has not developed, and a general vacuum of power has enabled the careerists to take over, with the military usually the senior partner. Heady uses Thailand as an example of bureaucratic imbalance, where dominance by a full-fledged bureaucracy has inhibited the development of other political institutions. He indicates that Thailand is "well adapted to its environment," since its behavior patterns emphasize maintenance of traditional social relationships rather than increasing productive output.

Polyarchal competitive systems in developing nations are quite similar to Western European and United States political systems, given the differences in developmental levels. Nigeria, the Philippines, Brazil, and Argentina are typical of this category, although all of these except the Philippines have periodically replaced civilian control by military regimes. High levels of political competition exist, with visible groups striving for public support; nevertheless, reasonably peaceful transfer of political power is possible. Because the government is seeking public support, its goals are short range, and it tends to be weak in regulation of and extraction from the populace. While the bureaucracy is instrumental, weak legislative and executive institutions may cause it to become deeply involved in the policy process from lack of direction.

Dominant-party semicompetitive systems differ from dominant-party mobilization systems primarily by the existence of at least some legitimized competition. In the latter case, the majority party is usually led by persons associated with the formation of the new nation, or it is so closely tied to the symbol of nationalism that opposition to the party or regime is near treason. Ideology reigns in mobilization systems, but does so less virulently in the semicompetitive system where opposition is tolerated. In this case it is hard to generalize about bureaucracy since India and Mexico remain the chief examples of the semicompetitive systems. In both of these countries executive political leadership has been strong and the bureaucracy instrumental. The Mexican bureaucracy seems more dynamic than the Indian, but Indian administrators may have more capacity for governing due to the long colonial heritage. In both cases the distinction between policy-making and policy application is blurred as bureaucratic specialists move into direct political participation.

Mobilization systems are largely African, with Tunisia, Egypt, Ghana, Guinea, and Mali being examples. Here, elites are young, aggressive, and committed to developmental nationalism, and there is usually a charismatic leader. The bureaucracy is often tightly controlled and loyal, powerful but neutral. Holding high status, it absorbs most of the country's intelligentsia. The party or military bureaucracy often is placed in positions within the civilian bureaucracy to control it although the need for expertise has increased the overall influence of "pure" administrators.

Communist totalitarian systems, Heady's last category, are also single-party states, but differentiated from dominant-party mobilization systems by the unity of ideological commitment to Marxist-Leninist theory and to-talitarian methods in the governance of the state. The ideology is so powerful and pervasive that most Communist states resemble other Communist states more than another non-Communist nation at the same level of development. The developing countries that fit this pattern (with the exception of Communist China, which is in a class unto itself) are Cuba, North Korea, and North Vietnam.

Communist bureaucracies are extremely complex, notes Heady, since the state must mobilize and direct all economic and social aspects of organized society. Control is through the party bureaucracy, paralleling the civilian bureaucracy. Within its ranks, its members experience a constant tension resulting from the necessity of having to be both true to the party line and right (at the risk of having their expert assessment of affairs cast doubt on their party loyalty). Dual accountability, on both the grounds of ideology and achievement, places heavy weight on the manager of the state enterprise and the staff specialist, who often respond by reducing their willingness to innovate and rely on hedging against both sets of constraints.

This brief outline of political regimes clearly indicates the variety of political and administrative relationships and the difficulty of fitting them into broad categories. The role of the bureaucracy is as diverse as the countries involved.

MODELS FOR STUDYING COMPARATIVE BUREAUCRACIES

The need for new conceptual tools became apparent, when political scientists began to analyze other cultures and develop generalizations about bureaucratic behavior in less developed countries. Structural-functional analysis proved the primary basis for what is now the flourishing study of comparative politics. Most of the leadership in the study of comparative bureaucracies has come from comparative politics. Thus the lead came from those who were striving to explain political systems as a whole and only considered administration or the roles of the bureaucracies as a necessary subsystem.

The use of structural-functional analysis focuses on the nature of the social functions that a system performs. In the broadest societal context these functions include cultural maintenance and transmission, goal seeking and setting, social integration, and environmental adaptation.[4] These systemic functions are carried on by the basic activities of the political system, such as converting inputs into outputs, and maintaining and adapting the systems capacity, as noted in Chapter 4. The significance of these somewhat abstract concepts is that they mark a turn away from traditional views of government which compared political structures, such as legislatures, executives, judiciaries, and interest groups, without considering the social functions they perform. The structural-functional approach is particularly important in analyzing less developed societies, where a certain structure

such as the executive (prime minister, king, president) performs a number
of functions. Perhaps he makes, judges, and carries out laws. While certain
functions may be universal, the structures which perform them vary considerably from nation to nation. Public administration for many years has
been plagued by the tendency to examine structures from only a historical
and legal point of view, often mentally abstracting them from their social
setting and considering only the organization charter or the position-classi-
fication plan. Hopefully, the field is well past this stage, as suggested by the
recent development of the comparative administration group and the new
journal, *Comparative Administration*.

Almond-Powell Model. The most influential, or at least the most popularized conceptual scheme extant in comparative politics is the Almond-Powell structural-functional plan.[5] A structure is an observable set of political
roles. The bureaucracy, for example, is made up of the roles of bureaucrats, plus the roles of those inside and outside the government as they interact with bureaucrats in their official capacity. The model divides the political activities or functions of the bureaucracy, or any structure, into
three levels. First is system maintenance and adaptation, which includes
political recruitment and socialization. In terms of the bureaucracy, recruitment involves obtaining a supply of top and middle level leaders or
career executives. Socialization involves being supported by a system
which inculcates attitudes favorably toward the bureaucracy.

A second level is related to systemic capacity, meaning the performance
of the system in its environment. Bureaucratic functions in this area can be
broken down as follows: regulative activities, concerned with the control
of citizen behavior and the suppression of demands; extractive functions,
concerned with the extent that the system draws resources from its citizens; distributive activities, involving the degree the system shifts resources; and responsiveness analysis, or determining how much the first
three functions are affected by citizen demands. The competence of the
bureaucracy is crucial to certain of these functions such as the capacity to
operate programs designed to extract or distribute resources. This suggests
the necessity of positive societal attitudes toward the government as a pre-
condition to effective administration.

The third functional level is conversion. The conversion process trans-
mits inputs into outputs. Inputs are demands and supports, symbolic as
well as material—such as for allocation of goods (a highway in a town),
deference to authority (enforce law and order), and behavior regulation.
Outputs are transactions such as goods distribution and behavior regulations. The conversion activities or functions which are crucial to under-

standing the overall scheme are: (1) interest articulation (expression of demands), (2) interest aggregation (combining demands into alternatives), (3) rule making, (4) rule adjudication, (5) rule application, and (6) political communication (the process of transmitting these activities within the system and to and from the environment). The first two functions are performed by interest groups and political parties in developed nations, by clan or tribe in less developed countries. Rule making, adjudication, and application refer to the familiar legislative, judicial, and executive rubric. In bureaucracy-dominated politics, these latter functions will be performed by the bureaucracy to a large degree. In the United States it seems evident that Congress no longer has primary responsibility for the rule-making authority, the latter having passed to executive agencies. Similarly, rule adjudication has, in large part, been transferred to the executive, as courts either refuse to or cannot review administrative actions.

In this model, political development occurs when existing structures and the culture cannot meet challenges or problems without structural differentiation or secularization. Structural differentiation occurs when roles become specialized or when new roles are created. Under pressures of change political institutions tend to become more specialized. A primitive society contains general interest groups and associations, while the United States Congress establishes specialized committees. Secularization is the process by which men become more rational and analytical and when decision-making processes linking ends and means become common. Secularization occurs when a Filipino leaves the barrio and his kinship ties for Manila, or when the United States established a budget system in 1921.

One criticism of the Almond-Powell scheme is that it merely substitutes a newer academic vocabulary for old concepts without adding analytical power. The model's language, however, is widely used now, and it is hard to believe that language can change without corresponding changes in the way political scientists view phenomena.

Prismatic-Sala Model. Another model which has implications for the comparative study of bureaucracy is Fred Riggs' prismatic-sala model. Also based on a structural-functional approach, it is a unique attempt to abstract the qualities of a transitional society into an ideal type, somewhat like Max Weber's ideal type bureaucracy.[6]

Using the analogy of optics, Riggs indicates that a less developed society is fused, meaning that its structures have many functions, while a developed society is diffracted, with specialized structures. Certainly, a very primitive society does not have separate parties and legislatures, but relies on a few structures as the chief and the tribe. A prismatic society has elements of both the fused and the diffracted. Some structures are multifunctional while more specialized ones are developing. New and old overlap. An administrative agency may display the new in the form of a classification plan, but will operate in an older and more traditional manner, perhaps employing on the basis of kinship ties. Formalism results, which means that the forms of development exist, but the practices do not.

Societal needs are exhibited by the existence of kaleidoscopic stratification in which both traditional and modern elites may exist. Hinterland folkways may ascribe status to age or religion, while in the metropolis, entrepreneurial groups may gain status and wealth. Kaleidoscopic stratification is also marked by polycommunalism or preoccupation with membership in a number of separate communities in the same society, with relatively little penetration, communication, or exchange among them. *Clects*, or groups combining the character of cliques and sects, develop. These are the forerunners of intermediate associations in a developed society.

The weight of bureaucratic power is greatest in prismatic society. New, functionally specialized bureaucratic organizations extend administrative controls over the corroding older power bases, both regionally and centrally. Civilian and military bureaucrats, using both old and new symbols, tend to dominate decision-making.

Riggs' prismatic public administration model is the *sala*, a Spanish word used in Latin America for government office. It is marked, as mentioned, by excessive bureaucratic power as well as by considerable inefficiency. The confusion of old and new values underlies the sala model. One result of this is mimesis, the combining of ritual and rationality. For example, the sala official naively accepts worthless technical advice. Since he cannot assess the cost of alternative means, he uses both the ritual form from the past and the technology of the developed nations. Trained health technicians practice both ancient sorcery and modern surgery, for example, or the agricultural adviser hires a witch doctor to bless imported hybrid seed.

Riggs' model is important for several reasons. First, it is based on considerable research in Southeast Asian transitional societies. Secondly, it is directly concerned with public administration and the role and influence of the public bureaucracy. Finally, it is an attempt to focus development administration on a pure or ideal type of transitional society rather than concentrating on the process of development. The difficulties are that it is easier to invent a vocabulary than to apply a model. At this date, the prismatic model provides insights but has had little use as a guide to empirical research.[7]

Weberian Model. The last model is that of Max Weber, the famed German sociologist, whose bureaucratic ideal type has proven so influential in social science research. The model was discussed in Chapter 4, so it need not be detailed here. The major problem of using this model in comparative research is that its roots seem to be imbedded in Western rationality and German Junker authoritarianism, even though it is true that despotic regimes of the past such as China and Egypt first developed the bureaucratic system. There is some question whether it can be applied to transitional nations in today's world—a question which was, of course, a motivating factor in Riggs' development of the prismatic model of bureaucracy.

In what is perhaps the best known attempt to apply Weber's notions to a developing country, Morroe Berger attempted to measure "professionalism" in the Egyptian civil service along a Weber-oriented bureaucratic scale. Berger concluded that Egyptian bureaucrats behaved in a different manner from Western administrators and that possibly both a Western and non-Western type of bureaucracy might exist.[8] Although his methodology has been severely criticized for lumping together behavioral and structural elements, his work seems to have spurred other attempts to modify Weber's classic scheme for more precise analysis of developing bureaucracies. Berger's study did not clearly deal with the politics of bureaucracy.

A Weberian definition of bureaucracy is the basis for Heady's analysis of regimes and bureaucracies, discussed earlier. In most cases, however, considerable modifications in the Weberian model are required for it to be useful in further comparative research.

The Case of Corruption. The phenomenon of corruption is a good case study in the application of these newer conceptual models. In terms of the Almond-Powell conversion function, it is merely interest articulation at the enforcement level. In developing nations, specifically the new states of Africa and Asia, and in United States urban political machines, demands of citizens are not policy-oriented, but rather personal and family-related. A combination of ethnic and familial ties of many cultures, the existence of wealthy elites denied formal access, the weak legitimacy of a system, and the use of government as an employment agency—all result in nonprogrammatic demands. These personal demands are often nonamenable to legislative relief or routine administrative action and lead to the provision of personal services and benefits at the output or enforcement level.[9] Corruption was endemic in earlier urban America, and was attributed largely to machine politics. More likely, however, it was only in part due to the nature of the political system and at least partially due to the personal needs of ethnic groups and poverty stricken persons too socially disorganized to demand choices between policy alternatives.[10] The situation appears to be similar in other countries at the same stage of development as the Philippines, suggesting that economic and social development does not automatically eliminate corruption.

This example suggests that comparative models can explain bureaucratic behavior at home as well as abroad. Some grasp of comparative models should be very helpful to American students of public administration. Certainly it would add perspective to American officials who are perplexed and distressed over the seemingly endemic corruption which exists in developing countries. "Pouring foreign aid money down rat holes" expresses their view. Students of comparative politics generally have more tolerance, understanding that what Americans denigrate as corruption may be acceptable in other cultures. In addition, even when they do not completely accept it, they realize it may be functional for the particular political system. Riggs suggests that a rational, impersonal, efficient bureaucracy in a developing society may aggrandize political power at the expense of developing political institutions such as the legislature and particularly the party system. The lack of spoils for the party may weaken its potential development. The ironic result is that ultimately weak political institutions will deprive the bureaucracy of the political support to develop the administrative incentives necessary for high level performance.[11]

Other students of comparative political development take similar or at least neutral stands regarding the existence of corruption. Bert Hoselitz regards it as helpful in the early stages of development when societal integrating devices are necessary. Nonrational, particularistic methods of recruitment then form a means of linking a new administrative state with traditional roles.[12]

When viewed from a comparative and functional viewpoint, it is much more difficult to regard corruption as a black and white issue. It depends upon the cultural context and on the functional needs it fulfills. This way of viewing administrative and political questions is much more complex than using simplistic, culture-bound models, but it is essential in order to understand the administrative process in a given country.

It is now possible to consider two different bureaucracies, France and the Philippines. One is a developed European power with a long history and a classic Weberian-type bureaucracy, while the other is a developing country in Southeast Asia. The focus will be on the adaptability of the administrative system to social settings and the controllability of the bureaucracy by other political institutions.

FRANCE

The French bureaucracy is a classic example of a Weberian bureaucracy, ruling powerfully and faithfully with equal disdain for politician and citizen. The shape of the French administrative system emerged around the time of the French Revolution, when the king's household fell into possession of the nation as a whole. After a struggle with the executive, the officials of the royal household gradually consolidated their positions and a permanent set of bureaucrats with their own strongly held values and beliefs emerged. As the state became depersonalized the bureaucrat became its agent, transferring his allegiance from the king to the nation. This classic experience is in marked contrast to the experience of more recent developing countries that lack the long tradition of allegiance of a trained corps of servants to the crown.[13]

The bloody overthrow of the French monarchy in 1789 was followed by a drastic and sweeping set of changes in the country. Napoleon came next, followed by alternative terms of constitutional monarchies and republican governments. After 1870 the Third and Fourth Republics suffered a succession of crises, culminating respectively in the German occupation and de Gaulle's Fifth Republic. Bloodshed has been common. The abortive Paris Commune in 1871 resulted in an estimated 30,000 executions. Since 1789, France has been a constitutional monarchy three times, an empire twice, a semidictatorship once, and a republic five times.[14]

These violent changes have weakened the French political system, and much of the strength and alleged imperviousness of the bureaucracy can be attributed to a need to compensate for this weakness. French parties are notably ideological and their unusually large number produces fragmentation. Consequently, the French parliament is an especially weak legislative body. The diversity of party ideologies reflects centuries of division in French society between clerics and anticlerics, monarchists and republicans, radicals at both ends, and labor and a combination of conservative peasants and business.

These divisions, writ large in parliament, have proven unbridgeable in the past. Frenchmen give more than casual support to the French philosopher Emile Alain's radical doctrine that "the government deserves distrust without revolt and obedience without commitment." [15] The student-worker uprising of May 1968 suggests that, as in the past, distrust may rapidly give way to revolt in France.

The unwillingness and inability of the French parliament to compromise differences arises from these historical cleavages and also from the nature of French socialization patterns. These patterns, to be covered in more detail, place a high value on avoiding face-to-face contacts, on individualism and absolute equality, and on low levels of political socialization in the family. At this point, however, it is important to explain how the French political system has been able to maintain some equilibrium with no parliamentary stability.

The answer is through bureaucratic rule. For centuries the higher civil service has been deeply immersed in policy-making. A combination of the need for new regimes to call on existing expertise to keep governmental wheels turning, insure popular acceptance of the value of special training and skills of the administration, and maintain the cohesiveness of the bureaucracy itself has made this political role possible; political instability may have made it necessary. Such policy involvement has been facilitated by the lack of restrictions on civil service politicking. Many senior members have returned to the service after a period of time in political life, often serving as ministers in some short-lived cabinet.

This stability has proven largely functional according to most observers. The bureaucracy has been able to provide at least a modicum of permanence. Its strength probably lies as much in acceptance by political leaders as in administrative aggrandizement.

This picture of the bureaucracy as the linchpin of the fragmented French political system has been less clear since the beginning of the Fifth Republic in 1958. De Gaulle established a strong presidency resting on popular support and, according to Henry Ehrmann,[16] largely gathered into his own hands many of the functions of government, such as rule making and rule application, which previously were the province of the legislature and the bureaucracy. At times this received approval (when the country and the parliament wanted de Gaulle to settle the Algerian war); other times it was attacked as an infringement of the republican nature of the state. The effect on the bureaucracy was not entirely clear.

Some expected de Gaulle to rely heavily on the bureaucracy, particularly in those areas with which he was not directly concerned. He did increase the number of civil servants and their role in decision-making. In fact, many of the cabinet members under de Gaulle were careerists, as they had been in previous years. Even so, some senior bureaucrats in important ministries were peremptorily overruled by de Gaulle. Given his term of office and popular mandate, they fell into step when they might not have been as compliant under a weaker executive.

One case in point was that of state aid to religious private schools, involving the implementation of legislation enacted in the late 1950s after a savage political struggle lasting several years.[17] About 20 percent of French schools are Catholic, as is 92 percent of the population. As it was felt that many Catholics were "dechristianized," most of the political left opposed the legislation. Despite the attempts of secular administrators in the Ministry of Education, contracts between the private schools and the state are now in effect. These contracts call for state funds if minimum standards are met. Administrators were not able to defeat the drafting of the bill or the approval of it, nor were they able to do more than hamper the final effectuation of it. There was only some short-lived bureaucratic foot-dragging in approving contracts.

The other case involved de Gaulle's decision in 1962 to seek direct presidential elections through a questionable use of the new constitution that would bypass parliament and place a referendum directly before the public. While some high-ranking bureaucrats apparently considered the procedure illegal, they did not oppose it. Opposition might have been expected since direct election would increase the power of an executive and would thus tend to decrease their own freedom of action.

Bernard Brown, in commenting on these examples, notes that "most sophisticated Frenchmen take it for granted that the 'grand corps' (Conseil d'Etat, Cours des Comptes, Inspecteurs de France) governs the nation regardless of the outcome of delays in parliament. This view is not borne out by our two studies." [18] In both cases, de Gaulle was in office and his presence, as suggested earlier, may have made the bureaucracy more subservient than in prior years.

Almond-Powell Analysis. At this point the discussion of France will be fitted to the conceptual model of Almond and Powell to let the student judge how well a model can fit fact to theory. System maintenance and adaptation, one of the three classes of functions, takes place through the socialization and political recruitment process. In France, socialization of the nation is incomplete. Major cleavages are largely associated with one class or view, such as Catholic, Communist, or Socialist. Many Frenchmen develop all their social and political views from one direction. Cross pressures are much less frequent than in the United States, since the relatively fewer organizations to which the Frenchman belongs do not overlap, but tend to duplicate views and "pile up" the same orientations.

The major source of socialization is the family. The extended family provides the net of relationships which determine most French social practices and attitudes. French family rearing patterns are authoritarian, close and demanding, but, according to Henry Ehrmann, leave the child a private world of his own as long as overt behavior conforms to parental demands.[19] This may explain the likelihood of the Frenchman's "obeying without commitment." Overt behavior suffices, involvement is not necessary.

Avoidance of face-to-face contacts is another aspect of French behavior which is instilled during early life. So are the deep strains of egalitarianism and individualism typical of Frenchmen. The French tend to distrust compromise and bargaining, partly because they conflict with the desire to remain individual, equal, and apart. Furthermore, there is a definite lack of family political socialization to a party.[20] All of these factors combine to prepare the Frenchman for a life of political alienation.

The educational system tends to strengthen this socialization pattern since it is highly authoritarian, very centralized, and places a very high emphasis on individual competition through national examinations which allow the successful candidate to proceed with further education. Generally, the higher classes are considerably more successful in the examinations, which tends to strengthen the intraclass bonds and weaken interclass mobility. Not surprisingly, recruitment to bureaucratic office is from a relatively narrow elite.

French public officials, as a group, are an elite cadre representing and speaking for the state. They expect and receive deference for this reason and perceive themselves as public *officials* rather than public *servants*. The service was even more elitist before World War II, when top careerists were limited to certain departments and were required to pass difficult examinations, spend a certain time in grade, and obtain a certain level of education. Generally these senior civil servants came from the Paris School of Political Science *(Ecole des sciences politiques)*, a wealthy school for the sons of upper-class Frenchmen noted for its legalistic and conservative viewpoint. These conservative views of an elite group contemptuous of the general public allegedly led to the bureaucracy's receptivity to the Vichy regime in 1940.[21]

Begun in 1945, the National School of Administration *(Ecole nationale d'administration)* opened competition for top positions to a broader range of students and gave some scholarships to those in poorer classes. Promotion to upper ranks was widened to include all lower ranks, with the highest positions being awarded equally to graduates of this new school and to persons promoted from within. It appears that promotion from within has helped the lower and middle echelons of the bourgeoisie, but not the sons of farmers and industrial workers. This may reflect deeper divisions in French life than administrative reforms can cure.[22]

In contrast to the United States, there is little recruitment to the public service above the entry level. Only those initially drawn from examinations immediately after college are likely to reach the top. Closing off lateral entry further restricts the chances of unrepresented classes to enter the bureaucracy.

Political system capacity is another function in the Almond-Powell model. These authors devote some attention to France as an example of a developed democratic political system, but with limited subsystem autonomy. They refer to the tendency of social groupings in France not to associate with each other. The political institutions of party, interest group, and mass media operate as Catholic or Communist parties, interest groups and media.[23] Working together with the agencies of political socialization such as peer groups, families, and work groups, these forces tend to wall off social groups, such as Communists or Catholics, from contact and communication with other Frenchmen.

Almond and Powell suggest that France has a relatively low capacity level compared to other industrialized Western nations, such as the United States. Political crises, such as aid to Catholic schools, are resolved after major struggles marked by immobilization for some time and crisis-style relief.

French evasion of taxation, cynicism regarding law enforcement, and noncompliance with the law, and general alienation from the institutions of the Fourth Republic suggest low support levels and limited extractive, regulative and symbolic capacities.[24]

Tax evasion and cynicism about legal institutions would normally be associated with inability of the central bureaucracy to penetrate the populace. Popular alienation from purely political institutions also apparently extends to the rule of *l'administration*. Alfred Diamant notes that ". . . Frenchmen have gotten used to the rule of *l'administration* but have not learned to like it, merely to live with it. He rebels against the service but not against the political system." [25]

The French distributive system is not so easily explained. Prior to de Gaulle, the weakness of parliament and successive cabinets had resulted in the more powerful interest groups such as big business and small merchants having ready access to the legislative assembly and the bureaucracy at the expense of weaker groups. The bureaucracy is not impervious to interests although it is justified in the eyes of many Frenchmen only because it assures absolute rationality and equality. Under de Gaulle the bureaucracy was under even more pressure from interests, as parliament became less of a major political force.[26]

Almond and Powell suggest that the distributive system rewards some groups relatively well, and others not as well, and that the responsive capacity is low and intermittent which would be typical of such a distributive system. All systems, however, reward certain groups more highly than others, so this explains little. Actually, the French system in some respects has a relatively high output level and it is unlikely that these outputs are given only to special elite groups. Table 8-1 compares the United States, Great Britain, France, and the Philippines on certain indices of distribution.

TABLE 8-1

Comparison of United States, Great Britain, France,
and the Philippines on Selected Indicators
of Government Distribution

Indicator	United States	Great Britain	France	Philippines
Expenditure of central government, social security, and public enterprises as a percentage of GNP	21.0	38.8	40.0	9.2
Inhabitants per physician	780	935	1,014	5,555
Students enrolled in higher education per 100,000 population	1,983	460	667	976

SOURCE: Bruce Russett et al., *World Handbook of Political and Social Indicators* (Yale University Press, 1964), Table B. 2, pp. 294–98. Data as of late 1950s.

France spends a higher percentage of her gross national product on "public goods" than do any of the other countries. In addition, despite the elitist nature of the educational process, France has many more students in higher education than England, although less than the Philippines and the United States. It is difficult to make a flat empirical statement that France does or does not have greater distributive capacity than similar countries.

In France the conversion process (the third functional level) has been somewhat ineffective, according to Almond and Powell. The ideological nature of French social divisions has made it hard for the process to work as parties do not aggregate demands,[27] interest groups articulate ineffectively or on single class demands, and the mass media does not penetrate to the public.[28]

De Gaulle's prestige blocked off the input structures of parties and the legislature. Thus there was a tendency for unresolved demands to pile up until some major crisis, such as Algeria, was broken by extra-constitutional measures, such as de Gaulle's Fifth Republic. The communication function was dominated by de Gaulle, but not used to build mass support for a party or other permanent institution.[29]

Interest articulation is weak since groups are widely regarded at best as partial representations of interests. This makes them somewhat illegitimate, resulting in weak trade unions and non-business groups. The reason for this weakness is partly historical. Rousseau's "general will" is flaunted by partial interests, and Bonapartism's ideal of plebiscitarianism argues against any secondary institution standing between the individual and the state. The other factor is, of course, the socialization process which teaches Frenchmen to trust only themselves to protect their interests.

As has been mentioned, in recent years de Gaulle stripped away much of what little rule-making power the parliament possessed, and added it to the executive branch's existing rule-making power and existing rule-application powers. Apparently this satisfied the bureaucrats who were never strong supporters of parliament, although they were under more effective control with a president than under weak cabinet government. But since de Gaulle did not concern himself with all issues, a random pattern of bureaucratic weight in the rule-making and rule-application power has evolved. In some important issues, such as aid to Catholic schools, de Gaulle was content to let parliament work out the details and the bureaucracy's role was simply that of rule application.

The French bureaucracy is distant, centralized, arrogant, and nonrepresentative, yet it is also prestigeful, powerful, and perhaps uniquely suited to the French temperament. How does this work? First, a short look at the bureaucracy's internal operations and attitudes is in order.[30]

Internal Bureaucratic Operation. A major emphasis of the French bureaucracy is, and has been for some time, that of maintaining the security and prestige of the service. The French civil service has long been a separate social class and a separate occupation which gained job security through employee safeguards granted in early years. As the Frenchman identifies a profession with an employer, the civil servant identifies his profession as serving the state. In so doing, he takes on a bit of its sovereignty.[31]

This emphasis on employee safeguards has been furthered by the existence and acceptance of unions which were given full recognition in 1946.

Civil servants now believe that there is no significant protection unless the slightest risks in or most remote contingencies of a man's career are covered.[32]

Entrance to a top career position requires rigorous training. The National School of Administration gives a three-year course for newly selected members of the top career service with law the primary discipline. Recent changes allow other studies such as political science and history to provide entry. This course includes an internship for practical training, temporary placement in private industry for study of industrial management, and concentration on one of four areas: general administration, economic and financial administration, foreign affairs, or social administration.

In return for accomplishment and career commitment, tenure and status are legally guaranteed to the bureaucracy. Tenure can be revoked only after legal hearings at which the member is judged by his peers. The civil service itself largely determines advancement and other status matters. Salaries are adequate with substantial fringe benefits such as retirement and family allowance.

The predominate characteristic of the system is the emphasis on the individual. He is a generalist, not a specialist, and his rank in the service is not contracted or changed. As he moves up in the service he must receive additional training. While prerequisites of rank and status are officially justified as advancing the efficiency, prestige, and stability of the service, they represent, in effect, no little amount of bureaucratic effort to improve their own position, to consolidate past gains, and to protect officials.

Conflicting views of public interest among highest level bureaucrats mirror the tensions within France between change and the "stalemate society" of the past.[33] Many of the younger bureaucrats who have reached high levels believe that the public interest rests upon a transformation of society in terms of technical and economic progress. Characteristically, they are convinced that an administrative elite must be the guiding force that reveals to France her destiny, and this elite must educate various economic and social groups to their true interest. In cases where haste is necessary, it must compel them to move forward and drop their quarrels.

Older members of the high civil service tend to visualize the public interest as maintaining harmony and stability. The state must act as arbiter to assure the continuation of the old values of order, national unity, and state sovereignty. Tradition is the highest value.

These views sometimes fuse. Both are paternalistic and authoritarian. Both see politics as unnecessary to the achievement of societal ends and are products of the French bureaucratic mind.

Ehrmann believes that the administrative system stabilizes conflicting values. The Frenchman's irrepressible individualism leads him to believe that no one but himself can protect his own interests. He tends to shun co-operative ventures in an almost anarchistic way, but he is wedded to a very strong tradition of equality and thus lends himself to an accommodation with bureaucratic rule. No matter how despised the state, it safeguards the uniform rulings that guarantee equality of treatment—the more so as increasing centralization limits the citizen's responsibility for face-to-face contacts. Thus, while Frenchmen may deride officious or rigid administrative decisions, these rules safeguard equalitarian standards and let him retreat, reassured, to his private world with his family.[34]

Impersonal, national controls relieve the necessity for the Frenchman to become involved with others. Thus does bureaucratic behavior with clients strengthen the French tendency to avoid face-to-face contacts with others, particularly outside his own class.

This pattern prevails inside large French organizations, according to Michael Crozier.[35] French bureaucracies are marked by a strong emphasis on hierarchy which pushes decision upward. When these decisions cannot be made on a routine, impersonal basis, however, immobilization occurs. Because of the French aversion to face-to-face contacts and case-by-case intervention, the supervisors or middle managers cannot settle the problem directly and it is appealed upward. If the crisis is severe enough, extralegal actions resolve it, such as one-day worker strikes. This kind of bureaucratic behavior is true of the political system in a broad way as conflicts cannot be resolved without extralegal events. In this respect, Crozier points out, the French bureaucracy is not the antithesis of the legislature, stable and impervious compared to unstable and inconsistent parliaments. Rather, the two systems are deeply interrelated—the bureaucracy representing the French control over routine matters and the legislature representing the helplessness of French society in the face of needed change.

As Alfred Diamant noted, ". . . the republic passes but the administration remains." [36] Most American observers regard this as essential for systemic stability. Perhaps, though, the phenomenon is not essential as much as inevitable. It is yet another example of the way that social institutions are shaped by the particular needs of the culture that cradles them.

THE PHILIPPINES

Social Life. The Philippines are in a state of transition from a rural, traditional society to a more urbanized, developed society. It is a unique blend of Eastern and Western cultures—Asian, Spanish, and American.[37]

For some three centuries Spain ruled the Philippines. With Roman Ca-
tholicism the dominant religion of the country, there prevailed a strong
tradition of central control over province and rural life, and a belief in deference to legitimate authority. The United States tradition superimposed a
political and administrative style on native institutions and practices that
resulted in a governmental structure much like that of America. Civil service rules, budgetary practices, and many of the operating principles and
practices appear very American, but they are laid in the bedrock of Philippine cultural values and social behavior.

The nation is very rural. As recently as a decade ago, only 13 percent of
the people lived in cities with populations over 20,000. The attraction of
Manila and other cities is changing this. Some of the urban drawing power,
however, is diminished by the high level of unemployment, which has been
as high as 8 percent and averaged over 6 percent during the 1960s.[38] It is
estimated that by 1975 40 percent of the labor force will still be in agriculture; thus, the rural base of the Philippines will be retained. Population is
growing at an annual rate of about 3 percent, and the 1969 total of 36 million is up from about 27 million in 1960. The tropical climate and the fact
that the remaining population is scattered widely over some 7,000 islands
make the problem of changing the practices of past years a difficult one.
Life is leisurely, centered on the extended family and the land.

Filipino rural society falls into two classes: a small elite group of mercantile or large land-holding interests and the mass of the population who either own very small plots of land, or, more often, are tenants farming a
small piece of land.[39] In urban areas, the Chinese mercantile class is important, as are developing industrial and commercial classes. The country is
marked by a devotion to the family with strong regional and kinship ties
and religious unity in the Catholic Church. Philippine culture is not as traditional nor ascriptive as many other less developed societies since there is
considerable upward mobility which is supported by the success of those
members of a small, growing middle class. There are great extremes of
wealth, but the relatively fluid class structure reduces potential conflict.
Wealth is seen as a function of power, a valued resource, and power comes
from "luck" or fortunate social relationships. One can aspire to power and
wealth with a little "luck." Often politics is the key to power.

The French avoid face-to-face contacts to protect individualism and a
personal inner world. The Filipinos pile up a great number of close personal relations as a form of personal security. Their entire set of social relations revolves around the family, kin, and barrio (neighborhood or district).
Individualism is protected by a strong emphasis on smooth interpersonal

relations. It involves strict avoidance of conflict, a pleasant smile and amiable disposition, "going along" with other persons, reliance on euphemisms in stating necessary facts, and the use of middlemen (pakiusap) for delicate arrangements. It is directly opposed to what Filipinos call the "brutal frankness" of Americans.[40]

Reciprocity is a very important element of Filipino social life.[41] It combines with the close ties of traditional Filipino society to develop a web of interpersonal relationships which bind individuals closely together. Patron-client ties are one example. Particularly important is utang na loob, or the debt of gratitude. This debt usually comes from outside the community and kin. While not a legal contract, it places the recipient in a dependent position and he is expected to reciprocate the gift quickly. If he does not, the social sanction of hiya (shame) is overwhelming. Between equals, a luncheon may repay a contract between parties. Between unequals, a job in the bureaucracy may call for a permanent set of small repayments by votes or running errands. The debt of gratitude is always personal rather than strictly contractual or based on a calculated quid pro quo.

The Filipino also has a "bargaining-negotiation" life style which sees authority as something to defer to, yet as personal and reciprocal. Relationships are based on power, which can be traded, manipulated, and bargained for, often through the use of pakiusap. All action in favor of another creates obligations which can be drawn on by the donor as needed.

This behavior is more typical of the rural lowlander than of the emerging middle class in Manila or of urban dwellers in general. It is still the dominant form of social relationships, although a growing industrial base in factories is now developing a Western subculture. Here management values reward efficiency rather than traditional personal ties. A workman who wants to succeed begins to adapt himself to newer impersonal ways—he resists relatives who attempt to use or exploit his new position. Excusing himself, a worker may beg off by claiming inability to resist the new system, but some Filipinos are delighted that there are convenient ways to avoid traditional relationships.[42] The Philippines are changing, but traditional and ascriptive ties still dominate the operation of the political and administrative system.

The Political System. Again using the Almond-Powell scheme, the outlines of the Philippine political and administrative system can be placed into its social setting.[43]

The Philippine system maintains itself through patterns of socialization which transfer family and kinship ties into the political sphere. Relationships between the bureaucracy and legislators on the one hand and the citizen on the other are personalistic, carried on by middlemen. Power and status are sought and bargained for. Patterns of actions and expectations, developed early in the family and the barrio, are carried into political life. These relationships involve jobs, projects for the municipality or province, or favors, rather than broad policies such as land reform.

Political recruitment pulls the better educated, upwardly mobile Filipinos into bureaucratic and political roles. Bureaucratic positions are sought by a wider range of candidates than are political positions. Most politicians are lawyers with undergraduate degrees from the more prestigious universities, while administrators tend to come from less prestigious universities. Although high administrative positions are filled by examinations, there is some tendency to classify positions as "temporary" or "professional" so that political jobs may be awarded to protégés of prominent legislators or the president. Generally, recruitment to the bureaucracy is "formalistic." The facade of merit is maintained, but positions at all ranges are the subject of bargaining between the president, administrator, and legislators.

Some recruitment takes place from bureaucratic to political roles, as top civil servants move from bureau chief to political appointments. Some cabinet posts go to bureaucrats, many of whom have moved up through the ranks, having received original appointments as well as promotions through political machinations and the intervention of patrons. Some ex-civil servants have become senators after moving into national electoral politics. The top Philippine bureaucrat's future promotion and present program responsibilities call for political support rather than intrinsic merit. In cultivating this support, his appointment and program become part of a bargain to which the president is a party. The president thus often regards the matter as a case of politics rather than program commitment and his support is weakened. The bureaucrat then must go outside the executive branch for support, weakening any program loyalty further and causing him to lose control of his subordinates whose appointments are likewise the subject of negotiation. This is a vicious circle which makes it most difficult for administrative effectiveness to receive sufficient attention. Given the Filipino orientation toward power and status, however, recruitment into either political or administrative roles is perhaps inevitably a matter of bargaining and negotiation rather than of "merit," as in the West.

For the reasons mentioned here, the capacity of the political system is relatively low although perhaps not in comparison to most countries at the same stage of political and economic development. The system is responsive, but to personal and regional job and porkbarrel demands rather than to programs or policies from a victorious political party. The public favors land reform, for example, and political candidates advocate it. After election, however, legislators lose interest because powerful interests are opposed and reelection is more related to their ability to bargain for jobs and for public works projects in their provinces.

Distributive capacity is weak in some regards, not in others. Most labor legislation, for example, was passed only because of United States pressure in giving aid to the Philippines to combat the Huk rebellion in the early 1950s. A basic threat to internal security was required to move the system. On the other hand, there is a highly developed system of higher and secondary education. The Philippines have an extremely high number of students in institutions of higher education (see Table 8-1). Many graduates are unemployed or underemployed leading to a potentially unstable condition; even so, many Filipinos have used education as a basis for class mobility.

In some respects, the regulatory and extractive capacity of the country is declining.[44] Income tax receipts have declined as a percentage of gross national product, and indeed in 1959 only about 9 percent of the gross national product was spent by the central government on all national enterprises. The Philippines also have a relatively small number of men in the armed forces even though the Huks, a rural guerrilla movement, were a major internal threat not too long ago and still are occasionally active. Regulation seems largely a private matter controlled by social relationships. Government services to rural areas are declining and government corruption may be increasing, as is public cynicism. This makes the task of penetration and program accomplishment even harder.

The political conversion process follows closely the personalistic social life of the Philippines. Interest articulation is not done by interest groups as in Western democracies. Rather, interests are personal requests arising from traditional social relationships, organized preferences from occupational and economic groups, and implicit or explicit expectations of nonpolitical groups such as the church. Interests are articulated by bargaining between the politicians and the local leader or patron, speaking for residents. Votes are traded for money or jobs. Some major groups do exist, such as sugar and tobacco blocs, newer industrial interests, veterans, and chambers of commerce. Contributions to campaigns and retainers to law firms of politicians provide the basis for protecting their interests. Since programs are not tied to the political process, older elite groups have maintained their control. Legislators or local leaders dispense money and jobs without fear that voters will demand programs threatening the hegemony of these traditional groups.

One source of interest articulation is the bureaucracy. For example, the Bureau of Animal Industry "takes every opportunity to make clear the role of better animal breeding and production in the national interest." [45] In this respect, members of the bureaucracy serve as spokesmen for the special interests of their bureau program.

Individuals rather than interests are aggregated into the political system. During elections, coalitions form to support or oppose particular candidates, changing from year to year. These shifting coalitions make up the national parties. They are collections of local personalities to which the individual Filipino gives allegiance in return for personal benefits. Because elections are the chief aggregating force in Philippine politics and determine the persons who will dispense jobs and money, an enormous amount of money and time is spent on them. It is estimated that 8 percent of the gross national product in 1961 was spent on the presidential election in campaigning and buying votes.

The conversion processes of rule adjudication, rule application, and rule-making are carried on through institutions very similar to those in the United States. The president is very powerful and takes an important part in the rule-making power, but cannot work his will in all cases. He too must bargain. He controls patronage and many projects, partly through his party and partly through consultation with powerful families in various regions. However, he has no greater mandate than the nationally elected senators and has had difficulty in being reelected.

The legislature is independent and by no means limits itself to rule-making. Indeed, rule-making is relatively unimportant compared to rule application, where personal projects and protégés can be manipulated. Thus, the legislature continually intervenes with the bureaucracy for special preference and carries on a constant bargaining process between the president, the bureaucrat, and itself.

The bureaucracy is completely instrumental. It seems to have relatively little impact on the rule-making process, partly because it is perceived as having little expertise or legitimacy, merely acting as an employment agency. Policy initiatives from the bureaucracy are the exception, not the rule.

Communication about the political system through the mass media frequently displays a very negative view of the political system as venal and corrupt. This view is strongest in Manila and the urban areas, while in the barrios "intermediaries" interpret national news to the resident. Hence, the rural population tends to know more local than national news. Jean Grossholtz argues that the skepticism toward government conveyed by communication patterns is healthy in a developing country since it reduces the level of demands on the system. It seems that in the Philippines, however, this might further limit the prospects for program-based politics in favor of even more personalistic demands.

The communication process is generally effective as a developmental or modernizing factor, as it slowly modifies ascriptive and kinship motives to national concerns. Local bargaining with municipal authorities for fishing rights is seen as equivalent to bargaining with a national legislator for favors and jobs. Thus rural social patterns are nationalized in ways that leave the negotiation-bargaining nature of the barrio writ large. The bureaucracy may not be helped in its necessary aim of penetration to local areas to begin economic and political development, even if modernization takes place.

The Administrative System. The political and social system of the Philippines determines the shape, effectiveness, and practice of the administrative system. Heady lists several of the major administrative habits of the Philippine bureaucracy worthy of consideration.[46] The first is the tradition of centralism. It results in a domination of regional decision-making by central functionaries who are often not overly familiar with field conditions. Local government in most provinces is badly underdeveloped, with the most rural barrios still operating much as they did under Spanish rule. Patronage, decision-making, and public works projects are determined centrally, caused by and reinforcing the strong centralist tendencies in the Philippines.[47] This pattern may be changed by the new emphasis on barrio autonomy.

The second major Philippine administrative habit noted by Heady is a reluctance to accept responsibility. This is due in part to the following: the pattern of deference to superiors and the reluctance to take action without clear approval from above; fear of losing face if things should go wrong; and the inability of untrained officials to clarify and implement complex and sometimes controversial tasks.

Mentioned earlier was the prevalence of personalized values underlying action. Appointments to positions on the basis of family or kinship ties are common, even expected. There is a good deal of deference to superiors and finally a tendency to do whatever is necessary to avoid conflict, preserve social amenities, and refrain from antagonizing people. Promotions of a relatively incompetent person for fear of damaging his self-esteem if he is passed over are not uncommon. The use of the civil service as an agency to reduce unemployment contributes to this personality syndrome.

A final point is the resistance to change. The tenacity of old institutions and customs is hard to break. This is typical of most transitional societies where old and new intermingle in complex patterns. Traditions such as centralism, despite attempts at change, remain strong.

So deep is the tradition of personalized and reciprocal obligations that Weberian concepts of a rationalized bureaucratic model may be entirely inapplicable in the Philippines. *Utang la noob*, combined with *hiya*, provides a powerful set of incentives for particularized rather than universalistic responses of those in authority. The public official is caught between traditional and modern pulls in determining public policies and a great deal of personal conflict develops.[48] If he is in a high position and speedily processes an applicant's papers, the benefited client may regard this action as a gift which he must reciprocate. Gifts and presents are not considered immoral. The line between bribery and *utang la noob* is thin and often rationalized. However, if the gift is presented after the act, rather than contrived as a bribe or payment before the act, it is considered appropriate. The overlapping of traditional and modern cultural patterns causes this type of ambiguous bureaucratic behavior in many cases.

A specific example of Philippine administrative behavior may put some of the previous comments into perspective. This case involves a simple request made in 1961 to drill one additional well on the island of Luzon with money saved from an Agency for International Development grant.[49] Four thousand pesos from a total allotment of 109,000 pesos were saved after the original twenty wells were drilled. The Department of Public Works and Communications (DPWC) requested authority to spend 2,800 pesos of the savings for the additional well. The paperwork and processing time to approve the request took 273 days from May 1961 to February 22, 1962, and involved nineteen clearances and endorsements. Yet, there was never any substantive objection raised to the expenditure. The department held the change order 107 days at various times; the National Economic Council (NEC) took 106 days, used mostly by the auditor; the general auditor had the request 51 days; and AID had it nine days.

Similar delays occur even in "efficiently administered" bureaucracies such as the United States and the reasons advanced by the concerned departments are familiar. The NEC suggested that the Bureau of Public Works in the DPWC followed the wrong procedure. The undersecretary of the DPWC argued for administrative decentralization so that department heads would not have to sign papers. Another DWPC official simply said there was "some oversight" and argued for a manual of procedures to prevent misapplications of rules for minor matters such as this. Another party blamed the bureau for misplacing papers, while another suggested that there is no reason for the auditor general to approve such matters. The auditor general disagreed, stressing that pre-audits prevent unwise expenditures. One unnamed low-ranking employee gave perhaps the best explanation:

Obviously nobody was sufficiently interested in the request to follow up. . . . In Philippine public administration, you have to speed up the process by personal follow-up or by contacting your friends or relatives who could help you secure prompt action on your papers. Or you may have to rely on the assistance of congressmen or other influential politicians sometimes. If there was enough personal follow-up on this request, it would have been approved, perhaps, in a month's time.[50]

This brief account underlines the Philippine bureaucratic expectation that personal or particular attention is necessary to accomplish anything. The need for top department heads to attend to small matters highlights the deference to superiors and the centralism which appears in requiring high level approvals and central (Manila) approval rather than perhaps field or regional sign-offs for a small project. A reluctance to accept responsibility also shows through.

The strengths and weaknesses of the Philippine bureaucracy might be summarized at this point. Two major weaknesses exist. (1) Deficiencies exist in skilled manpower for development programs. The Philippines lack an effective career pattern, professionalization, and suffer from overstaffing, nepotism, and low salaries. The government lacks administrative leadership. Not surprisingly, it cannot penetrate to the barrio. (2) An ambiguous attitude toward change and development marks the service. This comes from the Philippine mixture of ascriptive and modernizing goals. Deep corruption is a direct example of this. A formalistic approach to administration is taken where modern or progressive programs are advances, but actual behavior remains the same, responsive to traditional forces. Laws are passed, neither enforced nor designed to be enforced. In the recent past, attitudes toward decentralization of power to the barrios indicate this ambiguity, for power was formally delegated but in reality there was little change.

The weaknesses of the Philippine bureaucracy are intimately related to its strengths. First, despite the gloomy progress shown here, there appears to be slow development of the bureaucracy toward higher standards of effectiveness and increased rationalization of the administrative structure.[51] President Marcos has taken some hopeful steps toward local autonomy in the barrios, elimination of corruption, and economic reforms in planning.[52] Secondly, the weakness of the bureaucracy in carrying out programs is also a strength. Much of the weakness is simply due to the subservience of the bureaucracy to the popularly elected political institutions and to acceptance of the mores of Philippine life. The danger is not bureaucratic usurpation but ineptness and inadequacy. Democratic controls over the administrative system are strong. At this point in time, the Philippine system is not unlike the United States' at an earlier point in time. Its limitations mirror Philippine society, its strengths are those of the political system.

SUMMARY

This chapter has focused on the comparative study of bureaucracies in order to place public administration into a broader, more universal setting, and to suggest that knowledge can be expanded by the use of some of the new conceptual tools developed in comparative political analysis.

Public administration, as Dahl commented, will not reach toward any universal generalizations until all, or at least most, administrative systems can be compared and classified. Then, and only then, can the unique aspects of each culture be examined to determine how much the universal generalizations must be modified in the light of each country's experience. One chapter cannot do justice to the complexities of comparative administration, nor can it authoritatively delineate the issues. It can point out the necessity for a comparative viewpoint.

NOTES

1. Robert Dahl, "The Science of Public Administration: Three Problems" in *Public Administration Review* (Winter 1947), pp. 1–11.
2. A large number of books, articles, and monographs on this subject have been written in recent years. Princeton University Press sponsored a number of the earliest studies of which the most germane work is probably Joseph LaPalombara, ed., *Bureaucracy and Political Development* (1963). More recently, a spate of works by Duke University Press, working with the Comparative Administration Group of the American Society for Public Administration, is focusing on comparative administration in developing countries. The first book in this series was Ralph Briabanti, ed., *Political and Administrative Development* (1969).
3. Ferrel Heady, *Public Administration: A Comparative Perspective* (Prentice-Hall, 1966), Chapter 6. These categories are very weak at the boundaries and countries are not always easy to place. Since Heady's book was published, Nkrumah in Ghana has been overthrown. A more competitive system may result.
4. Talcott Parsons and Edward Shils, eds., *Toward a General Theory of Action* (Harvard University Press, 1951).
5. Gabriel Almond and Bingham Powell, *Comparative Politics—A Developmental Approach* (Little, Brown, 1966).
6. Fred Riggs, *Administration in Developing Countries* (Houghton Mifflin, 1964).
7. *Ibid.*, pp. 277–79. Others have attempted to apply this model to specific countries. See James Brady, "Japanese Administrative Behavior and the Sala Model" in Nimrod Raphaeli, ed., *Readings in Comparative Public Administration* (Allyn and Bacon, 1967), pp. 433–50.
8. Morroe Berger, *Bureaucracy and Society in Modern Egypt* (Princeton University Press, 1957). See also his article "Bureaucracy East and West" in *Administrative Science Quarterly* 2 (March 1957), pp. 518–30.
9. James Scott, "Corruption, Machines, and Political Change" in *American Political cal Science Review* 63 (December 1969), pp. 1142–59.
10. *Ibid.*
11. Fred Riggs, "Bureaucrats and Political Development: A Paradoxical View" in LaPalombara, pp. 127–31.
12. Bert Hoselitz, "Levels of Economic Performance and Bureaucratic Structure" in LaPalombara, pp. 173–76. See also Heady, pp. 71–72.
13. Brian Chapman, *The Profession of Government* (London: George Allen & Unwin, 1959), pp. 9–44.
14. Heady, pp. 41–45. For a detailed chronology of events see Henry Ehrmann, *France* (Little, Brown, 1968), pp. 346–48.
15. Ehrmann, p. 12.

16. Most of this section is from Ehrmann, pp. 255–71.
17. Both of the following cases are from James Christoph and Bernard Brown, *Cases in Comparative Politics*, 2nd ed. (Little, Brown, 1969), particularly the conclusions, pp. 181–84.
18. *Ibid.*, p. 183.
19. Ehrmann, p. 58.
20. Philip Converse and Georges Dupeux, "Socialization into Apathy: France and America Compared," *Public Opinion Quarterly* 26 (Spring 1962), pp. 1–23.
21. John Pfiffner and Robert Presthus, *Public Administration* (Ronald Press, 1967), pp. 72–75.
22. T. Feyzioglu, "The Reform of the French Higher Civil Service Since 1945," *Public Administration* 33 (Spring 1955), pp. 76–77. See also Ehrmann, pp. 132–34, who claims "the new school has had a considerable impact on administrative developments. But as an instrument of social promotion it has largely failed" (p. 133).
23. Almond and Powell, pp. 259–60; 263–66.
24. *Ibid.*, p. 265.
25. Alfred Diamant, "The French Administrative System: The Republic Passes but the Administration Remains" in William Siffin, ed., *Toward the Comparative Study of Public Administration* (Indiana University Press, 1957), pp. 182–217.
26. Ehrmann, p. 268 and Chapter 7.
27. According to Arthur Banks and Robert Textor, in France party aggregation of interests is "ambiguous," while they articulate interests "moderately" compared to "negligibly" in the United States and the Philippines. *A Cross Polity Survey* (M.I.T. Press, 1963), pp. 93–94. This suggests that French parties may be more like large interest groups in the United States.
28. Ehrmann suggests that the parochial press, such as the *Communist Humanite*, has declined. Even so, the major national press does not cover controversial political news for fear of antagonizing readers and many pay no attention to political news. Ehrmann, pp. 155–56.
29. The following portion is from Ehrmann, *passim*.
30. This section is from the following sources: Roger Gregoire, *The French Civil Service* (Brussels: International Institute of Administrative Sciences, 1964) and a review by Frank McCarthy in the *Philippine Journal of Public Administration* 10 (October 1966), pp. 339–413; Jerzy Langrod, "General Problems of the French Civil Service" in Raphaeli, pp. 106–18; Pfiffner and Presthus, pp. 72–75; and Heady, pp. 43–44. Of all the works cited, that by Ehrmann seems to have the greatest weight, as well as being of the most recent vintage. However most of the works which highlight the operations of the bureaucracy do not at all refer to or fit into the Almond-Powell scheme, while those broadly concerned with the political system do not cover administrative aspects except as necessary to illustrate some broader point. In addition, there is considerable divergence of opinion among authorities.
31. Gregoire, p. 29.
32. *Ibid.*
33. Bernard Goulnay, "Higher Civil Servants in France" in Mattei Dogan and Richard Rose, *European Politics* (Little, Brown, 1971), pp. 501–13.
34. Ehrmann, pp. 12–13.

35. Michael Crozier, *The Bureaucratic Phenomenon* (University of Chicago Press, 1964), pp. 251–63.

36. Diamant, "The French Administrative System. . . ."

37. The following works were helpful in preparing this section, although not cited directly. Jose Abueva and Raul de Guzman, eds., *Handbook of Philippine Public Administration* (Manila: Bookmark, 1967); David Wurfel, "The Philippines" in George Kahin, ed., *Governments and Politics of Southeast Asia* (Cornell University Press, 1964); Jean Grossholtz, "Land Reform and Rural Development in the Philippines; Political Imperatives and Political Impediments," a Southeast Asia Development Advisory Group paper (The Asia Society, 1967); Edward O. Stene and Associates, *Public Administration in the Philippines* (Manila: Institute of Public Administration, University of the Philippines, 1955); and the American Assembly, *The United States and the Philippines* (Prentice-Hall, 1966).

38. Figures from *United Nations Statistical Yearbook, 1968*. See also David Wurfel, "The Philippines: Decline or Progress?" *Proceedings of the First National Colloquium on the Philippines* (Western Michigan Institute of International Area Studies, 1969), pp. 13–20.

39. Jean Grossholtz, *Politics in the Philippines* (Little, Brown, 1964), p. 86.

40. Frank Lynch, "Lowland Philippine Values; Social Acceptances," in Lynch, ed., *Four Readings in Philippine Values* (Manila: Institute of Philippine Culture, 1962), pp. 100–108.

41. Mary Honsteiner, "Reciprocity in the Lowland Philippines" in Lynch, pp. 121–48.

42. *Ibid.*

43. This section relies, unless otherwise noted, on Grossholtz, *Politics in the Philippines, passim.*

44. Wurfel, *Proceedings.* Wurfel here is certainly pessimistic about the future of the Philippines. Most of this paragraph is from this article.

45. Grossholtz, p. 252.

46. Ferrel Heady, "The Philippine Administrative System—A Fusion of East and West" in Siffin, pp. 253–78.

47. For an interesting discussion see Riggs, pp. 363–93. See also Ladd Thomas, "Centralism in the Philippines: Past and Present Causes" in *Social Research* 30 (Summer 1963), pp. 203–19.

48. Willis Sibley, "Philippine Politics and National Development: The Provincial and Local Levels" in Wurfel, *Proceedings*, pp. 21–28.

49. Raul de Guzman and Frank Landers, "Change Order No. 1" in Guzman, ed., *Patterns in Decision-Making* (Honolulu, Hawaii: East-West Center Press, 1963), pp. 433–48.

50. *Ibid.*, p. 458.

51. Remedios Felizmena, "Civil Service Examinations and Appointments Revisited" in *Philippine Journal of Public Administration* (January 1964), pp. 32–45.

52. Wurfel, *Proceedings.*

9

PUBLIC ADMINISTRATION— CHANGE AND THE FUTURE

Most of the central themes of public administration have been discussed in the first eight chapters. This final chapter has been reserved for a view of the past, present, and future state of public administration. It is always difficult and often disastrous to project the future. In turbulent, fast changing times, it is difficult to give an adequate description of the present. Indeed, one is not even sure of the past's meaning, since it seems increasingly to be an irrelevant guide to the present. Even so, serious questions are at stake, and they cannot be ignored by an unwillingness to make tentative predictions.

This final chapter will first take up basic American values, relate them to more specific values undergirding public administration, and show how they now seem to be under considerable pressure. The chapter will then move into a discussion of the basic issues confronting the study and practice of American public administration. Finally, new directions in public administration, particularly the "New Public Administration" will be examined as a guide to what the future may hold for public organizations.

DEMOCRATIC VALUES IN AMERICA

The basic American values which induced social action in the eighteenth and nineteenth centuries developed out of the Western philosophical tradition, adapted to the American environment.[1] Perhaps the most important of these was the belief in a fundamental law. This fundamental law is based on: the Judeo-Christian belief in a higher or divine law, and the natural law tradition of Western philosophy which included, by the time of John Locke and the American Revolution, individual liberty from the excesses of the state.[2] Individualism was another value, exalting the free and responsible person, such as the frontiersman, small farmer, and worker. A third value was the almost divine "mission of America." Liberty had been established to flourish in an empty continent, free of the troubles of Europe. It was a symbol to the world of the blessings of liberty and faith in God.

Two other values grew from these three: constitutionalism, a direct derivative from the concept of natural and divine fundamental laws; and the American belief in the inevitability of progress, which developed as the link between individualism and the fundamental law. As men understood the laws of God, and as a society placed these moral immutables into rules of social conduct, civilization advanced.

These values largely made up the "liberal" tradition in America. This tradition was based on natural laws and natural rights, lack of class distinctions, lack of ties to a past, belief that political questions were decided in a constitutional convention, and the continuity of our political tradition.

By the twentieth century, a Christian humanism developed which somewhat modified these values. Scientific progress was exalted, reducing the weight of divine providence in social thought. A social ethic also developed which blunted the worst excesses of individualism. Conflicts between individualism and the development of a mass society also appeared. Yet, these early values still remained the heart of American social and political thought. The fundamental values of public administration are derived directly from them.

Public Administration Values. The administrative or bureaucratic state has never been very well legitimized in America. It came relatively late in our nation's life, with no constitutional mention of it. Founding-father support is largely limited to Federalist Papers Nos. 70 and 72 by Alexander Hamilton. Even here the main emphasis is on an "energetic executive," the president. However, even without explicit constitutional authority, implicit values have developed. Dwight Waldo has enunciated a number of them.[3]

Efficiency was a basic value of public administration. This involved a widespread acceptance of business values, the "Gospel of Wealth," in America near the turn of the last century. The Progressives linked efficiency and democracy to reform government, in terms of popular control and the positive welfare state, operating efficiently in terms of the business ethic. A belief in the mission of America thus underlay the value of efficiency, since government efficiency, long lacking, would show that democracy could be joined to the positive state.

Another value of public administration was a belief that the "good life" was the administered life. Individualism in a mass society required special attention by government to preserve equality and liberty, so that the free individual could enjoy the fruits of his labor. A bureaucratized, collectivist, efficiently administered life was necessary to preserve the highest values of individualism. While early Progressives and members of the bureaus of municipal research might have been shocked by these terms, this was the thrust of their reforms. The good life was to be created by the administrative state which included the use of experts, an administrative class, and a planned society.

A third public administration value is a belief in science and rationalism. Administrators and scholars relied on the following philosophies: positivism, with facts only for the basis of decision; pragmatism, or the valuation of ideas on the basis of their results; and utilitarianism, or the greatest good for the greatest number. This mental framework has specific implications beyond the simple view that science and technology are essential to build the good society. It justified the development of professional bureaucracies as the most rational administrative system. Centralizing power in the chief executive, as in the public administration model of organization, is the rational embodiment of executive efficiency and the principles of democratic control. A belief in principles of administration and in a science of administration grew out of this faith in science, as did the belief in the separation of administration from politics.

Values Under Pressure. Many of these deeply held American values have been badly shaken by events in the last forty years. The trauma of the Great Depression changed the views of many persons about the ability of a purely "free enterprise" economy to assure progress and the good life. The economic system was only righted by the savagery of World War II.

These doubts have been increased by the many and varied social changes occurring since World War II. The Cold War with the Communist world has led America toward a garrison state. High levels of military expenditures, the protracted tensions and frustrations of the Cold War, and the bloody, divisive, and fruitless war in Vietnam have raised serious questions about the inevitability of progress and the divine "mission of America." Hopes were raised by civil rights advances in the early and mid-1960s, elevated even further by "Great Society" programs such as the "War on Poverty," then shattered by the apparent failure of these programs. The Vietnam war, and the reaction of American youth to it, seemed to indicate that we were to have political stalemate and inflation, not guns and butter.

Another source of doubt concerned the likelihood that technology and science could indeed assure the future. Damage to the seas, skies, rivers, and wildlife resulted in apocalyptic predictions of ecological disaster, far from the traditional American view of a rosy tomorrow. Where technology seemed potentially useful in combating societal problems, such as wiretaps against organized crime or data banks to process social strategies, it raised profound questions of personal liberty.

In short, basic American values are under stress. They do not, of course, evaporate immediately and one never knows precisely how and in what ways they have weakened. Although some values have been under attack since 1930, our societal belief system has not entirely shifted from laissez faire to the welfare state. Still, it does appear that in the early 1970s Americans are considerably less sure about the nation's future, the likelihood that things will get better and better, and what "better" is.

If basic American values are shaken, subsidiary administrative values should show rapid changes. This, indeed, has happened. Recounting just how these values are under stress and the direction which change may take is one purpose of this chapter. Before this can be done, however, it is necessary to venture briefly into the basic philosophical underpinnings of public administration.

Changes in Philosophic Basis for Public Administration. Most students of public administration, or at least administration in general, follow the empirical or logical positivist tradition.[4] This means, simply, that they insist on a radical division of reality into facts which can be examined and value judgments or moral propositions which cannot be verified. Facts can be roughly divided into empirically verifiable observations, such as "he works for Organization A," and formal conventions such as mathematics or formal logic which are true by general agreement. To a logical positivist, a statement is verifiable if it can to some degree be confirmed or rejected by observation. He regards most philosophic issues, particularly metaphysics and epistemology, as idle speculation, and thus of no use to the scientist, or the philosopher who wishes to contribute to the advancement of science. Moral judgments are, of course, important but nonscientific and of little interest to the researcher as a scientist. They may be of great moment to him as a citizen, but this is a different matter.

Most social scientists now study behavior, or the way that people actually conduct their lives. They eschew consciousness, introspection, and intuition in their subjects, and report "what actually happens," to the extent that this can be determined. This commitment to the study of facts and dismissal of values first became important in public administration with the Hawthorne studies (Chapter 4) of worker behavior under varying conditions. It was most consciously noted in the works by Herbert Simon on decision-making in *Administrative Behavior*[5] and in his co-authored textbook *Public Administration*.[6] Here is a conscious effort to avoid "oughts" such as desirable administrative structures and to emphasize concepts imported from psychology, sociology, and economics.

In the last quarter-century, most of the studies of administrative practice and behavior have been, to a greater or lesser degree, behavioral. Following Simon's lead, much of the movement toward a science of administration has rested on the research of persons in disciplines outside political science, mostly sociology, economics, business administration, mathematics, and social psychology.

While Simon and other logical positivists still continue their studies into behavior, the use of computers in studying human decision-making processes being the latest, a philosophical counterrevolution is gaining adherents. Most common among the New Public Administration younger scholars, it is based on the phenomenological-existential philosophic tradition.

Phenomenology is essentially the philosophical study of the development of the mind, and existentialism is a philosophy that attempts to analyze individual human existence.[7] Both concepts tend to blend into a broad humanistic philosophy. The recent interest in phenomenology is largely a reaction to an overemphasis on empiricism. This philosophy contends that the mind is not a passive receptacle for sensory observations, as empiricists such as Locke argued, but has an intentionality of its own, and selectively interprets data. Reducing all phenomena to simplified measurements is not possible, for this eliminates subjective data such as the values which positivists deliberately exclude. One cannot eliminate or dismiss another person's feelings in scientific research; the researcher must gain insight into his subject's feelings to understand the facts about him. For practical purposes, this approach rejects any simple division of facts and values.

Existentialism, from Kierkegaard through Sartre, is a philosophy which places freedom of choice and individual dignity as the highest ends of human life. It insists that knowledge of the human condition, through an awareness of the tragedy of life, is the highest form of knowledge. Rejecting reliance on reason or on some superior being, existentialism posits the necessity of each person to choose how he will live and how he will behave, in a random unpredictable universe. Every man is ultimately responsible for his decisions. Reliance on the directives of superiors, as Nazi bureaucrats did in destroying the Jewish populations, is not enough. Every man is free to make, and is responsible for, his own decisions. This precedent was set in the Nuremberg trials, and is one of the slogans recently used by militant demonstrators against the Vietnam war.

To many of the young scholars in public administration, the phenomenological-existential view has become very popular. Wesley Bjur argues that the New Public Administration thrust involves rejection of a positivist, rationalistic view of man in favor of a humanist view searching for new values.[8] He argues that the manager needs to apply a positivist view to facts, objects, and their relationships, but in dealing directly with people he must use a phenomenological-existentialist view to gain insight into their needs. People must be seen as a whole being, not dissected into elements such as social needs, occupational roles, or psychological drives.

Much of the existential emphasis is based on the feeling that the administrator needs a guiding ethic for his choices and that he can no longer rely on traditional rationales such as the morality of the organization or the expressed values of society.[9] Each person must establish his own set of values to guide his administrative behavior. These values will naturally be affected by a changing environment. As old values weaken, new values will appear and subsequently govern the choices and decisions made in administrative life.

Although interest in the phenomenological-existential approach is increasing, traditional intellectual beliefs dominate administrative action. Most scholars and practitioners, even the younger set of "administrative radicals," still believe in efficient administrative action as a necessity for the good life, and in science and technology if properly controlled. But the hold of these latter values is weaker. Phenomenology is being urged as at least a partial replacement for the empiricist-rationalist tradition. For example, it could account for differences in expert views about the effectiveness and impact of a given organization, since few experts value all aspects of an organization in the same way. Existentialism is being urged as a replacement for efficiency, at least in some aspects. Efficiency, or the selection of the best (least cost) means toward given ends, requires an acceptance of the traditional values of society and in particular the demands of the organizational hierarchy as legitimate societal values. On the other hand, existentialism requires each decision-maker to value his choice in terms of the "human condition." Since no one bureaucrat will have a value system perfectly compatible with organization demands, existentialism invites each man to disobey hierarchical orders which his values reject.

It is still too early to tell whether the phenomenological-existential approach has "staying power." As of yet there have been few concrete results which would indicate that it has been utilized. Some of the demonstrations and internal revolts of younger federal administrators, discussed later under the New Public Administration, suggest certain directions the newer values may take.

Future Values in America. The set of values which will guide the United States in the future is by no means clear. Yet, the pace of change is very rapid, and the country is well into a post-industrial, tertiary service economy. We are urbanizing and suburbanizing at a high rate. Americans are terrifyingly mobile, each person averaging a change of residence every five years. A nation of nomads, our home changes and travelling have further weakened any ties of place and status. Technology dominates our lives with a powerful centralizing, homogenizing force. Television, for example, has already standardized much of the educational process through programs such as "Meet the Press" and "Sesame Street." [10] While most Americans grow more affluent, however, substantial pockets of poverty and unemployment remain.

Rapid cultural changes are not necessarily associated with changes in underlying values. But as a pragmatic people, we lack ideological commitments to abstract values which are strong enough to survive many of the changes noted. Older values are eroding without any clear idea of what values are to replace them. Perhaps our only commitment is to transience, to the "throw-away society." [11]

Ernst Haas has a scenario of the world, developed by extrapolating all present trends into an indefinite future.

. . . Culturally, the world will be more and more sensate, preoccupied with empirical perception, secular, humanistic, utilitarian, and hedonistic. People will be less and less willing to defer gratification; they will be bent exclusively on immediate enjoyment of whatever they value. Elites will tend toward both egalitarianism and meritocracy. Scientific knowledge of all kinds will accumulate even more rapidly than it does now. Society will change faster and more universally in proportion to the application of this scientific knowledge through technology and its diffusion. Industrialization will be world-wide, though its benefits may not be; both affluence and leisure will increase in proportion, but population will also continue to burgeon, thus giving us a continuing race between food supply and people. Primary occupations will decline even more in importance, and secondary occupations will begin a downward trend. Education and literacy will spread more evenly throughout the world, and so will the capability for mass destruction through war. Urbanization will reach the point of the megalopolis, if not the necropolis.

The major technical revolutions of the next twenty years will include a vast increase in computers, data retrieval, and their application, so that instantaneous factual information will be available to decision-makers on almost everything—but also to the increasingly literate and aware public. Developments in biology may result in control over heredity, motivation, and the length of human life. The oceans will be increasingly explored and exploited, and the weather will be subjected to manipulation. New forms of energy will be developed, making man less dependent on coal and access to fresh water, with wide implications for location of industries. Some of the more obvious "social problems" associated with these trends—*not* nec-

essarily capable of being solved by learned behavior such as forecasting and planning—include unemployment, status deprivation, and society's inability to assimilate an excess of educated, aspiring counter-elites. The race for food will imply
agrarian unrest, and the reliance on cybernetic equipment will lead toward the
meritocratic rule of communications scientists and technicians. Since more work
will be done by fewer people, private life will become crucial; the home and the
communal pad will be new centers of activity. . . .

The role of government and foreign affairs in such a setting calls for a further
comment. As accepted values erode, we can no longer expect a consensus on notions such as the "national interest"; perhaps the post-industrial nation will no
longer be an object of value at all to its citizens. The government may become an
agency taken for granted as the dispenser of largesse and physical security that one
assumes to be his right. More and more people will be able to afford to behave as
spoiled children, and American society could become a loose network of self-indul-
gent groups profoundly indifferent to the issues that make up this book. But someone would remain to feed and exploit the data banks to design and deploy nonkill-
ing but lethargy-inducing missiles, to plan the curricula for the next generation of
adaptive gene selectors and ocean ranchers. The ruling meritocracy would inherit
government by default. . . .[12]

If this scenario actually came to pass in its entirety (parts of it are sure to
occur), demands upon the administrative state would be enormous. It may
be true, as Harry Girvetz notes, that the new governing elite will be gray,
faceless bureaucrats in a meritocracy at least partially analogous to Aldous
Huxley's *Brave New World*.[13] Is there any ethic which legitimizes the
elite's power? Certainly traditional American values do not. Here we see
some of the attractions of existentialism, a philosophy that focuses personal
and final responsibility on the individual for his choices in a way that society may be unable to do. But how can society be sure that it approves of,
let alone is aware of, the myriad of individual values which will be cited as
justifications for decisions? If the scenario is accurate, perhaps society will
not care.

These questions must be asked in an effort to force those involved in
public administration to contemplate the future. If such an effort succeeds
only in laying bare the poverty of the values undergirding present administrative action, it must be counted a success.

CHANGING VIEWS OF PUBLIC ADMINISTRATION

So far the discussion has been somewhat general with major concern for
the broader society and how changes there might affect public administration. It is now time to look more closely at certain aspects of public administration to assess how certain traditional issues and questions are affected
by changes in societal values.[14]

The Basis for Action. As mentioned earlier, the traditional and primary criterion for administrative action has been economy and efficiency. Administrative actions were justified if they were considered economical, meaning that as little money as possible was spent. The same value applied to efficient administration, which generally meant a low ratio of expended funds to achieve results. These terms, often used interchangeably, represented the highest praise that an organization could attain.

For most of the years since 1776, private business was taken as the model for administrative action. In recent years, however, the business escutcheon has become tarnished. To a considerable degree, it has become the scapegoat for the troubles that plague America, whether ecological, economic, social, or ethical. Ironically, at the time that government is moving into many of the spheres previously set aside for private enterprise, the criterion of efficiency is valued less when it might in some regards be more appropriate.

As noted earlier, efficiency was also linked by the Progressive movement to democracy, so as to justify the positive state. Now that the welfare state is increasingly in evidence, advocates of further government action no more justify their position on the claim that it will be "efficient," but rather that it will further equality. This is an old value, but new to public administration.

Thus, there seems to be no explicit, generally accepted rationale for administrative action. The business model is less valued and efficiency has fallen into some disrepute, although not so much so that the New Public Administration's value of "social equity" reigns unchallenged. The disintegration of the line between politics and administration has further muddied any guidelines the bureaucrat could look to. Democratic controls, legitimizing the hierarchy, have been challenged by other sources of authority such as the expertise of the professions. Some argue that democratic controls are invalid because they represent an oppressive force over organizational clients, and that the executive must develop his own personal moral basis for choice. No consensus exists.

Public Administration versus General Administration. Once there was at least a fuzzy distinction between public and private administration. Government undertook those services which required coercive controls over society. These were few and clear-cut, and everything else was left to the private sector.

In recent years there has been a major convergence of public and private in America at all levels of government. The Gary, Indiana, school district hired a private firm to teach its students, with the contract stipulating that payment was dependent upon the children achieving certain minimum scores on national grade level examinations. COMSAT is a corporation which controls the use of communications satellites for television usage. Both the federal government and private corporations own its stock. This convergence often spills over national boundaries. In the Philippines, a new rice was developed by a combination of public, private, and nonprofit corporations.

A dramatic example of the successful mixture of instruments is cited in the Philippines rice case. There the national government's semiautonomous central bank and rural private banks joined forces with provincial governments, with a special agency in the President's office, with commercial fertilizer companies, and with the national Agricultural Extension Service, the Church, and the 4-H groups to develop a successful delivery system for the "miracle" rice.[15]

Actually, the rice was developed earlier by the Rice Research Institute, a creature of the Ford and Rockefeller foundations in the United States. The Agency for International Development and the Philippines National Economic Council sponsored the initial experiment in two provinces.

On the other hand, sometimes decisions that would best be made publicly are "privatized." Urban renewal decisions in many American cities are often delegated to private businessmen and downtown merchants.

This convergence and mixing of the public and private sectors pose dilemmas for training and educating present and future administrators. Should schools of public administration stress policy questions and the politics of administration? Or should they put more emphasis on quantitative analysis and mathematical and econometric modeling, in hopes of turning out technocrats for the twenty-first century? Perhaps they should tackle business inventory and marketing problems. Another option is to attempt to transform professional specialists into administrative generalists on the assumption that their talents will generally be used in a semipublic or public agency. Under this assumption social workers, civil engineers, and forest rangers would be given graduate work in public administration to prepare them for organizational leadership.

The present trend is toward general schools of administration, largely quantitatively oriented. This does represent some recognition of the public-private blurring, but it is not clear that the skills necessary for corporate success are completely interchangeable with those of the public executive. Furthermore, the heavy quantitative emphasis assumes that one key set of skills marks the successful public and private executive.

Until the relationship between public and private administration is clarified (if, indeed, it ever can be), there is unlikely to be agreement on the type of graduate training.

The Politics-Administration Division. Anyone who has read this far by now has discovered that the old division between politics and administration has long since been discarded by both practitioners and administrators. If it had not, a book like this could not be written.

Exorcising this old myth does present certain problems, however. It becomes difficult to distinguish between public administration as a practical art and as a known science to be taught. If there is no area of administration where nonpolitical issues can be found, there is also no subject matter that can form the basis for principles of administration. A science of administration must then remain unreachable.

When Herbert Simon destroyed the old principles of administration in the late 1940s, he felt confident that new ones rested more firmly on the bedrock of scientific knowledge and that social research could be established. Little headway toward these principles, however, has been made.

At present, training administrators for the public service is still much like coaching artists rather than training scientists. Public administration faculties know what a good administrator is able to accomplish and how he does it, at least in general terms. Basically, he is an expert in human relationships, intelligent, aware of political and social reality, able to tolerate ambiguity, and has a sense of commitment to his program area. Unfortunately, these qualities cannot be extracted from his personality and environment as a whole; there is no way, for example, to teach tolerance for ambiguity. Graduate work can give candidates an awareness of the issues in government administration, can give them some early coaching in the complexity of the governing process, and can teach some technical skills such as cost benefit analysis. Graduate work cannot teach the principles which a manager can apply at work. It is even doubtful if students of administration can discover the underlying principles of organizational behavior in the near future—if we cannot find them, how can they be transmitted for managerial application? As indicated, they cannot be.

This is a more realistic view of the educational process, but obviously a more limited one and thus more sobering to those who like to believe that administration can be neatly packaged in graduate courses and inserted into future managers.

Removal of the politics-administration dichotomy can have some dangers. It may cause a premature abandonment of a search for broad generalities (not principles) which underlie administrative behavior in favor of a casual or resigned attitude that "it's all politics," or "managers are born, not made." If recognition of the pervasiveness of politics causes academicians to swing from a belief in some near absolute principles to a rejection of any regularities in organizational behavior, it clearly proves the old maxim that a little bit of knowledge is a dangerous thing.

Perhaps a greater danger, in terms of controlling the bureaucracy, is the potential politicization of all organizational behavior. Expressed another way, we may be seeing the bureaucratization of political life, as everything becomes a matter of administration in the brave new world. At the present time, many questions of high public policy are determined by the values of members of selected professions. For example, questions concerning euthanasia and abortion are often settled by the medical profession, since there are frequently no formal public standards. Standards for appeals from administrative rulings and judgments are modeled by bar associations. Social workers set welfare standards, teachers determine curricula. We are moving rapidly toward a meritocracy ruled by professional experts. The loss of a tenuous line between political decision and professional expertise may justify increased activism among the professionals. After all, the political process is slow and full of compromise, and it is very tempting for professionals to rely on shared values and a homogeneous lump of knowledge in setting and justifying public policy. Having torn down the wall between policy and administration, we cannot easily argue that expertise is not a perfectly legitimate form of politics.

NEW DIRECTIONS FOR PUBLIC ADMINISTRATION

Those bold enough to look to the future of public administration are usually forced to make broad generalizations about contingent events, extrapolating from what the past has been and the present seems to be to what the murky future may be. This leads to predictions such as "the death of bureaucracy" or the "professional state." These are at best highly conjectural. Rather than end with this kind of prophecy, it seems more appropriate to evaluate certain trends in public administration which may become major new directions for the field.

The first two directions are political economy and policy analysis. Both are, at present, largely of interest to academics. The third direction, the New Public Administration, is of interest to both practitioners and academics. Most of this final section will be devoted to it, since it marks a thrust vastly different from the present. After outlining these new movements, the reader can supply his own future, if he so wishes. If he still feels that the future is somewhat murky and ambiguous, he is in good company. But at least he will be acquainted with movements which, at this point in time, seem most likely to illuminate the next decade or so in public administration.

Policy Analysis. The policy analysis approach moves from traditional political science concerns with institutions and more recent interest in processes and behaviors associated with government. It focuses on the analysis of public policies—specifically, the description and explanation of causes and consequences of governmental activity.

It is grounded in empirical rather than normative studies with very little attention paid to "oughts," or policy recommendations, and a great deal of attention to explanation. Hopefully, reliable research findings can be accumulated and general propositions about public policies developed.[16]

Associated with the work of Thomas Dye, Ira Sharkansky, and Richard Hofferbert,[17] among others, the policy analysis approach is somewhat controversial at present. It suggests to many a form of economic determinism since the major studies tend to suggest that the political system, and hence the administrative subsystem, has little independent effect on policy outcomes. Richard Dawson and James Robinson found, for example, that party competition had less impact on the level of welfare payments than did indicators of personal income, urbanization, and industrialization.[18] Social characteristics of the population seem to be much more important than aspects of the political or administrative system. This aspect of policy analysis has succeeded in sparking some vigorous counter research to prove that the political system is *not* the epiphenomenon of economics.[19]

It is not exactly clear how policy analysis will be tied to the interests of public administration.[20] It does mark an important turn in political science by focusing attention on actual system outputs. In the future much more attention may be placed on actually identifying the impact of these outputs on individuals and groups.[21] As of yet, however, there has been no linkage developed between academic studies of government policies and more detailed PPB analyses of specific alternative programs. At this point, academic and practitioner interests have been only theoretically linked.

Political Economy. Economics plays an important role in both new academic approaches to public administration. In policy analysis, many studies find that economic development is the best predictor of high levels of government output. In the political economy movement, the concepts and language of economics are formally and self-consciously introduced into political science. This movement is less clear at present than policy analysis, since at this point it is limited to some provocative works which suggest parameters of a new field and also begin to develop a vocabulary. A century or so ago, political economy meant a deliberate attempt to extend the

state's control into the regulation of economic affairs in order to maximize
the polity's power and wealth. It has a more limited aim now—to redirect
the work of political scientists into directions of more use to policy-makers
through the use of economic concepts. This is most obvious in the field of
comparative politics, where political science has been unable to give advice to regime leaders which helps them choose routes to economic development. Warren Ilchmann and Norman Uphoff make this point, and base
their argument for a political economy approach on the following concepts: political behavior and choice are determined by political resources;
leaders act to further their perceived goals and preferences; resource analysis requires disaggregation of the system into sectors (interests); political
values must be calculated at the margins; and calculations of values become soluble when applied to specific cases and regimes.[22]

It remains to be seen if political economy becomes more than a new academic jargon, or a form of systems theory or structural-functionalism.
More importantly, it remains to be seen whether new concepts can make
academic advice to policy-makers either more relevant or more palatable.
In developmental administration, for example, political economy places
some real burdens on the academic adviser. First, he must be able to
ground his advice on the assumptions that economic concepts can be applied to hard political and administrative choices. Secondly, he must be
willing to put his knowledge at the hands of the existing regime, for better
or for worse. Both of these assumptions remain to be proven.

THE NEW PUBLIC ADMINISTRATION

The New Public Administration (hereafter termed "the New PA") is the
set of attitudes and values which many young practitioners and academics
carry into their work and writings.[23] Presently there are relatively few persons who consciously consider themselves New PA'ers, but they have captured a good deal of attention in the literature, in the federal establishment
and at the national conventions of the American Society for Public Administration. At the risk of over-generalization, most of them could be characterized as more or less humanistic, dubious about technology, anti-rational-
ist, reformist, and generally doubtful of the ability of present organizations
to adapt to a fast-changing society. However, they are by no means united
philosophically.

One study examined a group of thirty-three young federal activists.
They had engaged in public protests against federal policies, ranging from
opposing the Vietnam war to urging welfare reform proposals. Their average age was 31; most were employed in the Department of Health, Educa-

tion and Welfare, working with programs in the "race and poverty" areas; most had graduate or professional degrees; and they ranged from entry level to the highest middle management or professional rating positions (GS-9 to GS-15).[24]

Highly motivated toward a "Kennedy role" of political commitment to activism and reform, they were attempting to change the system from within, were largely non-ideological, and generally distrustful of their agency's commitment to solve social problems.

What they were not is also of interest. They were *not* alienated from their agencies and actually found a satisfying work environment. Secondly, their protest was not a spillover from a shift in cultural values and increased radicalism among college students who then happened to become federal employees. Surprisingly, the protestors seemed to be potential bureaucrats who believed, with their "establishment" colleagues, that better funding and leadership could cure social problems.

The New PA'ers in the federal service were actually reformists, attracted by altruistic visions of service. They entered federal agencies and ultimately attacked the Vietnam war because it held up social programs. They literally stumbled into a protest role, aided by a critical mass of other employees who thought the same way and by the existence of peer groups in critical areas who provided social support.

What the New PA Believes In. There are three distinct values that most New PA'ers believe in. The first of these is the need for social equity in public administration.[25] Social equity means that administrative value neutrality is impossible and undesirable. Since variations in public services mirror groups' access to the agency or legislator, more powerful interests get greater benefits. Neutrality thus strengthens the inequity. The standard of "goodness" of a public service should be service equity, and so administrators should strive to direct any variations in services toward reversing the existing bias toward the well-to-do and the powerful. Finally, since reversing this inequity is the goal of administrators, isolation of them and/or their agencies from political or administrative responsibility works against redressing social inequity. Ultimately, by redirecting agency action on the behalf of hitherto powerless groups, progress toward equity in public services can be achieved.

The second important belief is a strong and widely shared view that organizational emphasis must be redirected toward the client.[26] Traditional relationships between an organization and a client vary a good deal, but generally powerless or lower class clients are considered children, or wards of the organization. They are subordinate to the organization, treated impersonally as objects requiring a good deal of supervision in the portion of their lives relating to the organizational mission.

The New PA model of organization-client relationships, at least for social purpose agencies, reverses this dependency relationship. Organization members must have a direct personal commitment to their client. The organization requires a structure designed with client needs in mind rather than management or professional desires. Finally, clients should judge the organization output and effectiveness. This latter point requires more than client advisory groups or even confrontations such as those between welfare mothers and the welfare department. It includes binding client evaluations of the agency. It may require a radical reversion to a private enterprise model in which a client is given "public administration" scrip which is good at a number of social agencies such as welfare, education, or health. By the voluntary choices he makes among agencies in purchasing services, he indicates his own set of needs as well as rewarding the more useful services and agencies.

A final basic element in the creed of the New PA is the belief in a "proactive" administrator. Not only must the new administrator challenge and confront his agency when its policies are wrong, but he must tilt the balance toward social equity in the programs he administers. Some advocate "sabotage" of the agency at the lower or more concealed levels in favor of advancing less favored organization members or clients.

An example of a successful protest may show how some federal employees have resisted their agencies. When HEW moved their Public Health Service (PHS) to the suburbs in Rockville, Maryland, a group of activist HEW employees banded together to oppose the move. Their opposition was based on the fact that Montgomery County (Rockville) at that time had no open housing law and that there was a lack of low income housing and of public transportation for low income employees to and from Washington. Seizing control of a dormant local of the American Federation of Government Employees, they used it as a forum for press releases and constant public pressure on HEW, finally taking the agency to court. They alleged impropriety, collusion, and abandonment by PHS of the central city problems it was supposed to solve. A number of changes finally occurred in federal practices. The General Services Administration, which makes office arrangements for federal agencies, issued a new set of site selection guidelines which promised to avoid relocations which worked a hardship on employees because of nonavailability of low cost housing or transportation. HEW also established a job guarantee plan to assist employees to relocate to another job if they were inconvenienced by the move to Rockville. About 10 percent of affected employees finally did take other jobs.[27]

There is no direct way to prove that employee objections caused these changes, but they obviously were closely associated with it.

Some young practitioners advocate even stronger action than this. A group of New PA'ers from HEW proposed a list of options for employees who opposed policies of the government or of their agency. They urge employees to refuse to participate in programs that they feel are unjust or immoral, arguing that throughout the government demands are constantly made on individuals to "obey an order, regulation, or law which is unjust" or which contradicts a "higher law—the individual's sense of morality, the Constitution, or simply the agency's goals." [28] Suggestions of what an employee can do range from controversial discussion groups to official protests, official slowdowns, and finally direct sabotage or confrontation of the agency. This may result, if necessary, in "creative job losing," that is, publicly being fired.

There are less open ways of acting on behalf of organizational clients and disadvantaged members. Proactive lower level employees can take advantage of the lack of complete top level control in many ways.[29] Among these are padding budgets and making transfers among agency accounts in areas where benefit to the powerless can be affected. Another way involves hiring temporary minority help, intending later to make the position or incumbent permanent. There are other ways to enforce personnel rules selectively to minimize employment discrimination.

These proposals for and acts of administrative activists are at the heart of the New PA. They represent an unwillingness to compartmentalize life into boxes of work, social concern, and private life style. The activist, existentialist new administrator seeks a job and organization where his reformist creed can affect clients, his organization, and his own life style.

A Look Ahead. What will be the impact of this New PA ethic on future organization? How can organizations be changed to conform to these new values? Indeed, should they be? These are not easy questions to answer. The last question might be dealt with first.

It seems likely that most persons favor, in the abstract, the ideal of social equity. The entire thrust of the past twenty years has been in this direction. Beginning with the 1954 *Brown* vs. *Board of Education* Supreme Court decision that outlawed the separate-but-equal dictum which tolerated segregation, moving through the reapportionment cases, the war on poverty, and recent state decisions outlawing inequity in school district wealth as a hindrance to equal education, slow, twisting, but constant progress toward social equity has marked political decisions in the United States.

The matter of client participation is a bit stickier, since organizations are seen as instruments of the duly constituted legislative body rather than as the property of their clients. The pattern has largely been set, however, by the efforts of the community action programs of the war on poverty, which required maximum feasible participation. In dealing with organizations established to help certain hitherto powerless clientele, it may be legitimate to rely on client feedback and participation in decision-making. It might be noted that the actions of the New PA activists in the HEW move to Rockville, and generally in the demonstrations and writings against agency policies, have not directly benefited clients or involved them in agency decision-making. It remains to be seen if abstract advocacy of "client power" will have an impact on actual agency policies when client and agency interests conflict.

The matter of a proactive administrator is the question most difficult to answer. Managerial activism is both condemned as empire building and condoned if the results are acceptable. It distorts legislative intent, but it may be seen as "standing up to politicians." The success and public acclaim of Robert Moses, New York's master builder and aggrandizer, who attacked bureaucrats and politicians alike as foes of progress, are instructive here.[30] Americans prize a man of action as long as they support his aims. In this sense, then, activist administrators may be justified as being at least partly in the mainstream of political and administrative tradition. They are subject to punishment if caught and if their aims are deemed unworthy, but any New PA'er worth his salt will take this risk.

The questions of the New PA thrust and the most likely way that organizations can be changed should be considered together. There are basically two ways that organizational behavior can be changed. One is from the demands and pressures of the outside environment, the other is from within the organization.

New PA'ers seem most likely to press their demands on the organization from within. Carl Hershey found they are well adjusted to organizational life, suffer little frustration, have few restrictions on autonomy, and receive adequate rewards.[31] They do want greater decision-making involvement, but generally seem to be incipient bureaucrats, perhaps a special type of social program zealot. They are willing to stay with their organization and to reform it in the direction of their goals. While some actions have in-

volved outside pressures through protests, the overall picture is that of inside reformers rather than outside attackers.

The direction of the inside demands can be outlined. Greater participation in decision-making for all persons within the organization, regardless
of hierarchical rank, will be demanded to legitimize top-level decisions
among the rank and file. In social program areas, clients may be formally
involved. This will increase participation and the stock of ideas and alternatives available to decision-makers, but will slow down action. Presumably, since clients are involved, this will be agreeable.

Some sort of counter socialization for members will be necessary to meet
the social demands for conformity present in every organization. Actual
protests or actions by the activists would provide one example; special contracts with new members or "counter organization" sessions another.
Much of the success of these changes depends on the kinds of people re-
cruited to the organization, with New PA types most susceptible to this
sort of counter socialization. The organization must tacitly allow counter
socialization, or the necessary reward system will not succeed.

Change generated from within the organization will be directed toward
modifying client relationships. In some cities, for example, rookie policemen are disguised as common vagrants or drunks and then required to
spend a weekend in county or city jail in an attempt to heighten their understanding of a prisoner's situation. The organization must sensitize itself
to client needs, partly by encouraging deeper and more lasting relationships between organization members and individual clients, and partly by
involving clients in the decision-making process. The question is whether
an organization can by itself give up power to clients for their use in increasing leverage for services.

Changes from within the organization can develop from an increased
sensitivity among members and greater openness in discussing organization
matters. Organizational development and sensitivity training are likely to
become more common—indeed, despite the difficulties with these techniques noted in Chapter 7, they must become more common if change is to
occur.

The antagonism of the New PA toward conformity and the compart-
mentalization of bureaucratic life will create considerable conflict within
the organization, perhaps leading to less formal and restricted patterns of
behavior. One of the demands of a group of young HEW employees was
that "privileges of class and status should be eliminated whenever they
create barriers among workers." [32] They made reference to the perquisites

of rank, such as a couch and rug, which reward those who are promoted past a certain level, and which tend to fix an expectation within organization members that conformity and "going along" will be rewarded. If the pressures of large organizations toward conformity are to be resisted, this is one obvious place to begin.

This discussion illustrates the ways in which organizations could be modified from within if the views of the New PA were to prevail. In reality, dramatic changes are extremely unlikely if they must come from within. Organizations tend to preselect members who are amenable to their demands and to reject those who might not assimilate organizational values. Those who join with quite different values either leave after a time or modify their views to coincide with the organization ethic. As noted, the thirty-three federal protestors were quite comfortable within their agency and had all the marks of potential bureaucrats.

What will likely happen is what usually happens. The organization persists, protest activities flag, and even New PA'ers become coopted. Their views make them likely candidates for eventual rewards in terms of positions and program responsibilities since they associate with agency goals. Once the responsibilities of office overtake a person, it is unlikely that he will work against his own self-interest in favor of client power or a reduction in status symbols. If he were able to, it is unlikely that he would have remained in the organization.

It seems far more likely that the pressure of outside environmental forces on the organization will cause the dramatic changes that the New PA, as well as other segments of society, want. Few organizations are dramatically changed from within—societal demands first must change.

Real power for clients does not come from negotiations with the organization, but from political clout obtained via ballot boxes and interest groups. Participation in decision-making may help self-actualize those clients who are involved, but real power to change organizational behavior comes from political mechanisms such as social service scrip or a guaranteed annual wage. Both of these give clients real bargaining power and actual sanctions over public organizations, similar to those which middle-class persons have exercised informally for many years.

Organizations are open systems and thus powerfully affected by societal forces. They can be modified somewhat by inside pressures and in some cases this may be sufficient. But for major changes in attitudes and behavior, reformers must count on societal changes. To the extent that the New PA represents a significant redirection of cultural values, organizations will change because the environment changes.

NOTES

1. Most of this material comes from Ralph Gabriel, *The Course of American Democratic Thought*, 2nd ed. (Ronald Press, 1956) and Dwight Waldo, *The Administrative State* (Ronald Press, 1948). Louis Hart, *The Liberal Tradition in America* (Harcourt, Brace, & World, 1955) was also of help. Waldo was the primary source for the discussion of administrative values. Other authors whose works were useful included Daniel Boorstin, *The Genius of American Politics* (University of Chicago Press, 1953); Richard Hofstadter, *The American Political Tradition* (Knopf, 1948); Robert Goldwin, ed., *Left, Right and Center* (Rand McNally, 1965), especially the essay by Martin Diamond, "Conservatives, Liberals and the Constitution." None of these gentlemen can be held responsible for my interpretations, although I have tried to be faithful to their sometimes varying views. See also Morton Frisch and Richard Stevens, *American Political Thought* (Scribners, 1971).
2. Some authorities do not consider the American political tradition a direct descendent of "natural law," at least in the European tradition. They prefer to consider the American experience unique, with our political theory derived from the pragmatic views of the founding fathers. Boorstin, Chapter III, seems to take this position.
3. Waldo. See also Albert Lepawsky, ed., *Administration* (Knopf, 1949).
4. The best study is A. J. Ayer, ed., *Logical Positivism* (Free Press, 1959).
5. Herbert Simon, *Administrative Behavior* (Free Press, 1947).
6. Herbert Simon, Donald Smithburg, and Victor Thompson, *Public Administration* (Knopf, 1950).
7. Nathaniel Lawrence and Daniel O'Connor, *Readings in Existential Phenomenology* (Prentice-Hall, 1967), particularly the introduction, pp. 1–11 and the article by Stephen Strasser, "Phenomenologies and Psychologies," pp. 331–451. Other helpful works include Robert Olson, *Introduction to Existentialism* (Dover, 1962); Jean-Paul Sartre, *What Is Existentialism?* (Philosophical Library, 1947); and Pierre Thevanez, *What Is Phenomenology?* (Quadrangle Books, 1962).
8. Wesley Bjur, "Communication" in *Public Administration Review* 30 (March/April 1970). Also see his unpublished papers "The Generation Gap and the Administrator," and "Toward Contextual Model Building."
9. Andres Richter, "The Existential Executive" in *Public Administration Review* 30 (July/August 1970), pp. 415–22.
10. Programs such as "Sesame Street" standardize education in that everyone is exposed to the same stimuli at the same time. They may not equalize education, for culturally deprived children may not benefit as much as middle-class children, and some may not even have access to television.
11. Alvin Toffler, *Future Shock* (Random House, 1970), chapter 4.

12. Ernst Haas, *Tangle of Hopes* (Prentice-Hall, 1968), pp. 220–23.

13. Harry Girvetz, ed., *Democracy and Elitism* (Scribners, 1967) in his introductory essay on elitism, p. 43.

14. A good work evaluating recent developments in public administration is Gerald Caiden, *The Dynamics of Public Administration: Guidelines to Current Transformations in Theory and Practice* (Holt, Rinehart, and Winston, 1971). See also Louis Gawthrop, *Administrative Politics and Social Change* (St. Martin's, 1971) for a discussion of the impact of change on administrative practices.

15. Milton Esman and John Montgomery, "Systems Approaches to Technical Cooperation: The Role of Development Administration in Documentation," *Public Administration Review* 29 (September/October 1969), p. 516.

16. A good overview of the policy analysis approach is found in Ira Sharkansky, ed., *Policy Analysis in Political Science* (Markham, 1970), pp. 1–18.

17. Thomas Dye, "Government Structure, Urban Environment and Educational Policy," *Midwest Journal of Political Science* 11 (August 1967), pp. 353–80; Richard Dawson and James Robinson, "The Politics of Welfare" in Herbert Jacob and Kenneth Vines, eds., *Politics in the American States* (Little, Brown, 1965), Chapter 10; Thomas Dye, *Policy Economics and the Public Policy Outcomes in the American States* (Rand McNally, 1966); and Ira Sharkansky and Richard Hofferbert, "Dimensions of State Politics, Economics and Public Policy," *American Political Science Review* 63 (September 1969), pp. 862–80.

18. Dawson and Robinson.

19. The best collection of works is James Wilson, ed., *City Politics and Public Policy* (John Wiley, 1968), particularly the article by Robert Lineberry and Edmund Fowler on "Reformism and City Politics in American Cities." See also James Clarke, "Environment, Process and Policy: A Reconsideration," *American Political Science Review* 63 (December 1969), pp. 1172–83.

20. One public administration textbook based somewhat on this approach has been written. See Ira Sharkansky, *Public Administration*, 2nd ed. (Markham, 1972).

21. For a direct application of policy analysis to the activities of government agencies, see the articles by Rufus Browning, "Innovative and Non-Innovative Division Processes in Government Budgeting" and by James Daves, Jr. and Kenneth Dolbeare, "Selective Service and Military Manpower: Induction and Deferment Policies in the 1960s" in Sharkansky, ed., *Policy Analysis in Political Science.*

22. Warren Ilchmann and Norman Uphoff, *The Political Economy of Change* (University of California Press, 1968). Their assumptions are found on pp. 277–78. Other important works on the use of economic concepts include Robert Curry, Jr. and L. L. Wade, *A Theory of Political Exchange: Economic Reasoning in Political Analysis* (Prentice-Hall, 1968), and *A Logic of Public Policy: Aspects of Political Economy* (Wadsworth, 1970); and William Mitchell, "The Shape of Political Theory to Come: From Political Sociology to Political Economy" in *American Behavioral Scientist* 11 (November/December 1967), pp. 8–20. Earlier works include Anthony Downs, *An Economic Theory of Democracy* (Harper & Row, 1957), and *Inside Bureaucracy* (Little, Brown, 1967), and "Why the Government Budget Is Too Small in a Democracy," *World Politics* 12 (July 1960), pp. 541–63, and Charles Tiebout, "A Pure Theory of Local Expenditure," *Journal of Political Economy* 64 (October 1956), pp. 416–24.

23. Since the New PA movement is new, most of the background for this discussion comes from papers presented at conferences. There are two books which are important. The first includes papers which came out of the Minnowbrook Conference, a 1967 meeting which initiated the name "New PA" and formalized the existence of such a movement. It is entitled *Toward a New Public Administration*, Frank Marini, ed. (Chandler, 1968). The other work is Dwight Waldo, ed., *Public Administration in a Time of Turbulence* (Chandler, 1971). The best short outline is Keith Henderson, *Emerging Synthesis in American Public Administration* (Asia Publishing Company, 1966), but it does not give sufficient weight to the more recent occurrences I am emphasizing.

Other papers or articles of interest and help in this chapter included the "Symposium on Alienation, Decentralization and Participation" in the *Public Administration Review* 29 (January/February 1969); James McCurdy, "Fiction, Phenomenology and Public Administration," a paper presented to the American Society for Public Administration in Denver, April 1971; Carl Stenberg, "The History and Future of Citizen Participation: An Overview," a paper presented to the American Society for Public Administration in Denver, April 1971; and Dwight Waldo "The Administrative State Revisited" in *Public Administration Review* 25 (March 1965), pp. 5–30.

24. Carl Hershey, "The Federal Protestor: Rebel or Revolutionary?" a paper presented to the American Society for Public Administration in Denver, April 1971.

25. This section draws mainly from George Frederickson, "The Case for Social Equity in New Public Administration," a paper presented to the American Political Science Association in Chicago, September 1971.

26. An important work in this area is Orion White, "The Dialectical Organization," *Public Administration Review* 29 (January/February 1969), pp. 32–42. See also Richard Collins, "Feedback or Organizational Change," a paper presented to the American Society for Public Administration in Denver, April 1971, where the idea of public administration scrip is presented at a New PA panel of organizational-client relationships.

27. Neil Lawer, "The Relocation of the United States Public Health Service" in *Public Administration Review* 32 (January/February 1972), pp. 43–49.

28. Mike Ambrose et al., "The Condition of the Federal Employee and How to Change It," Communications Section of the *Public Administration Review* 29 (July/August 1969), pp. 434–40. This credo has been widely circulated among the federal establishment.

29. Jerome McKinney, "Influence of Lower Level Officials on Policy Making," a paper presented to the American Society for Public Administration in Denver, April 1971.

30. Rexford Tugwell, "The Moses Effect" in Edward Banfield, ed., *Urban Government* (Free Press, 1961).

31. Carl Hershey, "The Federal Protester . . .".

32. Mike Ambrose et al., "The Condition of the Federal Employee. . . ."

INDEX